Shelton State Libraries
Shelton State Community College

Also by Clyde Prestowitz

Three Billion New Capitalists:
The Great Shift of Wealth and Power to the East

Rogue Nation:
American Unilateralism
and the Failure of Good Intentions

Trading Places:
How We Are Giving Our Future
to Japan and How to Reclaim It

THE BETRAYAL OF
AMERICAN PROSPERITY

*Free Market Delusions, America's Decline, and
How We Must Compete in the Post-Dollar Era*

CLYDE PRESTOWITZ

FREE PRESS

New York   London   Toronto   Sydney

Free Press
A Division of Simon & Schuster, Inc.
1230 Avenue of the Americas
New York, NY 10020

Copyright © 2010 by Clyde Prestowitz

All rights reserved, including the right to reproduce this book or portions
thereof in any form whatsoever. For information address Free Press Subsidiary
Rights Department, 1230 Avenue of the Americas, New York, NY 10020

First Free Press hardcover edition May 2010

FREE PRESS and colophon are trademarks of Simon & Schuster, Inc.

For information about special discounts for bulk purchases,
please contact Simon & Schuster Special Sales at 1-866-506-1949
or business@simonandschuster.com

The Simon & Schuster Speakers Bureau can bring authors to your live event.
For more information or to book an event contact the Simon & Schuster
Speakers Bureau at 1-866-248-3049 or visit our website at
www.simonspeakers.com.

Designed by Renata Di Biase

Manufactured in the United States of America

10   9   8   7   6   5   4   3

Library of Congress Cataloging-in-Publication Data

Prestowitz, Clyde V.
   The betrayal of American prosperity : free market delusions, America's
decline, and how we must compete in the post-dollar era / Clyde Prestowitz.
      p.   cm.
   Includes bibliographical references.
   1. United States—Economic policy.   2. United States—Economic conditions—21st century.   3. United States—Commercial policy.   4. United
States—Foreign economic relations—China.   5. China—Foreign economic
relations—United States.   I. Title.

   HC106.84.P74   2010
   330.973—dc22   2009048183

ISBN 978-1-4391-1979-2
ISBN 978-1-4391-3147-3 (ebook)

For my wife, Carol Ann Prestowitz, to whom I owe so much

The consequences of an economic defeat are much more difficult to nullify than those of a military defeat.

—Korekiyo Takahashi, Japanese finance minister, 1936

Contents

THE BETRAYAL OF
AMERICAN PROSPERITY

INTRODUCTION

Loads of Dung

Rome lived upon its principal till ruin stared it in the face. Industry is the only true source of wealth, and there was no industry in Rome. By day the Ostia Road was crowded with carts and muleteers, carrying to the great city the silks and spices of the East, the marble of Asia Minor, the timber of the Atlas, the grain of Africa and Egypt—and the carts brought nothing out but loads of dung. That was their return cargo.

—WINWOOD READE, *THE MARTYRDOM OF MAN*

What, you may ask, does the state of Rome and Roman trade have to do with the condition of the United States today? Anyone who visits Long Beach, California, will quickly understand the answer. The port of Long Beach is where most of the hulking container ships that carry the goods of Asia to the American market are unloaded. To the inexperienced eye, it is a vast expanse of cranes, stacked containers, and parking lots waiting to accommodate the millions of imported cars that roll off specialized Asian auto ships destined for the American consumer.

Long Beach is the Ostia of our day, the gateway to the great American market. Even more striking than the size of the port and the armada of ships is the contrast between the cargo that's off-loaded and that being loaded for the return trip to Osaka, Busan, Shanghai, Hong Kong, and Singapore. The imports are as numerous as the sands on the nearby beach, including everything from shoes and shirts to computers, autos, advanced telecommunications gear, and photo voltaic panels for generating solar energy. The exports, though, are few, consisting mostly of scrap metal and waste paper—this millennium's dung, you might say.

In 2008, our scrap metal and waste exports to China alone totaled $7.6 billion, exceeding our exports of each of the next three strongest categories: semiconductors, aircraft and parts, and oilseeds and grains. And even with all of those and our other exports included, the U.S. trade deficit with China runs annually at about $250 billion while our overall trade deficit is about $600 billion, even after declining by $200 billion as a result of the Great Recession of 2008–2009. Particularly disturbing is the fact that the United States has a trade deficit of about $100 billion in high-technology goods, and a substantial part of that is with China as well. In fact, China's biggest export to the United States in 2008 was computer equipment, at $46 billion.

It is easy to downplay the significance of this trade imbalance, as well as the startling difference in the nature of what we import and what we export, and focus instead on the fact that the United States will continue to be by far the largest economy in the world for decades and remains the world leader in many industries and technologies. But the trend lines are decidedly troubling. Each year the U.S. economy looks just a little bit more like that of ancient Rome, while at the same time the Chinese economy, and those of several other rapidly developing countries, look more like that of a younger, stronger America.

The question of course is, why? The short answer is that for some time now our "best and brightest" have been invoking false doctrines that are systematically undermining American prosperity. Leading among these is the economic orthodoxy of market fundamentalism, simplistic pure free trade, and hands-off government that, like the dogged adherence to the domino theory of the Vietnam era, has paralyzed common sense in dealing with competitive realities.

Reversing America's traditional national economic-development policies, U.S. leaders after World War II increasingly embraced consumerism and a faith in the efficacy of unfettered markets and trade that evolved over time into a new gospel of laissez-faire globalization— that tying the U.S. market tightly to others was best for both the United States and the whole global economy. Globalization, the argument went, was really Americanization and would lead inexorably to prosperity for all, which in turn would lead to global democratization and peace among nations, with America remaining the world leader. If this sounded too good to be true, it was.

In fact, there are a lot of varieties of globalization with some being advantageous and others disadvantageous. What we have now is a system in which U.S. markets remain relatively open to imports and foreign investment while many major foreign markets, like those of China and Japan, remain relatively restricted and controlled. To paraphrase Abraham Lincoln, the world today is half free trade and half neomercantilist (protectionist), and it is not clear that a world so divided can long stand. The popular orthodox notion that free trade will always be a win-win solution has been destructively simplistic. Win-win doesn't mean that there are no losers. It only means that the gains of some will outweigh the losses suffered by others, and it assumes (wrongly) that the winners will always compensate the losers. The usual interpretation of this is that the gains to be achieved by importing cheap goods for the great mass of consumers will outweigh the lost wages of the workers—a small group in comparison—who may lose their jobs as a result. The truth is more complicated.

Take the case of Walmart, whose imports from China are currently about $30 billion annually. Of course, Walmart has been expanding and hiring steadily in the United States over the past fifteen years. But the jobs it offers mostly pay close to minimum wage without, in many cases, health care or pension benefits. By contrast, many of the Walmart supplier jobs that left the United States for China paid above minimum wage and often provided both health care and pension benefits as well. So are "everyday low prices" really so good for consumers if the consumers happen also to be workers? Yes, I know that there are probably more consumers shopping at Walmart than Walmart supplier workers who lost their jobs. But keep in mind that the effect of those workers losing their jobs is to make other workers fear losing their jobs and to hold down or even reduce wages for all workers. The Dutch have a saying: *Goedkoop is Duurkoop*—cheap is expensive. Maybe everyday low prices can actually be quite expensive.

Or consider the popular "cash for clunkers" program that seemed to work so well in 2009. If you turned in a qualified gas guzzler, Uncle Sam gave you taxpayer dollars to go buy a new gas sipper. Of the ten most popular new sippers bought, five were Japanese and one was South Korean, and though the number 1 seller was the Ford Focus, by 2009 only 50 percent of the value of a Focus was produced in the

United States. That means that probably over half the cash paid for clunkers created jobs abroad instead of jobs in America. Again, cheap can be expensive.

Or, let's look at the apparently encouraging case of green energy and wind turbines. The Obama administration has trumpeted the urgency of creating green jobs and appropriated funds to promote wind farms. But in November 2009 when construction of a huge new wind farm in Texas was announced, it turned out that all the turbines—the actual windmills—were being imported from China. Texas would get some temporary construction jobs, but the long-term manufacturing jobs would be created in China, only adding even more to our trade deficit and international debt. More important, because with wind turbine production, as with so many industrial goods, the more you make the lower the cost of each, Chinese producers are likely only to widen their cost advantage over U.S. producers. That will stymie the growth of the U.S. factories and keep jobs from American workers. Again, cheap can be expensive and can undermine American prosperity.

Finally, you cannot talk about the flaws in free-trade and globalization orthodoxy without talking about "companies without countries." In the 1950s, when General Motors chairman Charles "Engine Charlie" Wilson famously said that "what was good for the U.S. was good for General Motors and vice versa," he was roundly criticized for seeming to identify a private company with the great United States. But his remark actually made good sense; in those days, American companies actually produced in America when American consumer demand increased, and that production increased the GDP and national income further, which in turn increased domestic demand for all the goods all the companies were producing. It was a virtuous circle in which what was good for the country was indeed good for GM and vice versa.

But over the past several decades, a host of U.S. corporations have gone multinational and can thrive regardless of the performance of the United States. The orthodoxy insists that while corporations compete economically, countries do not, and, indeed, should not, in order to avoid distorting the efficient operation of international markets. Thus trade must be entirely in the hands of global corporations. Moreover, unlike in the past when corporate leaders were also expected to fulfill obligations to the larger society, the loyalty of today's CEOs is expected not to be to their countries or local communities but only to the corporation's shareholders, and their sole mission is said to be to increase the value of the company's shares. While they may feel obligations to community and country as individuals, they do not, by and large, as CEOs. As Intel's former chairman Craig Barrett has said, "Intel can move wherever it must to thrive, but I sometimes wonder how my grandchildren will earn a living."

Important also is the fact that as heads of companies with operations in many countries, they must respond to the policies and pressures of those societies as well as to those of the United States. Indeed, one perverse aspect of globalization is that while U.S. CEOs and corporations are influential players in U.S. politics, they have no political clout in authoritarian countries like China, Russia, or Saudi Arabia. To be sure, they have some bargaining power because these countries want the technology and investment the CEOs have to offer. But in societies where discretionary administrative power is great and the rule of law weak, CEOs must maintain good relations with the powers that be. In a word, they must be deferential, and they can sometimes be more responsive to the wishes of the authoritarian countries than to those of the democratic countries.

In a 2009 White House meeting, a group of top American CEOs who have offshored much of their production told President Obama that to prevent retaliation against U.S. exports he must avoid inclusion of any "buy American" provisions in his economic stimulus package even though the measures being considered were all perfectly legal and permissible under the rules of the World Trade Organization (WTO). Moreover, at that very moment, China, Japan, and most of the major European countries that might threaten trade retaliation were already implementing "buy domestic" policies of their own. The CEOs were, in effect, arguing for sending more of our stimulus money to help create jobs overseas, while our trading partners were doing the opposite.

When I heard of this, I couldn't help thinking of how in the midst of the 1980s' trade frictions with Japan, then secretary of commerce Malcolm Baldrige had considered initiating antidumping actions against Japanese semiconductor producers illegally selling their computer chips below cost (dumping) in the U.S. market and threatening the future of the whole U.S. industry. Concerned about the impact of possible Japanese retaliation on American multinational companies as well as about the consequences for U.S. semiconductor users, Baldrige sounded out a number of leading executives before deciding to act. IBM Senior Vice President Jack Kuehler's comments had been particularly important. When asked whether or not some action should be taken, Kuehler had emphasized: "Not only should you act, you must act." Baldrige did act, and the result was not only a halt of the dumping but a deal that opened the Japanese market as well. This shift in CEO attitudes has come about largely because of where the big, global American companies are producing these days. Increasingly, it is not in America. Hence, we must be alert that when American CEOs advise the president or lobby Congress today, they may unwittingly be acting, in effect, as emissaries of foreign governments. In any case, we cannot be sure that they are speaking on behalf of America's overall prosperity.

So strong has the hold of this pro-globalization, free-trade orthodoxy become that some of our most respected economists have argued that it doesn't even matter what we as a nation make as opposed to what we import. As one former chairman of the president's Council of Economic Advisers told me, "They'll sell us cars and we'll sell them poetry." Indeed, most of our economists argue that we are moving into a postindustrial economy in which we will do high-tech R&D, software, and services such as consulting, travel and tourism, and design. Sophisticated financial services were also included in the list, but in the wake of the subprime debacle, the leadership role the United States will play there is now in question. Making dung might actually be better than that.

Wall Street was long the citadel of the orthodoxy, and its key points were the subject of great interest on December 7, 2007, when, exuding confidence, the vice chairman of Lehman Brothers rose in Washington, D.C., to address the Global Strategy Group, an assembly of about thirty of the world's leading geopolitical, economic, and social analysts and commentators, who meet regularly to assess global trends. And why should he not have been confident? He was an iconic example of the American Dream, a poor boy who had climbed to the top of one of the top banks in the world, and it was about to pay him a $12 million bonus.

In his remarks, the vice chairman forecast a continuing economic boom based primarily on what he called the uniquely innovative and efficient performance of the U.S. financial industry and its capital markets. One analyst raised questions about the future of the dollar. He noted that the Chinese and Japanese together had already accumulated over $2 trillion of dollar reserves as a result of their trade surpluses with America and so would be vulnerable to severe losses in the event of high U.S. inflation or a drop in the value of the dollar. He wondered if there weren't some danger of flight from the dollar as America's trade deficits and global indebtedness continued to grow. Not to worry, responded the vice chairman. The U.S. economy is strong, and U.S. capital markets are so attractive and efficient that foreign investors will indefinitely invest in them.

Another question was raised about the low U.S. savings rate. Won't that restrict the ability of America to invest in its future? Not at all, was the reply. The widely held perception of a low U.S. savings rate is false, said the vice chairman. In fact, he emphasized, Americans hold trillions of dollars of untapped equity in their homes, a vast store of savings not included in the comparisons.

I then asked a question about risks in the markets for complex financial products like mortgage-backed securities, collateralized debt obligations, and credit default swaps, the volume of which had ballooned in recent years to a total value of about $400 trillion, or nearly ten times the world's roughly $48 trillion GDP. But I could not shake his confidence. "Clyde," he said, "don't worry. We have stress tested our systems and positions in all possible ways, and we are solid. There is really nothing that can go terribly wrong." Less than a year later, of course, Lehman Brothers no longer existed.

The causes and long-term implications of the Great Recession of 2008–9 will be long debated, but it has already become perfectly clear that our orthodox economic theories are wildly off base. The crisis that brought down Lehman Brothers, most of Wall Street, and much of the global financial system has unmasked the long-running erosion of America's fundamental economic vitality. It has also signaled a shift away from the United States and toward China, the oil producers, and emerging-market countries such as India and Brazil. Chronic U.S. trade deficits of $600 billion to $800 billion annually over many years have turned America from the world's leading creditor nation to its largest debtor, thereby dramatically reducing U.S. bargaining leverage with our foreign "lenders." (Who argues with his banker?)

By normal rules of thumb, these deficits are also costing the U.S. economy somewhere around 10 million jobs, and they are an important reason why American men in their thirties are now earning less than their fathers did at the same age and why median family income is today not appreciably higher in real terms than it was in the 1970s. They also mean that just to keep running smoothly without a sharp rise in interest rates, the U.S. economy must have a gross inflow of foreign capital of about $5 billion per day. This puts its own pressure on the economy by raising the national debt. Present Congressional Budget Office forecasts show the U.S. federal debt rising to nearly 85 percent of GDP by 2019 even under relatively favorable economic conditions. Finally, consider that big dollar holders like China and the OPEC countries have recently been expressing serious concern about the state and future role of the dollar. For a long time, they believed the mythology about Wall Street and about the U.S. economy moving to ever more sophisticated services and high technology. But now they have begun to realize the extent of America's loss of competitiveness and that it does seem to make a lot of dung. They also fear that the U.S. trade and budget deficits will flood the world with dollars and create inflation that might lead to a dollar collapse.

This brings us to the irony of America's role as the world's sole superpower. Beyond our blind adherence to simplistic free-trade orthodoxy and market fundamentalism, America's prosperity has been undermined in another way in the post–World War II era. We have evolved from a country that wanted no foreign entanglements and saw the business of American government as business, into a country in which the business of government has become trading America's productive and technological base for geopolitical and military advantage.

To see a stark manifestation of this transformation, you have only to drive down the Pacific Coast from Long Beach to San Diego, where you will find the largest U.S. naval base on the West Coast and the home of the U.S. Pacific Fleet. Comprising 54 ships and 120 supporting commands, the base stretches over 977 acres of land and 326 acres of water and houses 20,000 military personnel along with 6,000 civilians. It is as impressive an example of American military strength as Long Beach is of American economic weakness.

In terms of warplanes, bombs, drones, and other exotic weapons, the United States enjoys unparalleled power and alone among nations can project its influence anywhere in the world—a capability with many benefits for America and the global community. But we Americans have paid a steep price for our military superiority by subordinating our prosperity to the demands of geopolitics. And I am not referring to obvious costs, such as the fact that the $1 million per year required to keep one American soldier in Afghanistan is $1 million per year that we are not spending on, for instance, upgrading our relatively slow 3.9-megabit-per-second (Mbps) internet speeds to the blazing 63.6 Mbps speed of Japan's internet. I am also not referring to the gallons upon gallons of oil that we must buy from Middle East countries to keep our navy moving, which is its own serious issue.

I am referring to something much more problematic. Take President Barrack Obama's November 2009 visit to Beijing: there he promised close technical collaboration and support for eventual U.S. safety approval to aid development of China's ARJ21 commuter jet. Why? Commercial jets are one of America's few remaining trade surplus products, and it is no secret that China is gunning for Boeing. Perhaps Washington thinks that by helping China make commuter jets, it can facilitate sales to China of bigger planes. But it also very much wants to sell some weapons to Taiwan without too much objection from Beijing, and it wants to obtain Chinese cooperation on a variety of non-economic issues—like North Korea, carbon emissions, and a host of other problems—and hopes that development assistance for the plane will serve these larger purposes.

This is but one form of what are commonly called "offset" arrangements. More typically, countries like South Korea and Poland—for which the United States provides a defense umbrella—stipulate as a condition of buying U.S. aircraft and weapons systems for their own armed forces that not only the production but also the advanced technology of the planes and systems be transferred to their factories. Such offset production in Poland, for example, now totals about $9 billion annually, translating into roughly 150,000 jobs. As a result of similar transfers over the years, Japan has developed a carbon fiber aircraft components industry that has largely displaced its U.S. competitors.

Consider also the flaccid response to China's currency manipulation. Recently Beijing has been intervening in currency markets, keeping its renminbi (RMB) undervalued to ensure that China's exports are relatively cheap. While this violates both WTO and International

Monetary Fund (IMF) agreements, no one has moved to stop it, and one reason is that Washington has long tolerated similar practices by Japan, South Korea, and other countries from which it wished geopolitical support.

A final and related factor further undermining American prosperity is the U.S. addiction to cheap energy and foreign oil. By eschewing both conservation and development of alternative energy we have become reliant on petroleum imports that now constitute a third of our trade deficit. We define our national security in terms of defending authoritarian regimes that happen to own major oil fields and that use the hundreds of billions of dollars we send them to finance terrorism and other activities that undermine not only our prosperity but also our security.

This brings us back to Barrett's question: how are our grandchildren going to earn a living in America if things keep on as they are? Implicitly, of course, the question is really about the fate of the American idea, of the American Dream, and of the world without American leadership. This is not an entirely new question, nor is the erosion of U.S. competitiveness a new story. Indeed, *Business Week* wrote in the early 1990s that "one could feel the erosion of America's productive capability." The scene at Long Beach—the exchange of waste for computers—evolved gradually over the past half century, accelerating over the past thirty years. It is a story that I have been trying to tell for much of that time. Nor have I been alone. Over the years, a succession of commissions, presidential advisory bodies, and studies of the National Academy of Sciences have warned of a potentially catastrophic erosion and even evaporation of the U.S. industrial-technological base and of the essential innovation ecosystem.

For many years, I and my colleagues in these and other bodies were criticized as "protectionists," "corporate statists," "antiglobalists," and "declinists," and our views were dismissed as being needlessly alarmist and outside the mainstream. But now it looks as if we may not have been alarmist enough. Our best and brightest have been betraying our productive base and overcommitting us geopolitically. Now we are at a crossroads where the future of America truly is at stake—not its future as a country, as a place on the map, but its future as a place of unique opportunity and hope and prosperity.

The question now is whether we Americans will have the insight and the determination to throw off the tyranny of orthodoxy. More of the conventional wisdom will not revitalize our economy or sustain U.S. technological leadership. It is a fallacy to believe that America will somehow dominate high-tech industries while the rest of the world concentrates on low- and medium-tech. The dynamics that have moved production of steel, autos, wind turbines, and the reading of brain scans abroad will also move biotech and nanotech and any other tech unless they are changed. We can't have more real estate and dot-com bubbles. We can't do a lot more stimulus spending without turning an already difficult financial situation into a disastrous one. We can't have zero percent interest rates forever. We will have to reverse the long prevailing dynamics and stop the offshoring of the production and provision of every tradable good and service. We will have to commit to making first-rate products and providing the full range of services in America, and to exporting something other than dung.

It has been our dominant way of thinking for so long that we tend to assume that our current economic orthodoxy is the "American Way." Nothing could be further from the truth. In fact, it is a reversal of the doctrine of national economic development that made us the richest country on earth in the first 160 years of our history. Beginning with Alexander Hamilton's proposals for the industrial and technological development of the United States through use of subsidies, tariffs, and patents, U.S. leaders pursued the "American System" of government-business partnership for national development of things like the Erie Canal, the telegraph, the transcontinental railroad, the aircraft industry, the RCA company founded by the U.S. Navy, and much more. As the dominant economy in the wake of World War II and facing the need to spur global recovery from the war and to support allies in the new Cold War, we reversed that early approach and rightly adopted trade and economic development programs that opened our markets and assisted our allies not only to recover but to thrive. But what was right and good then became increasingly less appropriate as the global economy and our own situation evolved. And it has now become apparent that we desperately need another change of course.

I have no doubt that we can now make the course correction needed if we put our minds to it. But if we are to do so, we must fully understand our present situation and how we've gotten ourselves into it. The Japanese have the concept of *tatemae* and *honne*. *Tatemae* is the way things are supposed to be, the outward presentation of things, the desired ideal. *Honne* is the way things really are. We Americans are accustomed to thinking of our country as number one in pretty much everything. That is our *tatemae*. Our present *honne* is quite different. Let me show you.

1

The Real State of America

America is in danger of going down the tubes, and the worst part is that nobody knows it. They're all patting themselves on the back as the *Titanic* heads for the icebergs full speed ahead.

—ANDY GROVE

The canary in our coal mine is the U.S. dollar. Since the end of World War II, the greenback has been the world's main currency for carrying out international transactions. Oil and virtually all other commodities and products in international markets are bought and sold in dollars. In addition, like gold in the nineteenth and early twentieth centuries, the dollar is the main currency in which most countries now hold their monetary reserves—an arrangement that greatly favors the United States. For example, in order to buy oil, people in other countries must first produce and export something in order to earn dollars, which can then be used to pay for the oil. Americans, on the other hand, have only to print more greenbacks to get their oil. Nor does America have to worry like other countries about its trade balances. If other countries import more than they export, they must borrow dollars to pay for the excess. But that can get expensive, and sometimes no one will lend to them. So they are forced to get back into balance. In the case of the United States, however, it is only necessary to print more dollars to pay for an excess of imports over exports. As long as the world will accept dollars, there is no need for America to balance its trade. This phenomenon is a crucial support of America's global military deployments. To pay for war in Iraq or Afghanistan or for fleets to patrol the oceans of the world or for troops in more than seven hundred bases around the world, America has only to print dollars—as long as the world will accept dollars in payment.

Recently and increasingly, however, the world is showing some unwillingness to accept dollars. In May 2007, Kuwait stopped pegging its dinar to the dollar in favor of a basket of currencies. Since then, the members of the Gulf Cooperation Council (Saudi Arabia, Bahrain, Oman, Qatar, and the United Arab Emirates) have been debating whether to link their planned new common currency to something other than the dollar. Indeed, former Federal Reserve chairman Alan Greenspan has noted that the OPEC (Organization of Petroleum Exporting Countries) countries are "already recognizing the value of shifting from petro-dollars to petro-euros." But it's not just OPEC. In the past few years, Russia, Thailand, Malaysia, and others have also reduced the dollar ratio of their reserves.

More recently, China, whose RMB is already a de facto currency in parts of Thailand, Russia, and Vietnam, and whose stash of dollar reserves now amounts to well over $2 trillion, has been calling for replacement of the dollar as the world's reserve currency by the International Monetary Fund's special drawing rights (SDRs), presently the unique internal currency of the IMF. At the same time, Beijing has been warning the United States against allowing any depreciation of the dollar and pressing Washington for a guarantee that the dollar will not depreciate further. China is also rapidly trying to diversify its holdings by using its reserves to buy oil fields and other commodity production sites around the world, to add to its gold stocks, and to buy companies and other assets.

The dollar was also at the top of the agenda at the October 2009 East Asia Leaders meetings in Thailand. As the dollar fell to new lows against almost all currencies, the new Japanese prime minister called for creation of an Asian currency that would replace the greenback. At the annual meeting of the World Economic Forum in 2010, French President Nicholas Sarkozy urged a new global currency solution.

In tandem with these developments, the September/October 2009 issue of *Foreign Affairs* featured an article titled "The Dollar Dilemma" in which University of California, Berkeley, professor Barry Eichengreen discussed how, as he put it, the world's top currency faces competition. He concluded that the role of the dollar will inevitably diminish in the future, but that it will for some time remain first among equals in a system of multiple national reserve currencies. On the other hand, the UN special advisory committee on reserve currencies chaired by Nobel laureate Joseph Stiglitz is calling for creation of a new global reserve currency.

FALL OF AMERICAN INFLUENCE

But it's not just the dollar that's falling. American power is falling as well. At the end of World War II, the United States was the dominant force in virtually every industry and technology and by far the richest country in the world. Indeed, it was the richest country the world had ever seen. It was also the strongest military power in the West at the moment of the outbreak of the Cold War. In light of this overwhelming economic superiority and the new geopolitical dangers, the country's leadership took a dominant role in crafting a set of international agreements to spur the economic recovery of Europe and Japan and also assumed primary responsibility for the military policing of all threats to the free world. The mandates of national and global security took precedence over concerns about industrial competitiveness.

Consequently, the United States fell into the habit—and the addiction continues today—of making economic concessions in order to obtain geopolitical objectives. To obtain rights for military bases overseas or votes in the UN or troop contributions to American-led military expeditions, Washington would grant special tariff exemptions to trading partners or acquiesce in the virtual exclusion of U.S. goods from foreign markets.

Innocuous at first, when America enjoyed overwhelming competitive superiority, this practice became increasingly disadvantageous as other countries caught up. Now that America has fallen behind in many respects, the habit is positively deleterious both for U.S. competitiveness and for U.S. security. Consider the new restraint and even self-censorship with which America now treats China as compared with the past. During a 2009 trip to China, Secretary of State Hillary Clinton never mentioned the words "human rights." This was in sharp contrast to the statements of such former secretaries of state as James Baker, Madeleine Albright, and Condoleezza Rice. Or take the speech of Treasury Secretary Tim Geithner at Beijing University on June 1, 2009. During the Q-and-A following his remarks, some students voiced concern over the possibility of a dramatic decline in the value of China's hoard of dollar reserves if prospective U.S. inflation should lead to dollar devaluation. They warned Geithner that America must make every effort to avoid such an eventuality.

Now keep in mind that no one in America ever asked China to pursue the closed-market, export-led growth strategies that have resulted in the accumulation of Beijing's dollar hoard. No one in America ever asked China to keep its RMB undervalued versus the dollar by intervening constantly in the currency markets to buy dollars. That China feels that it is stuck with too many dollars is at least as much China's fault as America's and probably more. But Geithner didn't even hint at that fact. Rather he somewhat timorously assured the students that the dollar was solid and that the U.S. government would keep it that way. The students laughed—yes, they laughed—in response. Geithner listened politely and made no reply.

Or take the U.S. Treasury's annual report to the Congress on exchange rate policies. Under IMF and WTO rules, countries are not supposed to keep their currencies undervalued in order to artificially promote exports. The Treasury is required by Congress to report every year on any such activity. It has been obvious to all observers for some time that China (along with others such as Taiwan, Korea, and Singapore) is pursuing such practices. Indeed, one of China's first actions in response to the outbreak of the recent economic crisis was to take steps to reduce the value of the RMB against the dollar. Yet in its statement to the Congress on April 15, 2009, the Treasury asserted that China was not engaged in any unfair currency manipulation. All informed observers knew this to be untrue. Further, they knew that China's policies could be damaging to the United States. Yet there was no outcry in the media and no uproar in the Congress. Nor during his November 2009 visit to China did President Obama publicly mention human rights or currency misvaluation. Indeed, he acquiesced to press conferences with no questions and to giving speeches that were not broadcast.

Indeed, rather than lecturing others, Americans are beginning to become accustomed to being lectured to by Chinese and other foreign leaders on the flaws of our form of capitalism. And if we look into the future, it is clear that we should expect much more of the same. China recently announced that it was investigating whether the U.S. bailout of GM and Chrysler constituted an illegal subsidy to U.S. auto exports to China. Now bear in mind that the United States exports virtually no autos to China.

In the geopolitical sphere, the U.S. relationship with Taiwan is of particular interest. For over half a century, a bedrock principle of U.S. foreign policy has been to maintain Taiwan's independence and to tie its economy tightly to that of the United States. Indeed, without access to Taiwan's semiconductor foundries and other high-tech centers, many U.S. industries, including defense industries, would be in deep trouble. Yet today Taiwan has become an extension of the Chinese economy. Taiwanese businesses have invested more than $100 billion in the mainland economy and more than a million Taiwanese live in Shanghai alone. Taipei and Beijing are negotiating to make the Taiwan dollar and the RMB mutually convertible, a step that would bind Taiwan closer to China while loosening its ties with America. Although the United States has on several occasions gone to the brink of war with China in order to protect Taiwan, it is today inconceivable that Washington would do so again or that it could be successful if it tried. Now let me emphasize that this is not necessarily a bad development. But it is nevertheless a measure of the shift in the balance of power.

Another indication comes from Japan. The long dominant and U.S.-dominated Liberal Democratic Party (LDP) was finally displaced in October 2009 after nearly sixty years of one-party rule. An immediate priority of the new prime minister, Yukio Hatoyama, has been to reduce the U.S. military presence in Japan, to call for greater development of ties with China and the rest of Asia, and to push for an Asian economic union that would have its own currency and that would not include the United States. Finally, the United States is slowly but steadily losing its freedom of action and even a degree of sovereignty. From the Declaration of Independence in 1776 to our refusal to accommodate the Barbary pirates of the early nineteenth century to our rejection of the legitimacy of the International Criminal Court, America has always insisted on controlling its own destiny. Yet in truth, over the past thirty years, without even a debate in the Congress or a cabinet meeting on the topic, the United States has ceded a significant degree of its sovereignty to China, Japan, the Middle East oil-producing countries, and other major funders of the ever-mounting U.S. debt. The fact is that Americans are not really paying for U.S. military actions in Iraq, Afghanistan, or Pakistan or other U.S. deployments around the globe, or even for tasks like the rebuilding of New Orleans.

While these enterprises are included in the U.S. government budget, the very low rate of U.S. savings and the chronic, large budget and trade deficits mean that they are actually financed by sending U.S-dollar-denominated IOUs to China and the other major international lenders. Thus, if America is pursuing policies that our debt holders find unacceptable, they have the means to put discipline on Washington. Of course, there is truth in the old adage that if you owe the bank $1 million, you may have a problem, but if you owe the bank $1 trillion, the bank may have a problem. Neither the Chinese nor the other major U.S-debt-holding countries can be sure that the United States won't generate inflation or act in other ways that might destroy a large part of their national wealth. So the nature of the relationship is one of Mutual Assured Destruction. Nevertheless, it signifies a major loss of U.S. freedom of action in both the economic and geopolitical spheres.

EROSION OF THE ECONOMY, INDUSTRY, AND TECHNOLOGY

Behind this erosion both of the dollar's position and of U.S. influence is the increasingly rapid erosion in recent years of the economic, industrial, and technological leadership on which U.S. prosperity has long been based. Once upon a time, the United States could mobilize quickly to overwhelm Germany and Japan with planes, tanks, and ships. It could build the world's most modern and extensive highway system, send a man to the moon, pioneer global aviation, and give birth to the information age. Its families could live a middle-class lifestyle, send the kids to college, and retire comfortably on one income. Now, we have trouble getting house trailers to New Orleans, and anyone who has walked through a foreign airport, made a cell phone call in Beijing, or Cairo, or Seoul, or stayed at a business hotel in any international city outside the United States knows that America is falling behind.

We are accustomed to thinking of the United States as having the world's biggest economy with the highest per capita income. While it is true that at $14.3 trillion America's is the largest national economy (more than twice the size of China and nearly three times that of Japan based on purchasing power parity, or ppp), it is also true that the European Union (EU) has the largest single economy with a GDP of nearly $19 trillion. In per capita income, the United States ranks number 8 behind countries like Sweden, the Netherlands, and Australia. If we look only at large countries, the United States at about $47,000 income per capita appears to be way ahead of others such as Germany ($35,000) and Japan ($34,000). But if we take income disparities into account, the picture changes dramatically. In the United States, the top 1 percent of earners account for 15 percent of total income as compared to 4 percent or 5 percent in countries like France and Japan. So if we exclude the top 1 percent of earners in all countries from the comparison, we find that 99 percent of people in countries like Germany, Japan, the UK, and France actually have a higher income than 98 percent to 99 percent of Americans.

This is even truer if you look at hours worked and at vacation time. At 1,804 hours per year, the average American is working about 300 hours more than his counterparts in other developed countries where statutory vacation times range from two to six weeks. Indeed, the number of hours worked per worker in America has steadily risen over the past thirty years while it has steadily declined in other developed countries. Thus, if time is money, the leisure hours of the other major countries more than close any GDP per capita gap with the United States for the overwhelming majority of the population.

The U.S. growth performance has also been somewhat less brilliant than widely imagined. It is, of course, true that the United States' GDP growth rates over the past twenty-five years have been well above those of the European countries and Japan. But one reason for this has been the fact that Europe and Japan have had stable or even shrinking populations, while immigration and high immigrant birth rates have driven substantial U.S. population growth. A second factor has been rising debt and associated asset bubble wealth effects. Since 1980, the United States has accumulated such large trade deficits that its net international credit position has shifted from that of the world's biggest creditor, to the tune of about $2 trillion, to that of its biggest debtor, with net debt of $2.5 trillion and borrowing growing at the rate of $400 billion to $800 billion annually. Think of this as resembling the performance of a highly leveraged corporation such as Enron, whose sales climbed rapidly and steadily, but whose financial viability eventually evaporated. Especially for the past ten or fifteen years, the dot-com bubble and then the housing and financial bubbles made everyone feel rich and engendered enormous buildups of debt that masked the true deterioration of the underlying economy. Thus, we really need to discount U.S. GDP by about 20 percent in order to account for the accumulation of debt. That would drop the United States well behind Japan and the major European countries in terms of growth and GDP per capita.

Over the past several decades, there has been much schadenfreude in America over Japan's so-called Lost Decade of growth during the 1990s. But in that decade, Japan accumulated trade surpluses and international investments that are now helping to fund its rising health care and pension costs. In contrast, the United States accumulated large debts that will make it much more difficult to fund health care and pensions for its now retiring baby boomer population. We might well ask who actually lost the decade.

As for productivity growth, after many years of lagging behind Europe and Japan, the United States surged ahead between 1995 and 2005 with a rate of about 2.5 percent compared to 1.5 percent for Europe and about 2 percent for Japan. This was largely attributed to the cumulative effect of years of investment in and wide adoption of information technology equipment and services. No doubt that played an important part. But it is also true that the United States changed the way it counted productivity to what is called hedonic scoring. For example, let's say that Dell sold computers last year with 3,000 megahertz of computing power. Now let's say you buy this year's model at the same price but with 6,000 megahertz. In theory, at least, you can now work twice as fast or do twice as many things as last year. So did you buy one computer or two? The Europeans and Japanese would say you bought one. But the U.S. statistical authorities would say two, meaning that they statistically increase the actual number of computers produced to account for the greater power of the new machines. Of course, this makes Dell appear to be very productive, and it also makes computer users appear very productive. This is not a case of one side being right and the other wrong. You can argue either way. But what you can't do is claim that U.S. productivity growth is better than that of Europe or Japan on any meaningful apples-to-apples basis without making the adjustment for the different scoring. In fact, there is not much difference in productivity between the United States and other top countries like France. Furthermore, productivity varies dramatically among industries. For example, Japan's overall productivity is lower than that of America, but in export industries such as autos, consumer electronics, and machine tools, it is much higher. Thus, in terms of international competitiveness, America may be falling behind despite a possibly higher rate of growth of overall productivity. Where America clearly does rank behind is with regard to income equality.

The Gini index measures the extent of the difference with scores from 0 (everyone has the same income) to 1 (all the money is concentrated at the very top of the society). With a Gini score of 0.37, the United States ranks highest among the OECD countries, which have an average score of 0.29, while Sweden's is the lowest at 0.23. By way of reference, top-scoring Brazil and Mexico are around 0.45, putting the United States closer to them than to its OECD peers. In short, it seems that more of the money in the United States is held by a smaller group of very rich people than in other major countries. Indeed, the very top 0.1 percent of U.S. earners receives about 8 percent of the country's total income as compared to about 2 percent in countries like France and Japan. Recall also the much higher costs Americans pay for health care, double or more than in other leading countries, and approximately 15 percent of Americans do not have health care coverage.

The bottom line here is that for all our pride in being the "wealthiest nation on earth," we Americans do not generally enjoy as high a standard of living as the average citizen of Europe, Japan, and several other Asian countries. We are not nearly as rich as we think.

But the devil is always in the details, and to get a more specific understanding of the U.S. condition, we must look at the details of critical sections of our economy.

Infrastructure

A couple of years ago, I was in Seoul, South Korea, and had to travel on to the city of Busan, at the tip of the Korean peninsula. Having never had the opportunity to see the Korean countryside, I decided to take the train ride along the spine of the country. I was traveling, of course, on a bullet train and it proceeded so smoothly at about 200 miles per hour through the tunnels and around the mountains that nary a ripple disturbed the surface of the water in my glass. Why, I wondered, can't I have a train like this between Washington and New York? If I could, I would abandon the energy-inefficient air shuttle instantly.

I was tired from jet lag and tried to sleep, but the passenger across the aisle was driving me crazy with his constant cell phone chatter. I had to suppress a strong urge to grab the phone and stuff it down his throat. But then I realized that this was really amazing and interesting and that I should be taking notes instead of becoming irritated and angry. Why? Because we were in the mountains and continuously passing through long tunnels, and the speaker never lost the call. Unbelievable, I thought. When I call my wife while driving from Washington's Dulles airport, I am sure to lose the call several times. As for calling from the so-called high-speed Acela train (less than 100 mph) from Washington to New York—forgettaboutit. Finally, the guy shut up and I heaved a huge sigh of relief and settled back to try sleeping again. But there was no way. He had switched the phone to video and was watching his favorite soaps at top audio—all the way to Busan.

Tired as I was, I couldn't help being impressed. You couldn't do that in America.

In his recent proposals for revitalizing the U.S. economy, President Obama has called for plans to develop high-speed rail lines in dense population corridors of 500 miles or less such as between Washington and New York or Los Angeles and San Francisco. This is part of his effort to create green jobs while also taking steps to abate global warming. High-speed rail is a great idea because everyone knows that such trains are far more energy efficient, sparing of greenhouse gas emissions, comfortable, and speedy than cars or airplanes for those distances. In fact, it is such a good idea that Japan began building its Shinkansen bullet train network in 1964 and now has 1,360 miles of special track carrying 300 million passengers a year at average speeds of 188 mph. France initiated its Train à Grand Vitesse (TGV) in 1981 and now carries 100 million passengers annually over 1,180 miles of track at 199 mph. Germany didn't get started until 1988 but now carries 67 million riders over 798 miles of rail at 186 mph. Spain also has a similar network, and China, which started in 2007, now operates trains at 186 mph over 588 miles of high-speed track. It is building out its network so rapidly that by 2012 it will have the world's largest high-speed system. The only American entry to date is almost embarrassing. The Acela (made in Sweden and Canada) operates (when it works) between Washington and New York and Boston at top speeds of 125 mph. But the track is so poor that the speed on many stretches is under 70 mph and sometimes as slow as 20 mph. It carries only 11 million riders. To make things more embarrassing, the *South China Morning Post* of October 25, 2009, reported that the planned U.S. high-speed line from Los Angeles to Las Vegas would be supplied by the South China Locomotive Corp.

Okay, you say, but trains are so nineteenth century. Our forte is high tech. After all, who invented the internet and email, and Twitter, and Facebook? Us, right? Yes . . . but, in a way that just makes the present situation in the United States look worse. Ten years ago, America's internet was the world's most extensive, fastest, least expensive, and most heavily used. Today, the United States stands at number 15 in the international broadband rankings. Its broadband penetration is a little over half that of Korea, well behind the likes of Finland, Australia, and Canada, and just about the same as France, the UK, and Japan. Its average speed of 3.9 Mbps compares embarrassingly to the 63.6 Mbps of Japan, the 49.5 of Korea, the 17.6 of France, and even the 16 of Germany. As for the prices, a month of that blazing Japanese broadband will cost you $.13 per Mbps. In Korea, you'd pay $.37, in France it would be $.33, and in Germany $1.10. All much better deals than the $2.83 you'd have to pay for the snail-like speeds of American broadband.

This would be funny if it weren't so important. The U.S. lag here literally means that there are whole classes of work and research being done in Korea, Japan, and even France that simply can't be done in the United States. For example, to do normal telecommuting requires about 2.0 megabits per second. Fine, Americans can do that. But videostreaming and high-definition television over the network require 15 to 20 megabits per second. No sweat in Korea, Japan, and France, but no can do in America. So anybody developing products or services relating to high-definition TV or videostreaming has to go outside the United States to get the work done.

The situation is pretty much the same with regard to cell phones. The United States ranks forty-second in cell phone penetration, but even more significant is the fact that it has fewer than a million 3G (high-speed third-generation) subscribers as compared with more than 40 million in Japan and the 10 million in the EU. This isn't just a matter of consumer convenience. It means that new kinds of businesses and products, such as banking by phone, can be developed in those countries but not in America. Or it means they can do things faster and more efficiently than the Americans can. The bottom line is that lack of adequate high-tech infrastructure is seriously impairing America's ability to compete, and especially to compete in the very high-tech sectors upon which most Americans think the future of their children depends.

Nor is the picture much brighter in the realm of traditional infrastructure. The Minneapolis bridge that collapsed in August 2007 was just the tip of the iceberg. The American Society of Civil Engineers estimates that more than one in four of the nation's bridges are structurally deficient or functionally obsolete. It would take $17 billion annually to bring all the bridges back into safe operating condition, but only $10.5 billion is being budgeted and spent. Interestingly, despite this serious assessment and shortfall, the society gives our bridge infrastructure a passing grade of C. So imagine what the D grade for the aviation infrastructure means. If you wonder why your flights are always late, and delayed, and why U.S. airports always look and feel so awful when you return from the bright, airy halls of Singapore's Changi Airport or Hong Kong's Chek Lap Kok or Shanghai's Pudong International, now you know.

The shortfall in needed upgrade spending on U.S. aviation infrastructure over the next five years is estimated at $40.7 billion. Then there are the dams, or maybe I should say there might be the dams. They get a D, too. The Society puts the number of deficient U.S. dams at 4,000 with 1,819 in the high hazard category. Moreover, this number is rising rapidly as a result of the fact that the average age of the 85,000 dams in the United States is fifty-one years. The drinking water infrastructure is in even worse shape with a D– and an annual investment shortfall of $11 billion just to replace aging facilities that are now leaking 7 billion gallons of drinking water a day, never mind the growth in demand for drinking water over the next twenty years. But it's the roads that cost the real money. A third of major roads are in poor or mediocre condition, and 36 percent of major highways are badly congested at a traffic cost to the economy of $78.2 billion a year—$710 for every motorist. But the current spending of $70.3 billion annually for capital improvements is far below the $186 billion the Society estimates is needed. So roads earn a D– as well. Add to these a D+ for energy, D– for levees, D for hazardous waste, D– for inland waterways, D for schools, D for mass transit, D– for wastewater, and C+ for solid waste. The total five-year investment shortfall for all of these comes to $1.176 trillion.

Americans' Health

A key element of any measure of standard of living is health. You cannot enjoy your wealth if you are sick or dead. Here the U.S. performance is woefully inadequate. According to the CIA Fact Book estimates, the United States ranks number 50 among nations in terms of life expectancy at birth. The U.S. figure of 78.11 years puts it just ahead of Albania and Taiwan and far behind the 82.22 years of Japan, the 81.23 of Canada, the 80.98 of France, the 80.20 of Italy, the 79.26 of Germany, and the 78.72 of South Korea. Particularly embarrassing for the United States is the fact that a far lower percentage of its babies survive than in other leading countries. The U.S. infant mortality rate of 6.26 per 1,000 births puts it number 46 in the international rankings, just behind Cuba and Guam and far behind the 2.31 of world leader Singapore, the 2.79 of Japan, the 2.92 of Hong Kong, and the 3.33 of France. Yet even though they are less likely to survive as infants and even though they die earlier, Americans pay twice or more as much as other leading countries for their medical care. Singapore, for example, spends only about 3 percent of GDP on medical care, and France spends about 8 percent, while the United States is now spending about 17 percent. And unlike most other countries, America leaves about 15 percent of its people without medical care, except for what they can get as a last resort in hospital emergency rooms.

What America Does Not Make

As a kid I often traveled by train from Wilmington, Delaware, where I lived, to Philadelphia, where my dad worked. Along the way the trains passed through the then thriving manufacturing town of Chester, which had proudly painted a sign in the railway station proclaiming that "What Chester Makes Makes Chester." Today, Chester is a sad derelict of a city, sunk in poverty and languishing next to the broken-down shipyards and factories that closed long ago. Today, Chester doesn't make anything, and there isn't much left of Chester.

Unfortunately, Chester is a metaphor for the United States and a pointer to many of the reasons for the rotting of the country's infrastructure and the hollowness of its apparent wealth. Like Chester, America doesn't make much anymore. Specifically, it doesn't manufacture the vast range of consumer and industrial goods on which its wealth and power were originally built. Like Great Britain before it, America has turned to nontradable services, home construction, and finance to earn its living as its manufacturing has migrated to other climes.

Keep in mind that manufacturing accounts for about three-fourths of America's corporate Research and Development (R&D) and pays average wages 20 percent above those in service industries. Manufacturing also has a job multiplier of 4 to 5, meaning that each manufacturing job creates 4 to 5 other jobs in the economy, as compared to a services industry job multiplier of 1 to 1.5. Manufacturing jobs also offer above average health care and pension benefits. And the sector enjoys productivity gains one third above the national average. Even more important, it is the source of most of the economies of scale that are the real drivers of wealth accumulation. It is, thus, a very good thing to have a significant manufacturing sector in your economy if you can. Unfortunately, it increasingly seems that America can't.

From 24 percent of GDP in 1980, manufacturing has fallen by more than half to less than 12 percent of GDP today. To some extent this is a natural development as all developed countries tend to create larger service sectors as their economies mature. But the relative shrinkage of the U.S. manufacturing sector has been extreme in comparison to countries such as Japan (18.3 percent of GDP), Germany (22 percent), France (15 percent), and even the UK (13 percent). The U.S. decline has been particularly brutal in the past eight years, during which it has lost about a third (from 17 percent to 11.8 percent) of its share of GDP as 40,000 manufacturing plants closed their doors. For instance, the American steel industry that produced 97.4 million tons in 1999 managed to do only 91.5 million tons in 2008 even as Chinese production rose from 124 million to 500 million tons over the same period. Between 2000 and 2008, 270 major U.S. furniture factories closed as the industry lost 60 percent of its production capacity and the market share of imports rose from 38 percent to nearly 70 percent. The U.S. machine tool industry—the backbone of any industrial economy and essential to defense production—produced only $3.6 billion in equipment, less than 5 percent of world production, down 30 percent from 1998, and only about half of U.S. consumption. In contrast, Germany, Japan, and even Italy currently produce more machine tools than the United States. Chemical plants are another essential element of an industrial economy. In 2008, 80 major plants costing in excess of $1 billion were being constructed somewhere in the world. None of them was being constructed in the United States.

There are many reasons for this long-running trend. The one usually mentioned in popular commentary—inexpensive labor—is the least important. Of course, that has played a role, particularly in industries like apparel that are very labor intensive. But machine tools, steel, and chemical plants are not labor intensive, and developed countries like Japan, Germany, and France have managed to hang on to them. These industries are leaving or have left the United States because the dollar is being managed both in Asia and in America to be overvalued versus many pegged or only partially floating currencies like China's RMB and Taiwan's dollars. Imports of products from these countries are thus artificially cheaper than they would be under truly open-market conditions.

The second major reason is the tax holidays, capital grants, free infrastructure, labor wage agreements, and regulatory exemptions that many countries use to entice investment by targeted global companies and that the United States does not match. The third reason is political pressure from countries like China who make it clear that if a global company wants to do business there it had best demonstrate that it is a *friend* of China. The fourth reason is corporate tax rates. U.S. rates are the highest in the world except for Japan's. The fifth reason is onerous and complex U.S. regulatory procedures. A sixth reason is the difficult labor union–management situation in some U.S. industries. Pure cheap labor is usually (not always) the last reason. Thus, the key to global manufacturing dynamics lies much more in the realm of policy than in the realm of economic fundamentals.

These dynamics have resulted in the dramatic loss of manufacturing jobs and in a depression of manufacturing wages. U.S. manufacturing wages that once were tops in the world are now tenth, and if we compare at nominal exchange rates, U.S. wages rank sixteenth in the world. Worse is the fact that this drop in manufacturing employment and wages also depresses wages economywide.

Those National Institute of Standards and Technology chief economist Greg Tassey has labeled the *apostles of denial* among orthodox economists and commentators have maintained that this is nothing to get upset about and is just the natural evolution of a postindustrial economy. Analysts like Michael Porter of Harvard Business School and the Council on Competitiveness insist not only that the U.S. economy doesn't need manufacturing, but, indeed, that its decline is an indicator of success. Thus, in one council report, Porter insisted: "We have to stop this notion of believing that manufacturing is essential. Such thinking is a real problem." Between 1998 and 2007, that argument seemed plausible. First the dot-com bubble and then the housing bubble masked the deterioration of manufacturing. On top of that, Wall Street's share of GDP grew to match the lost manufacturing share. America, argued the orthodox apostles, was moving to "higher ground" where its future lay in innovation, high technology, and sophisticated service industries like medical diagnostics and treatment, design, and investment banking. Indeed, in recognition of this expected development, a special category of U.S. trade statistics—Trade in Advanced Technology Products—was designated in 1989 to demonstrate how nicely the United States was shifting to a high-tech economic structure.

For the next twelve years, as expected, Advanced Technology trade statistics showed a respectable (though not huge) surplus even as the deficit in the rest of U.S. manufacturing plunged to new depths. But then, in 2002, Advanced Technology swooned as well, with a deficit of $17 billion. By 2008, that had grown to $61 billion as the dynamics of decline in traditional manufacturing began to repeat themselves in high technology.

High Tech Imitates Low Tech

Just as no chemical plants are being built in the United States today, so only 2 percent of all new semiconductor fabrication facilities under construction in the world in 2007 were under construction in the

United States. Thirty percent were being built in China, 25 percent in Taiwan, and 22 percent in Korea. Japan, Korea, and Taiwan dominate the development and manufacture of the liquid crystal display (LCD) panels that have become the world's preferred viewing surface. China's BOE Technology Group and Korea's LG Display Co. have both announced they will locate new $3 billion–plus LCD factories in China, and Samsung Electronics said it is considering a similar move. There are no LCD plants in the United States.

America is also losing out in the latest generation (300mm) of the semiconductor wafers that eventually are sliced and diced into the chips that go into your computer. In 1999, 36 percent of global production of such wafers was in the United States. By 2004, that was down to 20 percent and today it is around 15 percent. Recently there has been much talk of "green industries and green jobs" as part of the recovery from the economic crisis. But there is only one American company among the world's top ten producers of photovoltaic cells. Germany's Q-Cells is the world's leading producer, while Japanese and Chinese producers each have about 30 percent of the global market. In the area of solar concentration and collection equipment, the Germans dominate.

Similarly, the only U.S. company among the ten largest in the wind energy industry is GE with a share of only about 16 percent of a world market that is dominated by Danish, Chinese, and German producers. As for batteries, a series of U.S. government grants was announced in August 2009, totaling $2 billion to boost research by several U.S. battery producers. But this looked less than impressive in the face of an announcement by Toyota that it was forming a consortium with Sanyo and Panasonic not only to develop but also to produce advanced batteries.

Even more discouraging for those who have long argued that America's salvation lies in its unique innovative capacity was a recent report by the Information Technology and Innovation Foundation, which ranked the United States dead last among leading countries in improvement in innovation capacity and only number 4 in absolute overall innovation capability.

A recent headline in *Manufacturing & Technology News* read "America's Oldest Printed Circuit Board Company Closes Its Doors." The story reports that after fifty-seven years, Bartlett Manufacturing Co. can't make it anymore. Ten years ago, U.S. makers accounted for 30 percent of the global market. Today, that is down to under 8 percent and with the demise of Bartlett it will be substantially less. In 2008, total U.S. PCB industry revenue fell to $4 billion, down from $11 billion in 2000. Over that same period, Asian output has climbed from 33 percent to more than 80 percent of the global total. Says Bartlett chairman Doug Bartlett: "The U.S. industry has been crippled beyond repair. Our kids are going to be fluffing dogs and doing toenails while the Chinese are making leading-edge devices." In this, Bartlett echoes the concerns we saw expressed earlier by former Intel chairman Craig Barrett.

What bothers Bartlett and Barrett is what triggered the Defense Science Board to report that: "Urgent action is recommended, as the industry (semiconductor) is likely to continue moving in a deleterious direction, resulting in significant exposure if not remedied." This only echoed the 2003 report of the Pentagon's Advisory Group on Electron Devices (AGED) that said U.S. technological leadership "is in decline" and warned that the offshore migration of semiconductor chip foundries "must be addressed" because it "will potentially slow the engine for economic growth." It further emphasized that the Department of Defense "faces shrinking advantages across ALL technology areas" and noted that as U.S. industry shifts its production offshore, it "assigns those nations political and military leverage over the United States." It urged that the U.S. government needed to counter the "massive financial and tax investments" being made by foreign governments to lure U.S. companies to relocate their production away from the United States. AGED chairman Thomas Hartwick told Congress that "the structure of the U.S. high-tech industry is coming unglued with innovation and design losing their tie to prototype fabrication and manufacturing." This broken link leaves inventions "on the cutting room floor because they cannot be manufactured." Hartwick concluded that if dramatic action is not taken the United States faces the "destruction of U.S. innovation centers."

In 2004, the President's Council of Advisors on Science and Technology (PCAST) sounded similar warnings, noting that the loss of production capacity will quickly be followed by loss of research, development, engineering, and design capability as well. Said the council: "The continuing shift of manufacturing to lower-cost regions, and especially to China, is beginning to pull high-end design and R&D capabilities out of the United States." It warned that the "research to manufacturing process is not sequential in a single direction, but results from an R&D-manufacturing *ecosystem* consisting of basic R&D, precompetitive development, prototyping, product development, and manufacturing" all operating in such a way that the "new ideas can be tested and discussed with those working on the ground. Thus, locations that possess both strong R&D and manufacturing capabilities have a competitive edge." PCAST warned emphatically that "key elements of the innovation ecosystem" are eroding rapidly and said that only dramatically different U.S. government policies could halt and reverse the erosion.

This warning was echoed again in 2006 by the National Academy of Sciences. Its report—"Rising Above the Gathering Storm"—said the United States can no longer afford research in areas like telecommunications because it has lost its ability to compete in commodity products. A final warning along these lines came in a 2009 analysis of the defense industrial base by University of Texas professor Michael Webber. His conclusion is that among the sixteen fundamental defense foundation industries, the U.S. position is seriously eroded in thirteen, holding steady in one, healthy in only two.

THE SERVICES MYTH

In the face of the decline of U.S. manufacturing and high tech, many economists, business leaders, and policy makers have embraced the notion that America's future lies in the service industries.

But the numbers just don't work. While it is true that the United States had a services trade surplus of about $140 billion in 2008, that made only a small dent in the goods deficit of $840 billion. To get anywhere near a trade balance, the services surplus would have to grow by more than five times. But it isn't growing at anything like that rate, which brings us to the second point. It is not at all clear that services won't also go the way of manufacturing and high tech. Aside from travel, the big American service industry has been finance. But, as I have said, that industry just blew itself up and is going to have to contract as a percent of GDP. The real trend here is that noted by former Federal Reserve board member and Princeton professor Alan Blinder, who has forecast that as many as 29 percent of all jobs could be off-shored over the next few years. On top of that are the numbers we already have in hand for job shifts taking place domestically. Over the past ten years there has been a massive loss of 8 million manufacturing jobs. That has been accompanied by substantial job creation in the services industries, but the bulk of the new jobs are in retailing and food service, which pay far less with far fewer benefits than manufacturing.

The big news in services is India, not America. I recently had a brain scan at Suburban Hospital in Bethesda, Maryland. The radiologist was reading the scan from his offices in Bangalore. The accounting firm that handles my taxes recently moved its whole back office to Bangalore. Reuters news has moved much of its editorial operations to Mumbai. When you make airline reservations, chances are you're talking to someone in a suburb of New Delhi, and that is definitely true when you call the help line for assistance in fixing your computer. Or let's look at a comparison of IT services firms. Infosys and Wipro of India both have sales of about $2 billion compared to $25 billion and $15 billion respectively for U.S.-based EDS and Computer Sciences Corp. The Indian companies have profit margins of more than 20 percent while the U.S. companies are in the 3 percent range.

In view of this, whose future do you think more likely lies in services? In June 2006, IBM said India's. It held a meeting with Wall Street analysts in Bangalore, where it announced adoption of the Indian offshore outsourcing business model, explaining that it believed the talent pool of India and other low-cost countries would continue to deepen. IBM said it would be investing $6 billion to expand its Indian operations. Its head count in India, which was 6,000 in 2003, is projected to hit 110,000 in 2010. This compares to a U.S. head count of 120,000 and falling. In 2007, Accenture outdid IBM by actually increasing its Indian head count beyond that of its U.S. operations.

KNOWLEDGE IS POWER—FOR THOSE WHO HAVE IT

Discussions of U.S. competitiveness always eventually get around to the notion that America has the best universities and the most and best R&D in the world, and that if we just maintain and extend that, everything will be all right. Okay, it's true that of the world's top twenty universities, seventeen are generally agreed to be in the United States. That is definitely a huge asset, but not as decisive as you may think. For one thing, it is increasingly the case that at the graduate level these institutions educate as many non-Americans as Americans. The proportion of all U.S. university doctoral degrees awarded to foreign students is now more than 40 percent, up from 35 percent in 1987. In the sciences, math, and engineering, that number is now close to 50 percent for all master's degrees and more than 50 percent for doctoral degrees. This would not be a matter of much concern if, as in 1987, more than 80 percent of those foreign students remained to work in the United States. But that is no longer the case. Today, more and more return home after receiving their degrees. Now, there is nothing wrong about educating foreign students. Indeed, it has many potential benefits. Nevertheless, the excellence of U.S. higher education is increasingly being used not to underpin the future development of the U.S. economy, but that of other economies.

An important reason for this is that U.S. secondary education is not so great. All the comparative international tests show American students of whatever grade level performing far below the top levels attained typically by such as the Japanese, Koreans, Finns, and French. Particularly disturbing is the fact that U.S. students who score in the respectable 85th percentile in science and in the 55th percentile in math in the fourth grade, have slipped to zero in science and the 10th percentile in math by the time they get to the twelfth grade. Thus, European and Asian students who come to even the best American high schools find themselves from one to two years ahead of their American classmates. But it's not just that American students are often a bit behind their foreign peers. It is also that they avoid going for degrees in science and math because they know the jobs probably won't be there. As one Santa Clara University professor told me recently, "Enrollment in engineering is falling by 30 percent a year because the kids have figured out that most of the jobs in those disciplines are going to be in Asia."

As for research, the 2.68 percent of GDP the United States is currently spending on R&D is less than the 2.83 percent it spent in 1963–67 when it had virtually no economic competition from other countries. From number 1 forty years ago, America has fallen to number 7 in R&D intensity behind the likes of Japan, Korea, and Sweden.

Further, the great research centers of the past—Bell Labs, IBM Watson Labs, Xerox Palo Alto Research Center—have either disappeared or been turned into product development operations. U.S. basic research today is mostly done in universities where it is much less coordinated and connected to the industrial world. Because of the size of its economy, the United States is, of course, by far the biggest spender in actual dollars. But the trends are creating a much more competitive environment to which the United States has yet to respond.

The Globalized University

Another cause for serious concern is the state of U.S. higher education, the long-running excellence of which is increasingly not underpinning the future development of the U.S. economy. One reason is that many leading American universities have gone global in the same sense that U.S. corporations have gone global. Indeed, we need to remember that the universities are also corporations. Like any corporation, they need revenue, and while they don't have to make a profit, they have limited borrowing power and thus must break even over time. Most universities were strapped even before the present crisis. Now they are more so. It turns out that foreign students are not only a source of revenue, they are the best source of revenue. They pay full fare. No need-based financial aid for them. Many of their governments are so anxious to get the benefit of U.S. higher education excellence that they not only pay the full room, board, and tuition, they also pay all of the students' travel and living expenses. Furthermore, the students are typically coming from the ranks of the top 0.5 percent of the students in their often very large countries, meaning that they are really, really smart. Think close-to-perfect SAT or Graduate Record scores. If you picked the class solely on the basis of test scores, you'd fill it almost entirely with foreign students. So here the universities have the opportunity to enroll a lot of extremely bright students, none of whom need financial aid. What would you do if you were a university president? Take a lot of them, right? So they do.

But beyond this is also another powerful factor. The university presidents think of themselves as true globalists with a mission to educate the world. Indeed, many have opened campuses in other countries and commute between their various international establishments just as the heads of IBM, Intel, and other global companies do. They pride themselves on being citizens of the world and think of themselves as having a fiduciary responsibility to their global students and funders rather than specifically to U.S. students. Like their corporate counterparts, they also tend to be very responsive to authoritarian governments.

A final point about education is that it's not necessarily all it's cracked up to be. India was long known for having a large educated population for which there were few appropriate jobs. It wasn't until new economic policies came along in the 1990s that these people turned productive. Henry Ford's auto workers weren't better educated in a formal sense than any other Americans. But they became more productive by dint of working in an environment that gave them good tools and organization and that taught them skills on the job. China's workers today are not on average as well educated as U.S. workers. But the jobs are moving to China because the corporations can up-skill them on the line and make them highly productive. By the same token, just because the jobs are moving to China or elsewhere, American workers are to a certain extent being down-skilled as they move to more menial work in retailing or food service.

The bottom line here is that there is also no special education-genie that is going to bring salvation to America.

RIVAL TECHNOLOGY TIGERS

It is of the utmost importance to understand the revolutionary nature of the shifts under way in today's global economy. We are accustomed to thinking that developing countries with a lot of inexpensive, unskilled labor will focus on production of labor-intensive goods like apparel, shoes, and toys while we dominate capital- and technology-intensive industries. It is true that India and China do control many of the labor-intensive industries. But because of their large populations, even a small percentage is a lot of people. These countries each have 50 million to perhaps 150 million people who are highly skilled. They can therefore also compete in the advanced industries as well as in the sophisticated services and R&D. Thus, while the U.S. share of global R&D is steadily shrinking, China's and India's are rising.

China now spends 1.5 percent of GDP on R&D and is steadily increasing that effort with the aim of matching the entire EU by 2010. Much of this is being driven by U.S. and other global companies who are putting major R&D facilities in these countries. Since 1999, foreign corporations have established 1,160 research institutions in China while also making major commitments in India. For example, GM, Intel, Pfizer, Microsoft, and GE, to name only a few, have all established major labs and research centers in both India and China. This is in addition to their large and growing investments in advanced production facilities. Particularly important in this context is the fact that most of those foreign students getting their PhDs at top U.S. universities are Indians and Chinese. On top of that, both countries are making a prodigious effort to increase their numbers of scientists and engineers.

What lends all this particular power is the impact of the internet and air express logistics by the likes of FedEx and UPS. Anything digital can be delivered from India or China to anywhere in the world in two seconds. And anything made of atoms and molecules can be delivered in thirty-six hours. For all practical purposes these new challengers are across the street.

Nor can we afford to continue to tut-tut about Europe and Eurosclerosis. We have already noted the EU's superiority in such areas as high-speed rail, internet service, and technology for solar- and wind-sourced energy. Europe is also the leader, along with Japan, in nuclear energy, and the French Ariane rocket has become the world's preferred launch vehicle for satellites. The EU is now on track to grant nearly twice as many PhDs in science and engineering as the United States after 2010, and it has formally adopted the target of surpassing U.S. R&D spending by aiming to achieve a level of 3 percent of GDP for future R&D support across the EU. Of course, some of its members, like Finland and Sweden, already far surpass that. More important than the numbers, however, is the recognition of reality. First, the EU—like India, China, Korea, Japan, and most other leading countries—has understood that a nation cannot maintain a high standard of living without a technology-based growth strategy. Second, it has recognized its weaknesses and set out to correct them and to surpass the United States.

In short, the age of effortless American supremacy is over.

APRIL 2020

To consider what the continuation of this loss of competitiveness might mean, let's fast-forward to a moment in the spring of 2020 for a plausible scenario of how our power and prosperity may have changed by then. U.S. troops are long gone from Iraq, and Baghdad has become a kind of satellite of Tehran's anti-American Shiite regime. U.S. and NATO forces have also been out of Afghanistan for several years, and the Taliban is once more in firm control, strictly enforcing both sharia law and a ban on poppy growing and opium trading. Pakistan has managed to keep its Taliban-allied tribes under control, but only by dint of support from China in the wake of the U.S. withdrawal of military and economic support back in 2010. The United States' Fifth Fleet remains in the Persian Gulf, but only thanks to an annual subsidy from the government of Saudi Arabia.

The Seventh Fleet abandoned its Japanese home port, Yokosuka, in favor of new moorings in San Diego and Pearl Harbor in 2015 after the Sixth Fleet returned to Hampton Roads from the Mediterranean in 2012. The remaining U.S. bases in Japan, Germany, and Korea were also closed after that, bringing to an end three-quarters of a century of occupation and peacekeeping. The fate that befell the Soviet empire in 1991 (and before it the British, Spanish, Dutch, Venetian, and Roman empires) has now befallen the quasi-U.S. empire as well. It has become overstretched and simply can no longer pay the bills at home while also maintaining far-flung global deployments.

The Great Recession that followed the 2008 financial crash caused a dramatic shrinkage of world trade and a halving of the U.S. external deficits. For a while, as cash-strapped homeless Americans cut their consumption and the price of oil fell from $140 to $40/barrel, the U.S. trade deficit fell and it seemed that a more balanced pattern of global growth might emerge from the crisis. Massive government public works spending and the slashing of interest rates by all major countries had managed to restart growth. But once that happened, the old pattern of accumulation of external deficits by the United States and of dollar surpluses by the Asian exporting countries, Germany, and the Middle East oil-producing countries repeated itself.

Meanwhile, U.S. federal budget deficits soared, topping 10 percent of GDP. Economic stimulus expenditures, health care costs, a surge of baby boomers taking their Social Security, and the need to subsidize cash-strapped California and a number of other state governments had pushed federal spending to what for America were the unprecedented heights of about 40 percent of GDP.

By 2013, U.S. public debt had topped 100 percent of GDP. Foreign dollar holdings were now more than $10 trillion; inflation was beginning to roar as Washington printed more and more money. This, of course, occurred as civil war in Nigeria and the near complete collapse of the mature Mexican oil fields dramatically reduced global oil supplies and sent prices soaring to nearly $200/barrel. The situation was exacerbated by the lingering drought connected to global warming that reduced world food supplies and sent food and other commodity prices soaring as well. Countries with big dollar holdings, like China, Japan, and Germany, had begun to get extremely nervous about the growing likelihood that the value of their dollar reserves would be inflated away. For this reason, they had begun to conclude deals among themselves in nondollar currencies, thereby further reducing the value of the dollar, the U.S. standard of living, and the ability of the United States to remain the dominant power.

Then the Persian Gulf oil producers, led by Saudi Arabia, had announced they would no longer accept dollars for oil. Instead they wanted euros or yen or RMBs or Canadian dollars or Swiss francs or combinations of the above in exchange for a barrel of oil. The Asian exporting countries had quickly followed suit, and that had put the United States in a wholly new, humiliating, and extremely challenging position. It could not sustain its foreign deployments if it could not pay with dollars. Washington approached its allies for assistance, arguing that U.S. forward deployments were in the interest of friends like Germany, Japan, and Korea.

The negative response came as a surprise and a shock. But years of U.S. unilateralism had alienated even its closest friends. So America had to face the hard, cold fact that it was no longer a superpower, but only one of several powers that included China, India, the EU, Russia, and Japan.

The British had had a similar experience when they were forced to withdraw their forces and support from much of the Mediterranean in the 1940s because they simply could no longer pay the bills. Especially in 1956, Britain had been forced to withdraw from its occupation of the Suez Canal (in response to its nationalization by Egypt) when Washington threatened to dump the pound sterling on international markets, a move that would have bankrupted the UK. Now it was America's turn.

That scenario may seem extreme, but the point is whereas five years ago it would have been unthinkable, today it is not completely out of the question. Note that even in this time of the Great Recession, the United States runs a trade/current account deficit of more than $500 billion annually. This has to be financed by inflows of capital from China, Japan, Saudi Arabia, and other foreign lenders. Just to keep running smoothly and normally, the U.S. economy must have a net inflow of foreign capital of about $2 billion every single day of the year. But since some foreign and domestic capital also leaves the country, that means that there must be a gross inflow of foreign capital of $5 billion per day. Just a small decrease in that flow could result in skyrocketing interest rates and crippling of the U.S. economy.

So how did the United States morph from the world's dominant economic, industrial, technological, financial, diplomatic, and military power into a nation no longer in control of its own fate? And how can it regain its competitiveness and secure a powerful, if not so dominant, role in the new era that is breaking rapidly upon us? To answer those two questions is the mission of the rest of the book. But here is a summary of key points.

OUR OVERSTRETCHED ECONOMY

Six false doctrines have combined to put us in this dramatically weakened position. By far the most important has been our fixation on our geopolitical interests at the expense of our economic interests. In addition, consumerism, market fundamentalism, simplistic free-trade globalization, globalization of corporations, and our unquenchable thirst for cheap oil have all contributed mightily.

Buy-Buy-Buy

After 9/11 and again during the war to depose Saddam Hussein in Iraq, President George W. Bush called on Americans to support their economy by shopping and consuming more. This exhortation was in glaring contrast to the calls of other presidents during previous wars—for citizens to save more and buy more government bonds to help finance the wars—and thus dramatically signaled a fundamental shift in the U.S. economy over the past half century. Consumption has not only displaced investment as the main driver of U.S. economic growth. It has become virtually the sole driver.

By the early years of this century, the American household savings rate turned negative. It has rebounded a bit in the wake of the recent economic crisis, but household debt is still much too high. And, of course, the government's debt is a runaway train. This is not a recipe for competitiveness or for securing a good long-term standard of living when countries like China, Singapore, and Germany are saving from 25 percent to 50 percent of GDP and investing heavily in the latest infrastructure and technology while producing far more than they consume and earning more than they spend.

Market Fundamentalism

As I will demonstrate in this book, much of our current dilemma stems from the 1980s embrace by U.S. leadership of what financier George Soros has called "market fundamentalism." Ronald Reagan rode to the White House by repeating, "Government is not the solution to our problem; government is the problem."

This slogan had a foundation in the new academic theory of "rational expectations" and the efficacy of the unfettered market, which held that market participants consistently act rationally and that prices reflect the rational expectations of all market participants and are based on perfect information about what the prices should be. According to this thinking, the market can never be wrong over any extended period, and if it does become overheated, it will always adjust itself back to the appropriate level. Government intervention should be totally done away with as it distorts the smooth working of this self-adjusting market mechanism and does more harm than good.

The widespread acceptance of this philosophy led to substantial deregulation of markets and industries and a virtually religious taboo against anything that might smack of government management of business through an industrial policy. The spirit of the orthodoxy was captured by a popular economic aphorism at the time: "Potato chips, computer chips, what's the difference? They're all chips." Taken to the extreme, this argument was also used to justify the deregulation and diminished oversight of financial markets under the Federal Reserve chairmanship of Alan Greenspan, who devoutly believed that "the self-interest of lending institutions would lead them to protect shareholders' equity" and to police themselves through self-regulation. The 2008 financial crisis has revealed just how flawed this argument was.

Simple Unreciprocal Free Trade

Another key factor in undermining U.S. economic strength has been the similarly orthodox allegiance to unilateral free trade. This took hold in the wake of World War II. With U.S. industry emerging from the war as top dog in virtually every field, U.S. businesses, which previously benefited from high tariffs on imports, now wanted free trade. They came to believe that it was a sure route to continued dominance. The doctrine argued for an appealing win-win scenario whereby the United States opening up its markets would lead to both greater prosperity for America and recovery for Europe and Japan.

As it had been for Great Britain in the nineteenth century, the doctrine was now especially attractive to the United States. Essentially the doctrine holds that every country—based on its natural resources, the level of its technology base, and the skill of its workers—will produce some products or services better and more efficiently than others. So countries should concentrate on producing the goods they make best and trade with other countries for the rest. Under the assumptions underpinning the doctrine, this kind of trade leads automatically to the optimal level of production and consumption for each trading partner and also leads to the optimal levels for the global economy overall. A potential concern was that U.S. trading partners did not reciprocally open up their markets, but economists offered analysis that showed that this should not be a worry. Even if some trading partners decide not to play and instead protect their markets, the others are still better off by keeping their markets open and importing from the nonplayers. For a country with a wide variety of market-leading industries, which was also bent on fostering global recovery and attracting allies, this was a doctrine sent from heaven—as some of its proponents literally argued.

Although it at first seemed to work well and helped engender a so-called Golden Era of global growth from 1950 to 1975, the trade environment became increasingly problematic thereafter. U.S. trade went into deeper and deeper deficit, and many U.S. industries began to be displaced by imports with consequent unemployment and dislocations. But in the face of these developments, for reasons that I will explore—and refute—economists and policy makers continued to insist on the superiority of the U.S. open market strategy. The U.S. market remained relatively open to foreign imports while the foreign markets were relatively closed to U.S. exports. The eventual result was the loss of global market share by American producers and the offshoring of a great deal of American production overseas. This has resulted in more and more companies feeling less and less responsibility to their local communities and to the health of the American economy, with U.S. workers bearing the brunt of these developments. The effect on the overall U.S. economy is a matter of great dispute, and a key mission of this book is to resolve that dispute by showing how flawed the free-trade orthodoxy is in light of real-world conditions versus the idealized assumptions the theory is based on.

Sovereign Companies

As I noted in the introduction, in the 1950s General Motors former chairman Charles "Engine Charlie" Wilson famously said that he always thought that "what is good for the country is good for General Motors and vice versa." Although he was criticized for the remark, at that time, he was largely correct. American companies produced in America and exported abroad. If they increased production as companies, the GDP of the country also rose, and if U.S. demand increased, so did the domestic production of the companies. It was correct to think of the fate of U.S. companies and the fate of the U.S. economy as being tightly linked. Moreover, American CEOs tended to think that they needed to respond to all stakeholders in a company's fortunes, not just to shareholders, and to have an obligation to the welfare of the local community and the country as a whole. Also, as a result of close collaboration with the government during World War II, they tended to have a highly developed spirit of patriotism, viewing the government as a partner rather than as an adversary. These CEOs were rightly seen as champions of American competitiveness.

The situation has changed dramatically over the past several decades as a new shareholder-oriented management philosophy took hold. Globalization has also played a role. U.S. corporations have become multinational, with not only production but also R&D all over the globe. They can thrive regardless of the performance of the United States. Moreover, the CEOs believe they have a dominant fiduciary responsibility to shareholders and feel themselves to be under no particular obligation to their local communities or to the country. They may feel such an obligation as individuals, but not as CEOs. Moreover, as heads of companies with operations in many countries, they must respond to the policies and pressures of those societies as well as to those of the United States. Indeed, one perverse aspect of globalization is that while American CEOs and corporations are big players in U.S. politics, they are supplicants in authoritarian societies like China. Thus, they are often more responsive to the wishes of the authoritarian countries than to those of the democratic countries, and they often act as representatives of foreign interests in lobbying Washington. Their advice must be understood as in the primary interest of their corporations and as little beholden to national allegiance.

Energy: Cheap Is Expensive

As early as 1943 Secretary of the Interior Harold Ickes wrote, "We're Running Out of Oil." In 1948, America became a net oil importer and energy dependent for the first time since the initial arrival of settlers in Jamestown in 1607. The Interior Department proposed a $10 billion project to develop synthetic oil from Rocky Mountain shale. But the effort was quickly abandoned in the face of the ready availability of inexpensive oil from abroad. This cycle of concern, alternative energy project proposals, and retreat in the face of cheap oil imports has been repeated over and over again during the past sixty years. At the completion of each cycle the United States has become more dependent on imports, has accumulated a bigger trade deficit, and has sent more dollars to oil producers, of whom some are friendly but many are unfriendly. In either case, some of those dollars eventually find their way to al-Qaeda and other organizations whose sole mission in life is to kill Americans.

So the American oil addiction is financing America's bitterest enemies while also increasing the U.S. national debt, fouling the environment, exacerbating global warming, and ultimately diminishing U.S. welfare. This is not to mention the young American troops who become casualties in wars ultimately connected to oil. All this we do in the name of cheap energy. But with the Dutch, perhaps we should ask, "How expensive can cheap be?"

In his 1980s bestseller *The Rise and Fall of the Great Powers*, the historian Paul Kennedy notes that each of the three former great powers—Rome, Spain, and Great Britain—had created costly military forces and taken on far-flung geopolitical obligations even as they allowed their economic power to decline. Eventually they couldn't afford their empires, armies, and obligations, even many obligations to their own people. As Kennedy puts it, these empires were suffering from "Over-Stretch" and from it they collapsed.

As I have indicated, America today is seriously over-stretched. Indeed, we are in the odd position of actually paying our clients for the privilege of defending them or of borrowing from them to pay for that defense. We are protected for the moment by the unique role of the dollar, but this cannot last forever; it may not even last for another decade.

It is clear that if we are to avoid the fate of prior dominant world powers, we must quickly change many of our ways, as I shall discuss in my last chapter. Here I should like to make just one key point about the role of government. We need to stop kidding ourselves with the notion that government intervenes minimally in our economy. The fact is that government has and always will have a large role in it. Our problem is that while our government does play a large role, it does so without having sensible economic or industrial strategy to guide and control it. Our forefathers had just such a strategy, one brilliantly conceived. We need to reread our own history, and that is where the rest of this book will begin.

2

The Real Story of How America Got Rich

Manufactures are now as necessary to our independence as to our comfort.

—THOMAS JEFFERSON

Thank God I am not a free trader.

—THEODORE ROOSEVELT

The question of the best approach for growing the U.S. economy and how it should globalize is far from new. Indeed, it was the most burning issue confronting the founders immediately after the country's birth. Before their independence, Great Britain actively prevented its American colonies from pursuing industrial and commercial development, limiting them to supplying agricultural products, timber, and raw materials. After independence, the new nation's pressing question was whether it should imitate its former colonial master and attempt to participate in the Industrial Revolution that Britain was then leading or remain primarily an agricultural producer. The issue was hotly debated for a generation after independence, and the result was a hybrid system leaning toward the model that would bring the British empire to its glory: even more, it closely resembled the export-led growth model of today's China. Called the American system, it consisted of government policies and programs aimed at developing advanced infrastructure and protecting and subsidizing development of intellectual property and manufacturing industries. This, of course, was antithetical to the free-market, laissez-faire policies about to be adopted by Great Britain. But America was aiming to catch up and eventually surpass Britain. This sparked a century of competition between the world economic and military hegemon and the rising new power. Burdened by global wars and responsibilities, and blinded by increasingly outmoded doctrines, Britain eventually had to give way to the surging American productivity and power.

THE DEVELOPMENT OF THE AMERICAN SYSTEM

Central in the debate over this growth model was the issue of trade policy, which was also a hot topic in Britain, where the relative advantages of a free-trade strategy versus the protectionist mercantilism it had long practiced were being discussed. With the ratification of the U.S. Constitution in 1788, all tariffs on trade between the states were abolished, and the value of removing those state barriers to trade was widely accepted. Whether the country should also open up to free trade with foreign competitors was quite another matter. As those in England—where Adam Smith in his *Wealth of Nations* had made the argument for free trade the same year the colonies asserted their independence, 1776—the leaders of the new nation were deeply troubled about whether to abolish protective tariffs, in large part because they had proven so effective.

Today's widely accepted notion that Britain became the first industrial nation and the dominant power of the eighteenth and nineteenth centuries as a result of open markets and liberal, free-trade policies is a myth. Nothing could be further from the truth. That small island nation became a hegemonic power through unrelenting application of an aggressive, export-driven, protectionist growth model over a period of nearly four hundred years, starting with the reign of Henry VII late in the fifteenth century. Having spent his childhood in Burgundy, Henry had observed how that region had become affluent from the production of woolen textiles, and also that, ironically, the wool for the textiles came from England. He decided that England was in the wrong end of the business; it should be the leading maker of wool-based products. His solution was what came to be called mercantilism; today we often refer to it as the "catch-up" or "export-led" growth strategy.

Export duties were imposed on wool leaving England, to reduce the level of exporting, while tax relief was extended to start-up woolens manufacturers, who were also granted monopolies for periods of a few years in particular cities or provinces. In addition, efforts were made to induce craftsmen and entrepreneurs from Holland and Italy to come ply their trades in England. As English manufacturing capacity grew, the export duties were raised until England had sufficient capacity to process all of the wool it produced. Eventually, in 1587, Queen Elizabeth I embargoed all raw wool exports from England, thereby imposing what came to be called the Tudor Plan. Many historians have noted that this industrial policy of the Tudors laid the foundation for England's later greatness as it systematically sought to establish and maximize additional industrial sectors domestically. For several hundred years, the policy was simple: where possible, achieve a monopoly on the production of goods; where necessary, import the raw materials for doing so; and suppress imports of competing goods from foreign or colonial competitors.

The Navigation Acts were a major element of this strategy. Laws restricting shipping to England in various ways had been passed since 1381; in 1651, the first comprehensive Navigation Act was passed as a direct strike at the Dutch. It banned foreign ships from transporting goods from outside Europe to England and further banned ships of third parties from transporting goods from anywhere in Europe to England. Later versions of the act required all shipments to or from the colonies to pass through England. In addition, special duties were added to items such as molasses that came from non-English colonies as opposed to English colonies. In short, every possible means was applied to ensure that British ships carried as much of the world's trade as possible.

By the same token, every effort was made to ensure that the world's manufactured goods came from England. The spirit of this effort was well captured in the king's address to Parliament of 1721, which emphasized that "it is evident that nothing so much contributes to promote the public well-being as the exportation of manufactured goods and the importation of foreign raw material."

As in the case of shipping, a series of acts was introduced to assure the supremacy of English manufactures. Export of India's superior cotton calicoes was banned (by the ruling British colonial authorities) in order to promote export of English cottons. Tariffs were imposed on imported manufactured goods while manufactured exports were subsidized. The Wool Act banned the export of woolen cloth from the colonies to other countries. Other acts prohibited production of hats and finished iron products in the colonies. At the same time, subsidies were made available to promote the colonies' export of raw materials such as hemp, timber, and tobacco. Thus was every effort bent to create a global economic structure in which the rest of the world supplied inexpensive raw materials to England, while it monopolized the most profitable "high-tech" industries.

The key trigger of the Industrial Revolution, and the factor that made Great Britain its leader, was the dramatic increase of British exports. Between 1700 and 1750 Britain's home industries increased their output by 7 percent while export industries expanded by 76 percent. As E. J. Hobsbawm notes: "the country which succeeded in monopolizing the export markets of a large part of the world in a brief period of time, could expand its export industries at a rate that made industrial revolution not only possible but virtually compulsory."

A key factor in this achievement was British military might. Of the five great wars of the eighteenth century, Britain was on the offensive in four, and as a result had by 1815 a virtual monopoly on overseas colonies, worldwide naval power, and industrial production. The myth that England's supremacy was due to an entirely different strategy of free trade arose from the writings and later influence of Adam Smith, who founded Anglo-Saxon economics. Smith predicted that the mercantilist system would eventually become obsolete for Britain. He conceded that without it many British industries would not have gotten off the ground. But now that most English industries had become competitive, he argued, the subsidies, protection, and grants of monopoly afforded them were becoming counterproductive. They were encouraging complacency and inefficiency as corrupt inside payments and monopoly price gouging replaced innovation, industriousness, and diligence as the source of riches. The inefficiency, waste, and corruption that were proliferating in the system because of the increasing lack of competition and absence of market forces would surely lead to Britain's eventual decline. Therefore, he advised the removal of restrictions and subsidies, as well as minimal government intervention and a strategy of more open and competitive markets.

In this open market system, the individual's pursuit of his/her own profit would be the engine of growth, a powerful force that would maximize the welfare of the whole society as well as that of individuals through the intermediation of the famous "unseen hand" of the market. In other words, the economy would automatically tend to produce optimal results if it were simply left to be driven by market forces instead of by government intervention.

Because Britain was at that time the dominant world power and producer, Smith was not much concerned about competition from foreign rivals. Indeed, he portrayed a new world trading order, calling for countries to specialize in production so that each national participant in the world economy could concentrate on doing what it did best. His focus was on the immediate maximization of welfare, through increasing individuals' consumption of goods, rather than on long-term planning. A fundamental premise of his argument was that the sole purpose of production should be consumption, not the building of industrial strength. Here, though, he added an important proviso, one often overlooked by his later laissez-faire followers. He emphasized that "defense is more important than opulence" and noted that only a manufacturing country can win a war. This suggests that he did favor some government promotion of manufacturing. In this context he also praised the role of the protectionist Navigation Acts. But generally his focus was very much on the needs of the consumer and not on lending support to producers. The book was thus a powerful argument for a new kind of individualistic consumer-oriented market economics.

Less often considered are Smith's views on trade. He called for a new kind of complementary international trade structure in which each country would produce not only what it did best, but also trade for other goods rather than treating its trading partners as rivals to be imitated. Thus, for example, he argued that America should not enter into manufacturing but should rather supply raw materials to the superior British manufacturers. Tariffs on imports should be done away with in order to optimize the free flow of goods. While British manufacturers agreed with Smith about the United States staying out of manufacturing, his call for free trade and the abolition of tariffs did not, at first, gain similar traction. But as Britain's industrial dominance increased and became more apparent in the early decades of the nineteenth century, Smith's influence grew, resulting in a dramatic shift in British thinking that would ultimately help to undermine the nation's economic might. In the nascent United States, Smith's ideas were well known and heatedly debated by the founders. Some, led by Thomas Jefferson, embraced Smith's views; others, led by Alexander Hamilton, rejected them and favored imitating Britain's mercantilist approach to industrialization.

The Jefferson faction argued that property and wealth were and always had been the cornerstones of political power and that, therefore, if the new U.S. government was to establish a new politics more reflective of the will of the people, a relative equality of economic circumstances must be established. In order to do so, the economic power of the yeoman farmers should be enhanced, which would result in a political majority that would block the rise of any tyrannical elite. Reinforcing this check on tyranny would be powerful state legislatures, who could hold their own against a power-grasping Congress.

The beauty of the country's situation was that America offered a near-perfect opportunity for the realization of this vision. Land for farming was virtually inexhaustible. It was inconvenient that the Indians thought the land was theirs, but once they had been made to understand the white man's reasoning, the government could make an equitable distribution of it, and a national economy built on the prosperity of freeholding farmers would be created.

In Jefferson's formulation, the new American economy would be agriculturally based and the country would be best off trading freely for manufactured goods with outside producers. Thus Jefferson and his compatriots, including James Madison, Tom Paine, and Benjamin Franklin, were largely in accord with Smith's notions of specialization and free trade. Paine early described free trade as an engine of peace, a view that has echoed frequently in both British and American history. "Our plan," he wrote, "is for commerce, and that, well attended to, will secure us peace and the friendship of Europe." Franklin was not necessarily wed to the agrarian republican vision of Jefferson, but he did strongly embrace Smith's concept of open trade, arguing that "free trade never ruined any nation." Franklin's understanding of free trade was, however, what we would today call reciprocity, or "fair trade," with all players doing away with protectionism.

On the other side of the debate, Alexander Hamilton, with important support from George Washington, argued that the new nation needed a strong central government based on a firm financial foundation which should foster the growth of manufacturing industries. This would not only be the superior route to economic growth but also would provide for the national defense. Asserting that "a nation cannot long exist without revenue," he early called for a tariff on imports that would both finance the state and provide incentives to local manufactures.

One of Hamilton's first acts after he was appointed Secretary of the Treasury by Washington in 1789 was to propose a 9 percent general tariff, which was duly passed and signed into law on July 4, 1789. Though a plantation owner like Jefferson, Washington felt strongly that the new America needed a vigorous manufacturing base, an attitude that undoubtedly reflected his bitter experience during the Revolutionary War when the American army lacked cannon, clothing, and shoes. Thus in his first annual message, on January 8, 1790, he emphasized that a "free people ought not only to be armed but disciplined; and their safety and interest require that they should promote such manufactories as tend to render them independent of others for essential, particularly military, supplies."

By way of example, Washington ordered an American-made suit for his inauguration and stated that he consumed no ale or cheese "but such as is made in America." Thus, the father of his country underlined that the government had a responsibility to promote and buy domestic goods. Accordingly he promised the Delaware Society for Promoting Domestic Manufactures "to demonstrate the sincerity of my opinion by the uniformity of my practice, in giving preference to the produce and fabrics of America."

Vital in the support of American industry was Article I, section 8 of the U.S. Constitution, which states that "Congress shall have power ... To promote the progress of science and useful arts, by securing for limited times to authors and inventors the exclusive right to their respective writings and discoveries." This article was put into practice by the Patent Act of 1790; it was followed by Hamilton's *Report on Manufactures* in December 1791, which called for high tariffs to protect nascent American industry. The act also offered support for agriculture in order to encourage more exports and emphasized the establishment of patents to encourage and protect inventions. The report also called for Buy American policies to ensure a favorable balance of trade until domestically manufactured goods achieved the quality demanded by overseas markets. Finally, it foresaw allocation of substantial federal funds for the building of roads, bridges, canals, and harbors to facilitate both internal and external commerce. Hamilton was following the English mercantilist model closely.

Free trade, Hamilton argued, would be devastating to the young country's economy. With Britain using the Navigation Acts and a variety of tariffs and subsidies to favor its industries, the practical result of an American free-trade policy would be continued British dominance of all the leading-edge, rapidly developing new businesses. Things might be different if Britain changed its policies. "If the system of perfect liberty to industry and commerce were the prevailing system of nations," said Hamilton, "the arguments against a program of manufactures would have great force." But in the absence of equal treatment and reciprocity, the United States could become a "victim of the system" and be led into "a state of impoverishment." Hamilton also believed that in the long run a diversified economy would be more likely to grow rapidly and productively than would a narrowly specialized agricultural economy.

Hamilton countered the argument of free traders that tariffs would increase costs to consumers by noting that "the fact does not universally correspond with the theory. A reduction of prices has in several instances immediately succeeded the establishment of a domestic manufacture." Further, once established, a domestic manufacture "invariably becomes cheaper, being free from the heavy charges which attend the importation of foreign commodities." Thus, he argued that "a temporary enhancement of price must always be well compensated by a permanent reduction of it." In this way, Hamilton articulated what has since come to be known as the "infant industry" theory.

The debate over these issues continued in fits and starts for the next twenty years. However sympathethic he was with Hamilton's overall perspective, Washington recognized that, in view of the power of the Jefferson faction, some of Hamilton's proposals were politically premature and so he held back on enacting many of them. When Jefferson was elected president in 1801, the policy shifted toward his ideal of agrarianism. Eventually, however, a number of key developments brought about the hybrid mercantilist system that characterized the American economy from then until the end of World War II.

One important event was Eli Whitney's invention of the cotton gin in 1793, for which he duly received a patent under the strong new patent laws passed in 1794. While the cotton gin was revolutionizing the American economy, Whitney became bogged down in endless legal challenges to his patent and nearly went bankrupt. Eventually, however, he managed to finance the winning of his case with a government contract for the production of 10,000 muskets. In the course of fulfilling the contract he also developed the concept of interchangeable parts that, used in combination with power machinery and specialized labor, revolutionized production and became known as the "American System of Manufacturing" as it spread around the world. This system was perhaps the first example of how government contracting in combination with private enterprise could be used to spur innovation and productivity growth.

Another key factor was that British manufacturers began dumping their products at far below cost into the American market, a tactical maneuver to prevent U.S. manufactures from gaining ground. The British navy had also started boarding U.S. merchant ships and impressing their sailors into service. Objections to these practices precipitated the War of 1812, and the war glaringly demonstrated the limitations of the American economy in defending against major powers with strong manufacturing industries. As a result, Jefferson did an about-face, noting that the war experience had taught him "that manufactures are now as necessary to our independence as to our comfort." He promoted Buy American thinking and challenged free traders to "keep pace with me in purchasing nothing foreign where an equivalent of domestic fabric can be obtained without regard to difference of price." Other leaders, such as Madison, Monroe, John Adams, and his son John Quincy Adams, echoed Jefferson, and in 1816 the first really protective tariffs were imposed by Congress with a 30 percent duty on iron imports and 25 percent on cotton and woolens.

As president, in 1822 Monroe called for more tariff increases, noting that "whatever may be the abstract doctrine in favor of unrestricted commerce, that doctrine rests on two conditions—international peace and general reciprocity—which have never occurred and cannot be expected." Leaders of another more populist and agrarian faction of the Democratic Party, who might have been expected to take a different view, also agreed. Despite his being from the cotton-exporting state of South Carolina, John C. Calhoun called in 1816 for a tariff on cotton goods. And Andrew Jackson commented in the wake of the war he contributed so much to winning that "we have been too long subject to the policy of the British merchants. It is time we should become a little more Americanized, and instead of feeding the paupers and laborers of Europe, feed our own, or else in a short time, by continuing our present policy [of laissez-faire] we shall all be paupers ourselves."

At the same time, journalists and political economists took a more critical look at the teachings of Adam Smith and his *Wealth of Nations*. Among the most influential of these was Daniel Raymond, who was recognized as the "first systemic American economist." Raymond opposed Smith's preoccupation with the wealth of individuals, arguing that political and economic leaders should focus on the welfare of the nation and the overall society. He criticized Smith's notion that consumers should buy imports when they are cheaper than domestic products because he saw such buying as "destroying the unity of the nation by dividing it into classes and looking to the interests of individuals, instead of looking to the interests of the whole." Raymond further argued that individuals "ought not to be allowed to afford patronage and support to the industry of foreigners, when their own fellow-citizens were in want." Unlike later-day economists, Raymond did not assume that the winners from trade in the country would compensate the losers, or that a society was better off overall as long as trade produced net gains even if the gains were monopolized by a very few at the top of the society.

Thus, a new consensus emerged on the need for the development of what became known as the American System, a concept best articulated and promoted by Congressman Henry Clay of Kentucky. It called for free trade only in cases of "perfect reciprocity"; protection and subsidization of America's infant manufacturing industries; extensive government-led development of national roads, waterways, railroads, and other infrastructure; expansion of the country's borders; removal of the Indians; and settlement and development of the land. In particular, tariffs were not seen as a device for taxing consumers for the benefit of manufacturers. Rather, it was believed that tariffs would stimulate investment in the United States and eventually allow Americans to produce articles much cheaper than they could be procured abroad, by capitalizing on the economies of scale that would result from substantial population growth, thereby benefiting both American producers and consumers.

In response to President Monroe's request, Congress raised tariffs in 1824 and then raised them again in 1828 with the so-called Tariff of Abominations under which rates on dutiable goods rose to 61.7 percent, above even those that would later be imposed under the notorious 1930 Smoot-Hawley Tariff Act, so often blamed for worsening the Great Depression. Over the next few decades, tariffs declined from these punitive rates but were then raised again sharply during the Civil War at the behest of Abraham Lincoln, who might be called the Great Protector as well as the Great Emancipator. Lincoln wholeheartedly embraced Clay's American System thinking and argued that "the abandonment of the protective policy . . . must produce want and ruin among our people." From the Civil War until World War I, U.S. tariffs never fell below a 40 percent rate as leaders such as Theodore Roosevelt emphasized their support of the catch-up effort by saying "Thank God I am not a free trader."

Infrastructure and Industrial Policy

A crucial element of the American System was government backing of critical infrastructure and strategic industries. The first of these was the National, or Cumberland, Road. Begun in 1806, it created a paved connection from Cumberland, Maryland, to St. Louis, enabling travel from the Potomac River to the Mississippi River in four days. Another important early project was the Erie Canal, completed in October 1825, and a quick and huge success. The construction debt was paid off in twelve years, as the U.S. GDP doubled and New York became a world commercial and financial center.

By far the most important project of the American System catch-up program, though, was the Transcontinental Railroad. In 1850, Congress authorized land grants to the states of Illinois, Mississippi, and Alabama for construction of a rail line connecting Chicago to Mobile. By 1857, grants totaling 21 million acres had turned several railroad companies into America's first truly big businesses. Then, in the summer of 1862, Abraham Lincoln pushed through Congress the Pacific Railroad Act, which called for the chartering of two separate companies—the Central Pacific and the Union Pacific—to lay tracks from the Missouri River to Sacramento. After much delay and stupendous feats of engineering, the Central Pacific's engine Jupiter and the Union Pacific's engine 119 stood nose to nose on May 10, 1869, at Promontory Summit, Utah. The nation was tied together, coast to coast, by a ribbon of steel. Amazingly, although the government had loaned the companies more than $64 million, it earned more than $103 million in return and did so by the end of 1869. More significantly, the railroad led to the creation of huge new markets and cities and transformed the country into a true continental powerhouse of a nation.

Technology and Education

The promotion of technological innovation was also vital. On July 4, 1836, Congress passed a law creating the U.S. Patent Office with a commissioner of patents established within the State Department. An early beneficiary of this new office was a former professor of painting and sculpture at New York University, one Samuel F. B. Morse, who received a $30,000 congressional appropriation for an experimental telegraph line. Other inventions, like the sewing machine, the reaper, and the Colt revolver, were developed with strong government encouragement and protection.

Inextricably linked with the push for innovation was support for higher education. Jefferson had presented to Congress a proposal for a nationwide network of colleges to be built on land donated by the federal government, but it wasn't until Congressman Justin Morrill proposed a bill granting the states 5.8 million acres of federal land to be used for colleges, signed into law in July 1862 by Abraham Lincoln at the height of the Civil War, that the idea came to fruition. The land grant colleges (most of the state universities) founded due to the act revolutionized American education.

All of these measures worked together to produce unprecedented economic growth. Between 1820 and 1870, U.S. GDP increased tenfold as America's became the world's first "miracle" economy.

The Effect of Britain Switching to Laissez-faire

The wisdom of the crafting of the American System stands out in stark relief against the developments in Britain over the same time frame. In the 1840s British leadership decided to partially abandon its long-time mercantilist policies in favor of laissez-faire, nonreciprocal free trade.

Behind this fateful decision were the arguments of a London banker named David Ricardo. His 1817 treatise *On the Principles of Political Economy and Taxation* laid out a case against mercantilism and for nations adopting open markets and specialized production that built on Smith's analysis and extended it in several ways. The centerpiece of his contribution was the concept of comparative advantage, the notion that countries would optimize their welfare when they concentrated on producing what they did best and traded for the rest. Smith's argument for specialization was a step in this direction. But Ricardo took it further. His example of the trade of British woolens for Portuguese wine would become a classic.

Rather than trying to grow grapes in Britain or raise sheep in Portugal, both countries would optimize their benefits if the Portuguese imported their woolens from Britain and Britain imported its wine from Portugal. Moreover, Ricardo demonstrated that even if Portugal could do both woolens and wine better than Britain, the British were still better off by concentrating on woolens, because they were less inferior in woolens than in wine making. If they tried to take up wine making, they would suffer worse losses overall because their disadvantage in wine was so much greater.

Although it took time, this thinking, combined with the rapidly growing dominance of British manufacturers and of British commerce, led to the almost total abandonment of the mercantilist strategy (with a few major exceptions I'll discuss later) and the adoption of the new doctrine of laissez-faire. British leaders had come to the view that as the leading producers, transporters, and financiers of the world, they would automatically be the low-cost and dominant providers in a world of open markets and free trade, so switching to the laissez-faire model would be greatly to Britain's benefit. A number of initial tariff reductions were made in 1842 and 1845, but the big moves came in 1846 when the Corn Laws protecting agriculture were dropped, and in 1849 when the Navigation Acts were abandoned. These moves were followed by the unilateral removal of virtually all tariffs in the 1850s and early 1860s.

The new British ideal was a world in which the United Kingdom would import grain and raw materials at the lowest possible cost from the rest of the world and then export back to global markets the high-value-added manufactured goods churned out by the factories that had made Britain "the workshop of the world."

Although the British argued passionately, pushing the analysis of Smith and Ricardo, that the rest of the world should also switch to laissez-faire, the rest of the world absolutely did not embrace the new creed. No more than the Americans had been were the continental Europeans persuaded by London. The German businessman and writer Friedrich List, a onetime resident of the United States and fan of Alexander Hamilton, wrote extensive critiques of Adam Smith and David Ricardo along with proposals to apply the key elements of Hamiltonian thinking to the German Customs Union. List believed that Smith's focus on the individual and the consumer ignored the need to develop the entire national economy by expanding production. He further believed that Smith's emphasis on commerce and transactions missed the need for invention, long-term investment, and the potential for transformative shifts to dramatically better circumstances. There was, he felt, something terribly static about the Smith-Ricardian analysis. List argued that the preconditions for wealth and democracy are a diversified manufacturing sector subject to increasing returns to scale rather than the constant or diminishing returns of agriculture and raw material production. (Today he would include knowledge-intensive services in what he called manufacturing.) Thus, List contended, as had Hamilton, that a nation must first industrialize by means of developing infant industries and then engage in free trade with nations on an equal level of industrialization.

The upshot of all this was that the United States and the key European countries all rejected British laissez-faire. Germany introduced tariffs to protect strategic industries like steel in 1879. France adopted higher tariffs in 1882 and then raised them again in 1892 as Sweden, Italy, and Spain joined the party. Thus, by the last third of the nineteenth century, Britain had become the world's only fully free market, and a highly asymmetric global economic structure was established in which the world was half governed by free-trade doctrines and half by strategic catch-up policies.

The British move to laissez-faire turned out to be an historic pivot point after which, as the American System drove the U.S. economy to ever new heights, the British economy began a long decline.

America Becomes Number 1

The mid-nineteenth-century golden age of British supremacy was nowhere better symbolized than at the International Exhibition at London's Crystal Palace in 1851. It was dominated by British machine tools, British locomotives, British textiles, and everything else British. At this moment, Britain was by far the world's main industrial country, accounting all by itself for about 30 percent of total global industrial output. It produced nearly twice as much as the next largest producer, which by this time was the United States. British ships carried more than half the world's ocean freight. As the increasingly troubled United States moved toward civil war and Germany struggled to become a united country, Britain's economic supremacy seemed assured indefinitely. Yet between 1870 and 1900, America surged ahead of Britain in virtually every sector of the economy.

The blueprint of the American System began to reap vast rewards. The United States had evolved into an enormous, relatively unhindered market that afforded American manufacturers unprecedented economy-of-scale benefits which supported rapid increases in productivity. The railroads were the lynchpin of astonishing economic growth. Not only did they knit the regional markets together and by their own expansion create enormous demand for steel, coal, wood, and machinery. They also became the first modern business enterprises, and their model was copied to modernize one industry after another.

By 1870, America was laying track at the rate of 5,100 miles a year, more than the rest of the world combined. By 1896, there were 183,601 miles of rail, not counting another 60,000 in sidings and yards. This came to 42 percent of the world total for a country with just 6 percent of the global land area. The railroad system accounted for about 15 percent of national production, more than all federal, state, and local governments combined, and employed 800,000 men, or over 2 percent of the entire national workforce.

By 1880 the cost of traveling from eastern Europe to the American plains was $70, and between 1866 and 1869 more than 1 million new immigrants fled the poverty of Europe for the potential plenty of America, particularly of the American West where there was now accessible land for the landless. By 1900 the number of American farms had tripled from 2 million to 6 million while the area farmed doubled, and production of wheat, corn, and cotton outstripped the doubling of the population to make the United States the world's largest exporter of agricultural commodities.

Part of this dramatic rise in production was due to the increase in acreage, but much of it was also due to the sharply rising productivity. After 1860, widespread use of the mechanical reaper had more than tripled the acreage a man could harvest in a day, and the new land grant colleges helped develop new, drought-resistant seed strains and cures for animal diseases that also vastly increased productivity.

Yet even as agricultural production soared, it declined to less than half of total U.S. production owing to a vast wave of industrial development that has been called the Second Industrial Revolution. The new farms and the rapidly growing population needed more and more of the stream of newly invented machines—the thresher, automatic wire binder, combine, husker, typewriter, electric lightbulb, telephone, and refrigeration car—that emerged from America's industrial inventors. The railroads and the building boom drove demand for steel and wood, and all producers needed the tools and equipment that would allow mechanization and automation.

In 1870, Great Britain produced 40 percent of the world's steel, followed by Germany at 30 percent and the United States at 15 percent. By 1900, U.S. production had climbed to nearly 40 percent of the world total with Germany second at 25 percent and Britain trailing at about 20 percent. By 1913, the U.S. share had increased to nearly half the world's steel.

If we look more broadly at total manufacturing output we find the same dynamics. In 1870, Britain accounted for about 32 percent of total world manufacturing, with the United States second, at 23 percent, and Germany third, at 13 percent. By 1900, the United States was at 30 percent, with Britain at 20 percent and Germany at 17 percent. And by 1913, the United States accounted for 36 percent, Germany for 16 percent, and Britain for 14 percent. Most significant of all was the fact that by 1914, the American population had become twice as large as Britain's and 50 percent larger than Germany's, greatly enhancing the U.S. advantages in economies of scale.

American GDP stood at $518 billion by this time and was more than double that of Britain and over three times that of Germany, while U.S. per capita income was $5,307 as compared to $5,032 for

Britain and $3,833 for Germany. America had become the richest country in the world. And importantly, it had reached this height by using high tariffs and a catch-up strategy that resulted in 4 percent plus annual rate of GDP growth while free-trade, laissez-faire Britain could not maintain even a 2 percent annual economic growth rate. It had been argued in the old tariff debates that protection of infant U.S. manufacturers with initially higher costs than foreign producers would impose higher prices on consumers and inhibit the growth of the American economy. In fact, as they rapidly improved quality and exploited the potential for economies of scale, American manufacturers were becoming the world's low-cost producers even as they paid the highest wages, and American consumers were enjoying the lowest relative prices.

Not only did the domestic prices of American producers decline rapidly, but their exports soared as they undercut the prices of the higher-cost British producers. From 1875 onward, the United States had a trade surplus driven by rising exports of manufactures, and between 1870 and 1913, U.S. exports grew at a compound annual rate of 4.9 percent while those of Britain managed only 2.8 percent. As the twentieth century dawned, the United States completed the integration of its internal market, built the Panama Canal, and acquired an empire. American products seemed to be everywhere, as Europeans and others fell in love with American typewriters, sewing machines, phonographs, autos, elevators, telephones, and lightbulbs. Indeed, the English *Daily Mail* noted: "there is hardly a workshop of any significance in the UK that does not use American tools and labor saving devices." The British engineer Benjamin Thwaite went further to say that "British soldiers and sailors open new highways of commerce, but the American by his ingenuity is producing machinery that will undersell the Briton in every part of the world."

By the time of the Paris Exhibition of 1900, there was no longer any question that Britain had lost its industrial and technological leadership. British industrial output had fallen to only about 15 percent of the world total while that of the United States had passed 30 percent. Both America and Germany produced more steel, more iron, and more coal than Britain. In addition, Germany dominated the new chemical industry while America was a leader in the emerging electrical and automotive technologies. Britain lagged in all of these as well as in new developments in older industries like steel. Perhaps most indicative of the turn in British fortune was the fact that increasingly it was importing not only raw materials and components, but finished products as well. In other words, its producers had lost out in each and every link of the supply chain. Imports of finished manufactures as a share of total British imports rose from 7.3 percent in 1860 to 18.8 percent in 1900.

In the face of this dramatic loss of industrial leadership a modification of the hard laissez-faire model might have been expected, and there was a push to do so. Many of London's imperialist leaders were frightened by their country's relative industrial decline and launched a series of inquiries into its causes, because it struck at the heart of their power. "Suppose an industry which is threatened [by foreign competitors] is one which lies at the very root of your system of National defense, where are you then?" asked the prominent professor and defense expert W. A. S. Hewins in 1904. "You could not get on without an iron industry, or a great engineering trade, because in modern warfare you would not have the means of producing and maintaining in a state of efficiency, your fleets and armies." Indeed, the First Lord of the Admiralty warned: "In the years to come the United Kingdom by itself will not be strong enough to hold its proper place alongside of the United States, or Russia, and probably not Germany. We shall be thrust aside by sheer weight."

Leading imperialists began proposing the abandonment of laissez-faire free trade, with former Manchester manufacturer Joseph Chamberlain, who had become head of the Board of Trade and Colonial Secretary, leading the charge. He spoke of Britain as "the weary Titan, struggling under the too vast orb of its fate." But though Chamberlain strove mightily to unite the cabinet behind him on a proposal for a protective tariff, he failed to overcome the sway of free-trade orthodoxy.

One reason for the persistence of orthodox thinking and policies was that the decline of Britain's economic might was masked to a large degree by the exploitation of its colonial possessions. As they lost out more and more in the U.S. and European markets, the British turned increasingly to colonial and quasi-colonial underdeveloped countries to compensate for lost sales. Britain controlled large regions of the world as both formal and informal colonies, the biggest of which was India. And in those territories, laissez-faire by no means prevailed. These were, in effect, captive markets and suppliers. The English limited them to supplying raw materials to the mother country while they imported only its manufactured products. By the dawn of the twentieth century, half of Britain's cotton textile exports and one-third of its galvanized iron production was going to India.

Increased exports of coal also compensated for the decline in manufactured goods exports, so that total export numbers in pounds sterling were maintained, but, if you subtracted coal, the rest of the exports were falling off dramatically. To see what was happening, let's look at the progression of coal production, coal exports, and overall exports. While in 1870 coal production was 110 million tons and coal exports were 13.4 percent of total exports, by 1900 production had climbed to 225 million tons and exports to 25.9 percent of total exports; that is, manufactured exports had actually suffered more than a 10 percent decline even as world markets grew at record rates. British industrialists were losing market share in great gobs.

They cried "disaster," arguing that low-value raw material (dung perhaps?) was being substituted in British exports for sophisticated, technologically advanced, high-value-added manufactures that supported high wages as well as research and development. But the majority of British economists and the influential magazine *The Economist* countered that coal was as good as machine tools as exports go, and the bulk of the elite British leadership remained unconcerned.

A third major factor in the British economic equation at this time was the earnings from the so-called invisible exports of shipping, insurance, brokering, and financing. Despite its becoming the world's workshop, the fact of the matter is that throughout the nineteenth century, Britain never had a trade surplus in goods. It always imported more goods than it exported, but it balanced its trade figures by carrying the goods of others in its ships, as well as by providing the insurance and other financing and services essential to the smooth flow of commerce. Indeed, the fact that Britain long retained a virtual monopoly on global shipping, with British ships still carrying more than 50 percent of the world's oceangoing freight as late as 1913, afforded British producers a largely protected market in many parts of the world seldom visited by other than British ships. Until the beginning of World War I, for example, it was common for American shipments to Latin America to go first to England and then on to their final destination.

Owing to its position as the major naval and colonial power, Britain's dominance of shipping led naturally to the development of London as the hub of the world's commercial and financial dealings. Thus, even as its manufacturing and technology industries declined relatively, Britain's shipping and services grew, and the country leaned increasingly on them as a mainstay of its economy.

Even more important, the British economy was propped up by earnings from overseas investments. In the early part of the nineteenth century, Britain invested abroad at an average annual rate of about 2 percent of GDP, and by 1870 it had net foreign assets of about £700 million. In this period, more than half of its investment went to the rest of Europe and the United States. After 1870, as British industry stalled at home and lost market share in Europe and the United States, Britain's foreign investment soared to an average rate of 4.3 percent of GDP up to 1914 and even topped 10 percent in some years. Moreover, the direction changed so that more than half of this amount now went to the empire and other developing regions rather than to the United States and Europe. The return on these investments became—along with shipping, insurance, and commercial fees—the key to Britain's continued economic health.

In turn, the key to this investment flow was the establishment of the so-called Gold Standard whereby all the major countries adopted gold as their reserve money. Under this arrangement, central banks committed to exchange currency for a set amount of gold upon demand. All currencies were pegged at a fixed rate to gold so that the international price of gold, which was the same everywhere, determined national money supplies and established what was effectively one international currency. Britain had operated under a gold standard since about 1717, but it was only after 1870 that it persuaded most of the other major economic powers to join. Once that occurred, and the world was effectively operating with one central currency, the risk of exchange rate adjustment was removed for international investors. This, of course, greatly stimulated the international flow of capital, and bankers and investors loved it both for that reason and because it tended to be deflationary, thereby protecting the anticipated return on their investments.

In particular, the City of London (the financial district) loved it. London, like Amsterdam before it, sat as the great hub at the crossroads of world commerce and finance, and the gold standard only served to cement that position. Moreover, the City liked a strong pound sterling that was valued under the gold standard at $4.86 to the pound. While this preference was justified by the vast flow of money to London, it was not helpful to the increasingly struggling manufacturers facing protected and often subsidized competitors whose currency values in gold were less strong.

In view of the significance of shipping, commerce, and the empire to Britain's economic well-being, its defense and expansion became an even greater priority. Indeed, as its relative economic position declined between 1870 and 1900, Britain added 10 percent of the earth's land area to its holdings to create the largest empire the world had ever seen. And even as this economic balancing act became increasingly precarious, public support for the expansion of the empire was strong because the public was enjoying the delicious fruits of globalization. As John Maynard Keynes wrote in 1920,

> The inhabitant of London could order by telephone, sipping his morning tea in bed, the various products of the whole earth, in such quantity as he might see fit, and reasonably expect their early delivery upon his doorstep; he could at the same moment and by the same means adventure his wealth in the natural resources and new enterprises of any quarter of the world, and share, without exertion or even trouble, in their prospective fruits and advantages; or he could decide to couple the security of his fortunes with the good faith of the townspeople of any substantial municipality in any continent that fancy or information might recommend. He could secure forthwith, if he wished it, cheap and comfortable means of transit to any country or climate without passport or other formality, could dispatch his servant to the neighboring office of a bank for such supply of the precious metals as might seem convenient, and could proceed abroad to foreign quarters, without knowledge of their religion, language, or customs, bearing coined wealth upon his person, and would consider himself greatly

aggrieved and much surprised at the least interference. But, most important of all, he regarded this state of affairs as normal, certain, and permanent, except in the direction of further improvement and any deviation from it as aberrant, scandalous, and avoidable.

The Great War pushed the British economy over the edge, costing Britain more than £44 billion ($209 billion). By 1918 the war was consuming more than 30 percent of annual British GDP. Government debt, which had stood at £700 million in 1914, soared to £7,500 million by 1919. Debt to the United States alone rose to £900 million, and much of the stock of overseas investment had to be liquidated, including about $500 million of U.S. railroad and other securities. Before the war, total debt was about 35 percent of GDP. Afterward it stood above 200 percent.

Even worse was the impact on the longtime staples (steel, cotton textiles, coal, shipbuilding) of the British export economy as the United States, Japan, and others moved in to take over markets the British could no longer supply due to their focus on the war. In 1912, British cotton goods production had been 8 million square yards. By 1938, it was only 3 million, and exports had dropped from 7 million to 1.5 million square yards. Coal production in 1938 had not yet climbed back up to the 287 million tons of 1913, and shipping tonnage, which had been 12 million tons in 1913, was less than 11 million in 1938. New ship construction was only half what it had been in 1913. New industries like autos and chemicals were rising up to fill some of the gap, but these were not primarily export industries. For this reason they did not contribute substantially to helping Britain pay for its imports.

In the face of these daunting challenges, the British government at last took decisive action to change policy. The government took over the railroads, as well as the production of munitions, coal, flour, and many other products; by the end of the war, government entities were directly producing and distributing 80 percent of all food and controlling consumer prices. In the most dramatic step of all, import tariffs on a range of manufactured goods were introduced for the first time in a hundred years.

These changes would help to restore vitality to the British economy for a time, but the momentum behind the growth of the U.S. economy had become a juggernaut, with the war benefiting the United States even as it hobbled Britain.

America Tightens Its Grip

Britain's losses in the war, and those of the rest of Europe, were America's gains. For starters, Britain borrowed heavily from American banks for war funding, and once it had exhausted its credit with them, it turned to the U.S. government for further credit. Before extending aid, however, Washington insisted that Britain liquidate its remaining assets. From 1914 to 1919, London sold off about $8 billion of its American holdings and then borrowed another $5 billion from the U.S. Treasury. By thus depriving Britain of potential future gains on its U.S. investments and forcing it into a large net debtor position, Washington undermined future British wealth creation and power. Other countries, like France, also borrowed from America so that whereas in 1914 the United States had been the world's leading debtor, five years later it was the leading creditor.

Perhaps even more significant was the shift away from the gold standard. Before the war, most nations had adhered to this system, with their currencies backed by gold and pegged to its value. Once the war started, however, all governments except the United States went off the gold standard and issued paper money with no gold backing. The result was soaring inflation, wildly fluctuating exchange rates, and a huge flow of gold to the United States. Thus, America emerged from the war as the newly dominant financial power, and New York replaced London as the center of global finance.

The story was similar in the case of shipping. Before the war, America had virtually no merchant marine, and less than 10 percent of U.S. exports were carried by U.S. ships. This deficiency had been a source of concern in commercial and naval circles for some time, and during the 1912 presidential election campaign, the Democratic candidate Woodrow Wilson had emphasized: "Without a great merchant marine we cannot take our rightful place in the commerce of the world." With the war as an excuse, the government established the United States Shipping Board to direct and finance a major shipbuilding program. By 1918, the board was directing the launch of 3 million tons of ships annually—an amount equal to total world production in any prewar year. By 1920, American ships were carrying 42.7 percent of American commerce and the United States had displaced Britain as the world's leading maritime country.

Aircraft and aviation was another area of shifting leadership. Although the airplane had been invented in the United States, its further development had taken place much more rapidly in Europe under the direction of government-sponsored institutes. The outbreak of war demonstrated dramatically and concretely that European and particularly German aviation was far in advance of America's. In response, the 1915 U.S. Navy appropriations bill established the National Advisory Committee for Aeronautics, which became a key driver of U.S. aerospace technology, eventually morphing into today's NASA. The army also placed orders for aircraft that resulted in U.S. production increasing from a few hundred planes annually before the war to 14,000 in 1918.

After the war, the drive for leadership in aeronautics continued as the Air Mail Act of 1925 (the Kelly Act) gave private contractors rather than the post office the right to transport air mail. A year later, the military declared its intention of having a fleet of 2,600 planes by 1931, and this touched off another wave of investment in aviation, further stimulated by the Air Commerce Act of 1927, which financed building of airports and set standards for radio communications and aircraft design and construction. As a result of these efforts and the defeat of Germany, the United States also took over world leadership in this field.

Perhaps the most interesting story of shifting leadership, however, is that of radio telegraphy, which was also dominated before the war by Britain and its Marconi Radio Corp. At the Versailles peace treaty negotiations in 1919, President Wilson began to perceive that "we are on the eve of a commercial war of the severest sort, and I am afraid Great Britain will prove capable of as great commercial savagery as Germany has displayed for so many years in her competitive methods." In particular, he believed that communications technology would be the key to the future and wanted to use the new radio technology to break the British monopoly on cable traffic.

Navy officials were particularly worried about an attempt by British Marconi to buy from General Electric the exclusive right to manufacture and sell the Alexanderson alternator, the only key piece of radio technology still in U.S. hands. Wilson therefore directed Navy Secretary Franklin Delano Roosevelt to stop the sale. The navy pressured GE to halt negotiations with the British and assisted the company in a buyout of American Marconi, the owner of many key patents. It then orchestrated the formation of a consortium of other holders of important electronic technology including AT&T, Westinghouse, and United Fruit Co. A new communications giant was formed, called Radio Corporation of America (RCA), with the U.S. Navy as a 20 percent shareholder.

Owen Young, the GE lawyer who became the first chairman, said he "wanted to make America the center of the world in radio communications." RCA undercut the submarine cable rate of 25 cents a word with a new rate of 18 cents a word. By 1923 it was capturing 30 percent of trans-Atlantic traffic and 50 percent of trans-Pacific traffic.

U.S. GDP rose by 204 percent from 1914 to 1918 and by another 63 percent to 1921.

AMERICA BECOMES THE WORLD HEGEMON

The interwar years constituted an uneasy interregnum. The United States had morphed into the world's biggest economy, but Britain, still in control of history's biggest empire, remained diplomatically and militarily the world's leading power. So determined were Britain's leaders to regain the economic lead, at least in finance and commerce, and so strong was the myth of laissez-faire doctrine, that despite what should have been glaring evidence that laissez-faire had contributed heavily to British decline, they reversed the very successful emergency industrial policies instituted during the war. The government removed tariffs and industry supports in a reprise of the old, comfortable, albeit highly uncompetitive, laissez-faire.

Like London, Washington also reverted to prewar policies after 1918. But these, of course, were diametrically opposite to those of Britain. Washington raised tariffs by more than 40 percent with the Fordney-McCumber Tariff bill of 1922. This was a much bigger percentage hike than that of the later Smoot-Hawley tariff, which has long been criticized as a major cause of the Great Depression. Thus, we might expect that it proved a drag on the economy and especially on U.S. international trade with possible retaliation by trading partners, coming as it did during a global economic downturn. On the contrary, however, trade boomed and the economy picked up speed as we moved into the "roaring twenties." (You've probably never heard the boom being attributed to the effects of this tariff, have you?) A U.S. economic boom was powered by exports to the war-devastated European economies, rapid innovation and adoption of new technology like electricity and the telephone, and government support of easy consumer credit, which marked the beginning of the evolution of the American consumer society. As a result, in the decade of the 1920s, the United States produced more than the major countries of Europe plus Japan combined.

The American boom of course turned to a bust with the crash of the stock market in 1929 and the onset of the Great Depression. The United States temporarily lost some of its new dominance, suffering more than the other major countries—a setback due primarily to three factors. The first was a decision by the Federal Reserve to allow the money supply to shrink by a third. The second was a wave of global protectionism—of which the U.S. Smoot-Hawley Tariff Act was notoriously a part. This wave exacerbated a falloff in already rapidly shrinking world trade. The United States was hit harder than some other countries because, as a net exporter, trade was a bigger contributor to its growth, so the falloff caused disproportionate U.S. unemployment. The third factor was a premature tax increase after recovery seemed to be under way in 1936. The U.S. GDP fell by half between 1929 and 1932, and the value of manufactured goods production in 1933 was only a quarter of what it had been in 1929. American exports fell by 69 percent, and the U.S. share of foreign commerce fell even faster than total world trade, declining from 13 percent to 10 percent in 1932.

The catastrophe of the Depression was followed, of course, by a sustained economic recovery in the United States, which was driven largely by a willingness to experiment with far-reaching methods for government-industry partnerships and for government intervention in managing the economy, but was also greatly boosted by the stimulus of World War II. The most important of the new government measures was the Reconstruction Finance Corporation (RFC), established in 1932 by President Herbert Hoover. Based on the wartime War Finance Corporation, it was initially intended to loan up to $2 billion (keep in mind that the entire federal budget under Calvin Coolidge had been $3 billion) to large financial institutions under stress and to railroads whose bonds were held by insurance companies and banks. The idea was to shore up the credit markets, but the structure of the RFC was extremely flexible, and the RFC had certain extralegislative powers and lots of money.

When he became president, Franklin Roosevelt seized upon this new corporation and turned it into one of the most powerful government agencies of all time: through it passed most of the funding of the New Deal. Roosevelt didn't see the RFC as temporary or as restricted only to assisting the banking sector. He wanted an activist RFC to spread government capital and credit to as broad a base as possible. The first step was to use RFC money to buy shares in more than half the nation's banks and thereby enable them to join the new Federal Deposit Insurance Corporation. From there the RFC funded the Federal Emergency Relief Administration, the Rural Electrification Administration, the Resettlement Administration, the Federal Home Loan Bank, the Commodity Credit Corporation, and the Export-Import Bank.

With this as a warm-up exercise, the RFC was ready when World War II broke out to resume its old role as the war-finance arm of the government. In June 1940 Roosevelt authorized the RFC to make loans or purchase stock in any company that produced or transported war materiel. The RFC quickly created eight divisions for defense production. Thus the Rubber Reserve Company became the only importer of crude rubber. The Rubber Development Corporation helped produce synthetic rubber and became the nation's main source of rubber. The Metals Reserve Company bought and stockpiled strategic metals, and the Defense Plant and Defense Supplies corporations each invested more than $9 billion in plants and equipment for production of war supplies.

Through the Defense Plant Corporation, the government financed more than 80 percent of the new plant construction and plant conversion by the auto, aircraft, and other companies for wartime production. Washington came to own 90 percent of the country's synthetic rubber, aircraft, magnesium, and shipbuilding plants and facilities; 70 percent of the aluminum factories; half of the machine tool plants; and 3,800 miles of pipeline. By the end of the war, the RFC had spent $37 billion that not only helped win the war but also stabilized the economy.

In 1940, to run the wartime economy, the White House established the Office of Production Management, which morphed into the War Production Board and the Board of Economic Warfare in 1942. The war created 17.5 million jobs in the United States as the board drove war production to reach more than 40 percent of GDP in 1943–44. For example, steel production in 1944 reached 80 million long tons, or more than two-thirds of total world production. The merchant marine expanded from 11 million to 40 million gross tons as 5,545 ships were built in American yards. By 1945, the United States had 60 percent of the world's merchant tonnage. Having produced less than 14,000 airplanes total in the twenty years before the war, the United States was turning out 96,000 per year by 1944. On top of this was the incredible R&D effort that led to the atomic bomb, the computer, dramatic advances in aeronautics including the jet airplane, and the development of penicillin and numerous other drugs and biological agents.

By the end of the war in 1945, after a century and a half of "catch-up," of the American System, of industrial policy, infrastructure policy, protectionism, and continuous government intervention in the economy to encourage industrial development and direct war production, the United States emerged as an unprecedentedly powerful hegemonic colossus. It accounted for about half of global GDP, owned 70 percent of the world's gold, had a monopoly on nuclear power, was the world leader in virtually every technology and every industry, owned the world's main currency, was the leading world creditor to the tune of $3 billion, and had a trade or current account surplus of $5.8 billion. It had more than caught up. It was all alone in a realm no nation had ever before inhabited.

Then it took a new tack.

3

America Changes Course

The United States is organizing its own decline.
—GEIR LUNDESTAD, NORWEGIAN HISTORIAN

Having reached the top, America discovered not only that the view from the pinnacle was much different from that on the way up, but also that it revealed the need for new priorities. For one thing, there was no longer any necessity to catch up. The United States was number 1 in virtually everything. Of course, American preeminence owed a lot to the fact that much of the rest of the world was in ruins—ruins that only America could afford to repair. Global recovery thus became a major priority that was also linked to defense. The 1948 Communist takeover of China and the Soviet blockade of Berlin followed by the first explosion of a Soviet atomic bomb in 1949 and the start of the Korean War in 1950 all signaled the advent of the Cold War. With Britain but a shadow of its former self, the international balance of power and the security of its own citizens and of billions of other people around the world depended solely on America.

The building and maintenance of global alliances, securing of the rights for overseas bases, and the global deployment of powerful military forces became the overriding national priorities. And economics became the handmaiden of geopolitics.

Meanwhile, for most of the rest of the world, recovery from wartime devastation was the overwhelming priority. Especially for Germany and Japan, and later for the so-called Asian Tigers (South Korea, Taiwan, Singapore), developing competitiveness trumped geopolitics, which they were glad to leave to the Americans. Or perhaps it would be more accurate to say that becoming competitive was their form of geopolitics.

The structure of today's global economy, with its chronic trade imbalances, its tendency toward financial crises, its asymmetric economic growth policies, and its continuous low-grade economic conflict, was largely determined by the asymmetry between America's fixation on geopolitics and laissez-faire free trade and the neomercantilist emphasis of the leading countries of Europe and Asia on "catching up" and becoming competitive. Conflict between these priorities was not apparent in the first flush of the postwar boom. But in later years, under presidents Ronald Reagan and George H. W. Bush, bitter conflict arose as the early signs of American decline began to appear.

AMERICA'S POSTWAR STRATEGIES

As America in the postwar world adopted new international priorities, it no longer felt there was any reason to worry about its economic competitiveness. Indeed, as it exercised its new preeminence in the context of global responsibility, America made a momentous about-face, morphing from being the world's leading "catch-up," mercantilist nation into its leading apostle of free trade. Of course, assurance of national security was a key issue. That, despite a new emphasis on market forces, sometimes involved a kind of inadvertent industrial policy. But the primary economic concern now was to avoid sliding back into depression as wartime spending wound down and 15 million service men and women were demobilized and sent home. This triggered the most consequential of all America's postwar policies—the decision to vigorously promote domestic consumption as the engine of the economy's growth.

Let Them Shop Till They Drop

With much of the rest of the world in a state of near collapse, exporting higher volumes of U.S.-made products was clearly not a feasible growth strategy. So U.S. leaders focused on stimulating consumer spending at home. Americans themselves would provide the market for the goods and services that would keep factories and offices humming and put the returning servicemen and -women back to work. The federal government therefore used every imaginable device to encourage consumers to spend.

The economic rationale for this was well established. John Maynard Keynes had identified underconsumption as the root cause of the Depression and, in his famous Four Freedoms speech of January 6, 1941, President Roosevelt had not only identified the freedom from want as essential to American life but also emphasized the need for a "constantly rising standard of living." Of course, during the war people had been encouraged to "save now in order to buy tomorrow," and by 1945, personal saving was at 21 percent of disposable income as opposed to the 3 percent it had been in the 1920s. But those same public service ads that encouraged saving also spoke of "what we're fighting for," and in addition to democracy and a better world, emphasized a "steak in every frying pan," permission to "take a taxi to Brooklyn," and "the right to have cuffs on our pants."

To fulfill these objectives, the 1944 GI Bill provided veterans with grants for college or other education and training; it also made mortgages available with no down payment and low interest rates. Between 1945 and 1966, 26 percent of all new houses were financed by the GI Bill. In addition, the 1946 Full Employment Act committed the federal government not only to maximizing production and employment but also to maximizing purchasing power. All these measures and others led to the widespread adoption of the philosophy articulated by the journalist and New Jersey urban planner Ernest Erber that "the prosperity of this nation is built on spending, not saving."

Essential to this idea was the adoption of a tax and credit regime under which interest earned on savings and dividends from investments were heavily taxed, while interest on installment buying (credit card) payments and sales taxes were made tax deductible. These measures led to an explosion of consumer credit and borrowing. As William H. Whyte noted in *Fortune* magazine in 1957, thrift had become "un-American." Between 1945 and 1960, consumer credit increased by a factor of 11 and installment credit was up by a factor of 19. Debt rose faster than income. In 1950, the ratio of credit to disposable income was 10.4 percent. By 1960, it was 16.1 percent, and by 1970 it had reached 18.5 percent. In 1965 this Keynesianism reached an apotheosis when Keynes was named *Time* magazine's Man of the Year.

Further turbocharging postwar consumption was the enormous expansion of roads and highways whose centerpiece was the National Interstate and Defense Highways Act of 1956. Not only did it create a national web of 41,000 miles of high-speed roads, it also stimulated the expansion of suburbs, where increasingly larger homes could be crammed with more and more consumer goods. Owing to the lack of public transportation out to the suburbs, more and more families found they had to have two and often three or even four cars.

National Security Drives Industrial Policy

While the emphasis on consumer-led growth did not spell the complete abandonment of government support for industrial development and R&D, the rationale for this support was now based more on the need to bolster national security and military prowess than on any concern for maintaining industrial and technological leadership for its own sake. RCA and IBM provide good examples. Created by the government, as we have seen, specifically to beat British Marconi after World War I, RCA boomed as a military supplier during World War II, and again during the Korean and Cold wars. It then turned the cathode ray tube and orthicon, developed in part with Pentagon funding, into the TV cameras and television sets with which it dominated consumer electronic markets for many years. IBM was an even more significant case. In the 1950s more than half its total electronic data-processing revenue stemmed from government contracts for the B-52 bomber guidance system and Simulation Air and Ground Engagements (SAGE), the North American air defense system. Moreover, throughout the 1950s and early 1960s, well over half of IBM's R&D expenses were paid by the U.S. government. It was on the basis of this government largesse that the company created its revolutionary System 360. Introduced in 1964, it represented a quantum leap forward in computing technology and played a vital role in making the computer indispensable to the corporate world.

Powered by sales of the 360, IBM gained a 70 percent share of the global computing market by 1980. And it is really to this dominance that Intel and Microsoft owe their own commanding positions today in PC chips and software. By dint of their adoption as, respectively, the microprocessor and operating system providers of the early IBM PCs, they automatically set the key standards for the new industry. Intel benefited additionally from aerospace spending. The Air Force Minuteman project and NASA's Apollo lunar landing project not only were the main buyers of semiconductor chips in the industry's early days, but they also provided critical assistance with development and quality control. The truth is that in the 1950s and '60s virtually all firms in Silicon Valley were aided in some way by the U.S. government. The National Science Foundation had been established in 1948, and either it or NASA or the Pentagon or the CIA were involved in development of the technologies that led to the relational database, the computer mouse, the Apple Macintosh, Microsoft's Windows, the Sun Microsystems workstation, the flat panel display, and, perhaps most important, the internet, which began life as the Arpanet, the network of the Defense Department's Advanced Research Projects Agency (ARPA, also known as DARPA). Thus did Alexander Hamilton remain alive and well at the Defense Department.

THE SHIFT TO FREE TRADE

Outside the realm of national security, however, the U.S. government now began to act in ways that often greatly aided the foreign competitors of American industry. Take the case of the transistor (solid-state) radio. Japan's Sony Corp. is famous for beginning its conquest of the U.S. consumer electronics companies by beating them to wide commercial introduction of the product in 1957. Less well known is the fact that the technology was initially developed by AT&T, which demonstrated the first working model of a transistor radio in 1948. But at that time the U.S. Justice Department was trying to break up AT&T on antitrust grounds, and the consent decree that eventually resolved the issue prohibited the company from participating in any business other than telecommunications while also compelling it to license all of its technologies to any qualified applicant (domestic or foreign) at very reasonable rates. Sony got the keys to its kingdom for $25,000. Think about that for a moment. AT&T's research arm, Bell Laboratories, had spent hundreds of millions, and U.S. telephone users had paid billions to finance the generation of that technology. Sony, a company based in a Japan that was then compelling U.S. companies to transfer their technology to its companies as a condition of being allowed to enter the Japanese market, got it for almost nothing. To say this is not to criticize Sony. It was smart to do so, and its American competitors could also have gotten the technology for the same low license fees.

But imagine how the world might have looked if a U.S. president, à la Woodrow Wilson in the case of RCA, had taken the view that being the leader in transistors and in products based on them was a U.S. priority and had not only allowed AT&T to keep its technology but also urged it to use its vast resources to dominate the new markets.

In fact, the Japanese couldn't believe Washington wasn't doing exactly that. Had they been in America's shoes they almost certainly would have. They had spent years modeling their own Nippon Telephone and Telegraph (NTT) on AT&T and parceling out its technology to a select group of "NTT Family" companies in a position to dominate key markets. Not only was technology developed by NTT not available to foreign licensees at cut-rate fees, it wasn't available to non-"family"-member Sony. Nor did a foreign supplier at the time have any chance of selling something to NTT. The reason was that, for Japan at the time, catching up technologically to the United States was *the* top priority, and NTT was one of the main engines driving the catch-up machine. To this fact no one in Washington paid any attention.

Shortly after Sony stormed the U.S. market with its new radio, RCA was compelled to agree to a consent decree that forced it to make radio/television technology licenses available to domestic companies without charge. Not only did this discourage further research by RCA in these technologies, but it also had the further perverse effect of encouraging RCA to license its technology widely to foreign producers who turned it into the flood of America-bound electronics exports that eventually drowned the American industry, including RCA. There were two reasons for this. First, without the ability to maintain a technological lead or even to gain income from its technology domestically, RCA had to look abroad. But, at that time, Japan and many other major countries did not allow RCA and other leading U.S. corporations to produce in or export to their markets. Thus, the only alternative for RCA was to license its technology to foreign companies who did, at least, pay full royalties.

By contrast, in these years, the Japanese government (à la the mentioned president Wilson) adopted legislation aimed specifically at creating a consumer electronics industry equal to or better than America's. Until the late 1970s, that industry was built mostly around RCA technology. Indeed, RCA chairman David Sarnoff received Japan's Order of the Rising Sun from the emperor. Nor did IBM escape Justice Department consent decrees, which in its case compelled licensing that allowed domestic and foreign rivals to build "plug-in" computers that were essentially clones of the IBM products. Again, Japanese producers operating in a protected home market where, unlike their U.S. counterparts, they could largely escape competition with IBM, were the prime beneficiaries.

Although this aggressive antimonopoly activity was partly driven by the desire to curb the power of big business, it was also symptomatic of a broader shift away from America's traditional Hamiltonian emphasis on industrial development toward a focus on the virtues of Smith's unseen hand and free-market forces. Particularly striking was the complete absence of any consideration of the likely consequences of these actions for America's international trade and competitiveness. The United States was edging onto the same laissez-faire international path that Britain had trod after its ascendance as the world's dominant economy.

Why Follow a Loser?

Yes, I hear you. Given the decline and fall of the UK, why were U.S. leaders so eager to follow it onto a trail that clearly led to failure? Keep two things in mind. First, so powerful was the British elite's faith in their laissez-faire free-trade doctrine that they never blamed it for any role in their decline. Most British leaders firmly believed that, all things being equal, laissez-faire would produce optimal results. Any problems had to be due to something else. Blue ribbon commission after blue ribbon commission blamed the country's declining competitiveness on: the education system, from which only a small percentage of the population graduated and which produced only a very few scientists and engineers; the lack of entrepreneurial drive; the incompetence of British business leaders who, among other things, failed to create enough large-scale enterprises, and who were slow to innovate and to adopt advanced technologies and techniques; the class system; and, of course, the wars. (Sound familiar?)

The Americans also tended to believe these explanations, in part because there was some truth to them but also for two other reasons. First, the British explanation fed the American ego and confirmed many Americans in their low opinion of Britain and of British business. More important, however, having bought into the laissez-faire doctrine, the U.S. economists found it hard to see any other. Also, rather than attributing American economic success to much that Washington had done, they attributed it to good old American ingenuity, pioneering spirit, rugged individualism, and the operation of free markets. Indeed, they tended to see success as having been achieved more in spite of than because of any government intervention.

Early Steps on the Road to Free Trade

America had first set foot on this road at the 1944 Bretton Woods conference at which, along with Britain, it led forty-two other countries in drawing up a blueprint for postwar economic reconstruction. This plan called for the establishment of the U.S. dollar as the world's main money (in place of gold, the pound sterling, and other important prewar currencies); the creation of the International Monetary Fund (IMF) to oversee the setting of currency exchange rates and to help maintain a balanced global financial system; and the establishment of the World Bank, to provide lending for financing the development of underdeveloped countries. These policies contrasted sharply with the U.S. isolationism that had contributed so much to the failure of the post–World War I economic and peacekeeping arrangements. Indeed, it was expressly to avoid a repeat of those failures that in 1945–46 President Truman and his administration accepted the mantle of world leadership from the UK and not only spearheaded these initiatives but also pushed for both the General Agreement on Tariffs and Trade (GATT), as suggested by the Bretton Woods plan, and the founding of the United Nations. Later, in 1948–49, after some hesitation and amid the gathering clouds of the Cold War, the administration undertook four new programs: the Marshall Plan to assist the reconstruction of Europe, Truman's Point Four program for economic and technical assistance to developing countries, the formation of the NATO alliance, and, in 1951, the U.S.-Japan Security Treaty, by which the United States gained use of several important Japanese military bases. In return for the latter, the United States committed unilaterally (Japan made no reciprocal commitment) to defend Japan.

To be sure, there was opposition to some of these programs. For

example, Senator Robert Taft of Ohio and some of his Republican colleagues opposed the Marshall Plan, fearing it would be too expensive,
and former vice president Henry Wallace, along with some other Democrats, opposed it as a possible export subsidy for U.S. big business.
But the surprising thing is how readily this historic shift of policy was
accomplished. In truth, this shift had been under way ever since the
appointment of Cordell Hull as secretary of state in 1933. As a native of Tennessee and a champion of its cotton and tobacco interests,
Hull was a traditional Southern free trader. Like Britain's free-trade
champion Richard Cobden, he believed that mercantilist protectionism engendered conflict and war, while completely unregulated free
trade not only would stimulate economic growth but also foster democratization and peace among nations. His appointment to the State
Department, in the wake of the adoption of the prohibitively high
Smoot-Hawley tariff in 1930, coincided with the depths of the Depression, which many economists and financial analysts claimed had
largely been caused by the tariff. That view, of course, provided strong
support for the change of trade policy Hull had long been advocating.

Further support came from a shift in Washington personnel. The
practical, industry-development-oriented businessmen and bankers
who heretofore largely staffed the government's international economic policy positions were being replaced by a new breed of more
theoretical academic economists then migrating to Washington's brain
trusts. One of these, Claire Wilcox, who was later to become my economics professor, had led the organization of a petition by 1,028 economists against the Smoot-Hawley tariff. Like him, the other immigrants
to Washington mostly shared the views of Hull as well as those of the
leading British economists who had laid the foundations of Anglo-
American economics and whose works the new policy advisors had
avidly studied. They also came to wield as much influence over American economic policy as Britain's laissez-faire academic and financial
elite once had exercised over London's. Thus, the new brains—most of
whom, like Wilcox, had fought to prevent Smoot-Hawley—gathered
under Hull's banner to build a new world of British-style unregulated
free trade. Their first step was to undo Smoot-Hawley.

WHAT EXACTLY DID SMOOT-HAWLEY DO, ANYHOW?

In a September 20, 2009, *New York Times* article, ninety-four-year-old David Rockefeller invoked the specter of the 1930 Smoot-Hawley tariff to warn President Barack Obama against the imposition of temporary tariffs on imports of Chinese tires. Rockefeller stressed that the tariff had contributed greatly both to the advent of the Great Depression and to the outbreak of World War II, and suggested that Obama's tire tariffs risked leading to a similar catastrophe. This understanding of the apocalyptic consequences of Smoot-Hawley has become deeply ingrained in the public mind over the past eighty years and, as Rockefeller's article demonstrated, is regularly repeated at moments of trade tension to prevent any deviation from pure laissez-faire unregulated trade. Indeed, it is repeated so often and in so many clearly noncomparable circumstances as to have become almost trite. Nevertheless, it has been and remains the single most powerful rationale for the orthodox laissez-faire unregulated trade doctrine and policy.

It all started in 1928 when then presidential candidate Herbert Hoover promised struggling U.S. farmers to raise tariffs on agricultural commodities if he were elected. He was, and he duly proceeded to ask Congress to raise tariffs on a number of agricultural products. At the same time, however, he also requested a reduction on a broad range of industrial product tariffs. In the wake of the worsening economic situation following the stock market crash of 1929, the bill that finally came to Hoover's desk for signature called for dramatically increased tariffs across the board. Hoover opposed most of the increases and agonized over what to do as the likes of Henry Ford and the 1,028 economists urged that he veto the bill. But eventually, under enormous pressure from Republicans in Congress and from some business interests, he eventually signed it into law.

In the conventional version of the story, the American action triggered a wave of retaliatory tariff increases and competitive currency devaluations by other countries that cut world trade by two thirds. U.S. imports also fell by two thirds, exacerbating the economic slowdown in Europe and triggering bank failures there while a 61 percent decline in U.S. exports smothered American growth and turned a stock market correction into the Great Depression, which in turn created the conditions that eventually led to World War II. The conclusion is, as David Rockefeller assumes, that any deviation from unregulated trade, even if it is fully in keeping with all international trade agreements and laws, is an invitation to global cataclysm. In the alternative version, while Smoot-Hawley was not a smart move (because by cutting imports it made earning the money to pay off their loans to the net creditor United States more difficult for the debt-laden European countries), it was not the disaster of conventional mythology.

Yes, U.S. imports fell by two thirds, but only about half the imports were dutiable. The other half were duty free, yet those imports actually fell a bit more than imports of the dutiable items. So was it the tariff that stopped the imports and triggered the Depression, or did the reduction of the money supply by the Federal Reserve so squeeze credit that neither businesses nor consumers could buy imports of any kind? In just the past couple of years of economic crisis, we have seen U.S. imports fall dramatically with no significant increases in tariffs and an unprecedented increase in the money supply. So maybe in crises, people just stop buying. This possibility is only strengthened by the fact that although the almost equally high Fordney-McCumber tariff of 1922 represented a greater percentage increase in the tariff rate than the Smoot-Hawley tariff, it was followed by the boom of the 1920s.

As for other countries' retaliatory tariff increases, some of them actually were imposed before the adoption of Smoot-Hawley, and State Department reports from that time speak little of retaliation and a lot about protectionist pressures from within individual countries. The conclusion of this version of the story is that, while not helpful, Smoot-Hawley was no more than a minor cause of the Depression if for no other reason than the fact that trade accounted for less than 10 percent of U.S. GDP. Indeed, in perhaps the most sophisticated analysis of that period, University of California, Berkeley, professor Barry Eichengreen concludes that the tariff was probably mildly positive for the U.S. economy and mildly negative for the rest of the global economy.

One thing is for certain. In the 1932 presidential elections, the Democratic Party, with the strong support of most professional economists, targeted the tariff as a prime cause of the unemployment and misery then prevailing and helped themselves to the White House by blaming it all on Herbert Hoover, who had never wanted the tariff in the first place. Thus, regardless of the actuality, Smoot-Hawley was cast for all time as the ultimate bogeyman of trade policy, and by the late 1930s Hull had initiated a series of negotiations to begin negating the act by concluding deals for mutual tariff reductions with several key U.S. trading partners. Guided by the long-standing British philosophy that unregulated free trade is always and everywhere a win-win proposition, these talks were the harbingers of the coming conversion experience by which America would replace Great Britain as the high priest of free trade among nations.

"Born Again" on Trade Policy

While Hull and his minions had led the way, it was America's new perspective from the pinnacle of power and our postwar global responsibilities that eventually clinched Washington's full "born again" conversion on trade policy. Perhaps the most important element was the desire of American and most other world leaders to avoid the nationalism that had been a fundamental cause of the war. They hoped that Hull and his allies were correct in thinking that open trade could be a force for peace and cooperation among nations and were willing to give it a try. As the new world leader, the United States could also now see that a revitalized Europe and Japan or a stable Middle East offered potential long-term benefits that could justify making short-term economic concessions. With the advent of the Cold War, trading technology and access to the U.S. market for the right to station troops in a critical country began to look smarter than insisting on narrow reciprocity and on maintaining complete U.S. industrial and technological leadership.

This conclusion was greatly facilitated by the fact that American industry had become more dominant than any other country's had ever been. In a world of unregulated free trade, American CEOs, like their British predecessors in the nineteenth century, were convinced they could not fail to win every time. Similarly, American labor also thought it would be a big winner because it was far and away the world's most productive workforce. Thus by 1950, after nearly a century and a half, Alexander Hamilton was out, and Adam Smith and David Ricardo were in.

The Bretton Woods–GATT System

The GATT and the IMF were established as the essential institutions for the achievement of the new world of free trade and increasingly integrated global markets (the term *globalization* was not yet in use but that was clearly where Hull and other U.S. policy makers wanted to go). The GATT was actually not so much an institution as an accident. At Bretton Woods, the idea was to have an International Trade Organization (ITO) as an IMF and World Bank counterpart that would deal with all aspects of trade, including tariffs and quotas, investment, antitrust issues, and so forth. The GATT was initially meant to be only the part of the ITO dealing with tariffs and other border trade barriers. But strong congressional opposition to creation of the ITO led President Truman not to bother even proposing the idea. Instead, he pushed for the GATT treaty, which Congress had previously authorized him to sign under a congressional-executive agreement. So the GATT became the only game in town for reducing tariffs and regulating trade.

The key principle of the GATT was nondiscrimination, and its two main pillars were its articles on most favored nation treatment (MFN) and national treatment. Under the MFN provisions, countries had to extend the most favorable terms in existence with any particular trading partner to all trading partners. In other words, if my tariff is normally 20 percent, but I offer to reduce it to 10 percent for country A, then I have to offer 10 percent to all other GATT members as well. National treatment meant that contracting parties would not use national tax or regulatory policies to discriminate against the goods, services, or investments of other parties. In short, I'll treat your companies and persons operating within my borders the same way I treat my own.

Now what the GATT and its successor, the WTO, call "free trade" is not what Adam Smith or the British of the nineteenth century or most American economists mean by "free trade." For the economists, free trade means that a country unilaterally removes its tariffs and other trade barriers regardless of what its trading partners do. It means laissez-faire or totally unregulated trade. The GATT/WTO, on the other hand, is supposed to be a *reciprocal* trade agreement. I reduce my tariffs to you only if you reduce something for me. Moreover, the GATT/WTO formally prohibits or restricts subsidies, dumping (selling in a foreign market at prices below the cost of production and/or below the home market price), nontransparent regulation, and a wide variety of other practices, including particularly any action that might nullify or impair the value of negotiated reductions in trade barriers. This is in some respects more a mercantilist approach to trade than a pristine free-trade approach. Contrary to much current economic orthodoxy, it highly values production, employment, and the costs of adjustment that might arise from changes in trading conditions and arrangements. Thus, one can be a WTO free trader without being a conventional economist's free trader.

The IMF was designed to promote an open world economy by encouraging monetary cooperation, currency convertibility, international liquidity (all countries can earn or borrow enough to pay their international bills), and the elimination of exchange restrictions. These were all seen as vital to the expansion of foreign trade and investment. Note that last point about investment. Although in the early days trade was the main concern, from the beginning there was a notion of investment flows and of a globalization going far beyond trade.

The lynchpin of this postwar system, which came to be called the Bretton Woods–GATT system, was the establishment of the dollar as the major international reserve currency and unit of account in a so-called dollar-gold standard. Under the initial agreements, the dollar was to be convertible to gold (only by other governments and not by individual citizens) at $35 per ounce while all other currencies were pegged to the dollar at fixed rates that could, in principle, be adjusted in response to such things as shifts in productivity subject to IMF approval. Thus, the Japanese could exchange Y360 for a dollar, the Germans could get a dollar for DM 4, and the British pound brought about $2.80.

Under this system, a country running significant trade deficits could finance them by borrowing dollars from the IMF. But it would also have to accept IMF guidance on how to reform its economy to avoid deficits, a requirement that might entail a globally agreed formal shift in the rate at which it pegged its currency to the dollar. Countries accumulating large surpluses of dollars could turn them in to the United States in exchange for gold. In turn, significant reductions of U.S. gold reserves were expected to put pressure on U.S. authorities to increase interest rates and tamp down inflationary excess spending. The objective was for each country to keep its international payments in balance and thereby to maintain overall balance in the system. As we will see, a weakness of the system was that while it provided discipline for countries in chronic deficit, there was no discipline for chronic surplus countries. At Bretton Woods, Keynes had anticipated the problem and called for a mechanism by which tariffs could be imposed on countries with surpluses. But the idea was never adopted owing to opposition from the United States, which expected to be more or less permanently in surplus.

The key dispute regarding Bretton Woods was over the role of the dollar. Keynes again objected, arguing that the dollar's supremacy would give the United States a privileged position. All other countries had to produce goods or services and export them in order to earn the dollars necessary for buying in international markets. (Virtually all things tradable were priced in dollars.) Only America could purchase in world markets by simply printing dollars. In doing so it could accumulate chronic deficits, export inflation, live beyond its means, enable its firms to invest and gain control of foreign markets more easily, and more easily finance global military deployments. Of course, other countries could attempt to discipline America by turning in their dollars for its gold, but a lot of damage could be done before that happened and, as we will see later, that move was freighted with its own problems.

Keynes's counterproposal was for the creation of a new international currency—the bancor—to be used by all countries equally in settling accounts through the IMF. Such a currency would, of course, put everyone on the same footing. But it was just because of the privileges to which Keynes and others objected that the U.S. Bretton Woods chief negotiator Harry Dexter White and the U.S. Treasury wanted the dollar to be king. And because in 1944 White and the United States had a lot more chips than Keynes and the UK, the dollar became king.

A consequence of the establishment of the dollar as the world's key currency was that for international trade to recover, enough dollars had to be circulating outside the United States to enable foreigners to pay for their imports. The best way to get dollars circulating out in the world was for America to import lots of things, an aim that was facilitated by the switch to free trade. The U.S. government began reducing tariffs and opening the U.S. market as it championed not only rising domestic consumption but also rising imports.

MIRACLES IN THE REST OF THE WORLD

For Europe and Asia, the immediate postwar challenge was quite different: the reconstruction of productive capacity. The emphasis was on saving, investing, protecting domestic markets, and exporting goods in order to earn the dollars necessary to buy oil and essential international commodities. (Remember that the IMF had designated the dollar as the main global reserve currency and currency of exchange or account.) Catch-up was the top priority. France, Britain, and Sweden adopted many socialist policies and governments promoted national champions in key industries. Germany adopted a more market-oriented approach but used traditional close cooperation between government, industry, and labor to rebuild its major manufacturing industries by emphasizing export-led growth strategies. Yet despite the generally large measure of government economic guidance and emphasis on exports, these were highly democratic societies with strong labor unions and had to pay some attention to the welfare of consumers and workers. Moreover, for the most part, they welcomed and even sought foreign investment and, thus, participation by foreign companies in their economies without many conditions. So while the Europeans were far from being red-blooded American capitalists, neither were they case-hardened mercantilists.

Beginning with Japan, however, Asia became a completely different story. Japanese leaders completely rejected the free-market, free-trade Anglo-American doctrine and set out on their own version of the Hamilton road. They imposed a near ban on inward investment by foreigners, made any rarely approved investment conditional on technology transfer—getting new technological expertise from the United States or others—and forced most foreign companies that did manage to get into the Japanese market to do so in joint ventures. Japan also virtually sealed its market shut against imports of any product like steel, machine tools, rice, or pharmaceuticals that might compete with products made in Japan.

In those days, Japan was a country with a lot of low-cost labor and relatively little capital and technology. According to the neoclassical free-trade doctrine the United States had recently adopted, the Land of the Rising Sun should have been specializing in low-tech manufacturing while leaving the sophisticated stuff to America. Of course, it did produce a lot of low-tech stuff, but the main emphasis was to catch up and to surpass the United States in industrial and technological capability. As Naohiro Amaya, the former vice minister of Japan's Ministry of International Trade and Industry (MITI), once explained to me: "We did the opposite of what American economists said. We violated all the normal concepts. The American view of economics may help business to increase current production or to lower current costs. But research and development is necessary for the future, and it is a gamble. Businessmen are risk-averse. They hesitate to take the gamble on new developments. Therefore, if the invisible hand cannot drive the enterprise to new developments, the visible hand must." In this regard, MITI official K. Otabe also once noted that "if the theory of international trade were pursued to its ultimate conclusion, the United States would specialize in the production of autos and Japan in the production of tuna." But he emphasized that this would not be the case, because the Japanese government believed that the creation of certain industries is "necessary to diversify and promote the development of the Japanese economy."

Japan thus adopted what came to be called a neomercantilist strategy. As noted earlier, it managed to negotiate an initial peg of the yen to the dollar at what most economists thought was an undervalued rate of Y360/$1. It protected its domestic markets on the grounds of its need to recover and to develop infant industries. To boost savings, the government made consumer credit virtually impossible to obtain and built its economy to operate primarily on a cash-payment basis. The government provided little support for home buying, and companies organized their corporate compensation systems to encourage the saving of semiannual bonuses. An army of housewives was hired part-time as weekly collectors of household savings deposits for the Postal Savings system. These savings were then funneled into export and so-called target industries. The building of world-scale production facilities was also subsidized. The government found many creative ways to support growth. To cite just one interesting example, the Japanese shipbuilding industry was given the exclusive concession to import sugar into Japan, a highly lucrative grant given that the Japanese market for sugar at the time was highly protected and the domestic price was several times that of the world market price. Not only did this approach prove spectacularly successful for Japan, it also became the template for the rest of Asia.

The Golden Era

The years between 1947 and 1973 saw remarkable economic growth in the "free world" economies and have come to be called the Golden Era. Europe and Japan both enjoyed "miracles" of economic recovery, and U.S. GDP and productivity grew at a compound annual rate of about 3 percent for twenty-five years while household income more than doubled. Home ownership in the United States rose by 50 percent as ownership of autos and TVs also shot up. Moreover, the gains were equitably spread, with low wage earners substantially narrowing the gap between themselves and those at the top.

Manufacturing was the driving force of this U.S. wealth creation, accounting for 22 percent of GDP, 22.3 percent of employment, and most of productivity growth. The big industrial companies were mostly unionized, and union members comprised 25 percent of the workforce. Most families had one breadwinner whose earnings easily supported a rising middle-class lifestyle. And despite the emphasis on consumption, savings still accounted for 9 percent of disposable household income, household debt was 12.4 percent, and the federal budget deficit was $14 billion.

During this period Washington moved ahead with its effort to expand global free trade. By 1967, several multilateral rounds of negotiations under the aegis of the General Agreement on Tariffs and Trade (GATT) had succeeded in dramatically reducing tariffs and other barriers to trade among the major countries. But in these deals, the United States conceded a lot more than it got. A good example is the 1947 Geneva Round of GATT negotiations in which the United States offered Britain tariff reductions on half of total imports from Britain with cuts of 36 percent to 50 percent on 70 percent of these items. In return, Washington asked for reduction of Britain's Imperial Preferences that discriminated in favor of imports from the empire. In the end, Britain kept the preferences and also pocketed the American concessions. President Truman and the State Department decided that for political reasons "a thin agreement was better than no agreement." Another example is the 1954–55 negotiation with Japan in which the United States made substantial tariff cuts on 56 percent of total imports from Japan while receiving major tariff cuts on only 1.6 percent of U.S. exports to Japan.

Nevertheless, these results were deemed a great success by economists and policy makers intent on promoting both recovery from the war and the binding of allies to the United States. The U.S. attitude was well expressed by a State Department official who noted in 1953 that "the U.S. trade surplus is a serious problem and we must become really import minded." President Truman added that "our industry dominates world markets and our workmen no longer need fear the competition of foreign workers." Indeed, in 1953 the President's Advisory Board for Mutual Security called for unilateral elimination of tariffs on autos and consumer electronics because "U.S. producers are so advanced no one can touch them." At the same time the State Department instructed its officers abroad to promote foreign exports to the U.S. market. I had personal experience of this as a young Foreign Service officer serving as vice consul at the U.S. Consulate in Rotterdam in 1965. Even at that twenty-year removal from the war and the need for recovery, one of my primary responsibilities was to promote Dutch exports to America. The fact that the Netherlands had a big trade surplus with the United States was of no consequence.

To be sure, there were some doubts about the wisdom of such unbalanced economic agreements. Former president Hoover feared in 1953 that "thousands of U.S. villages and towns will be deprived of their employment and their schools, churches, and skills will be greatly decimated." Treasury Secretary George Humphrey feared that "a great wave of competition from plants that we built for them [our trading partners in Europe and Japan] will bring vast unemployment to the United States." But Cold War concerns over national security trumped these objections. For instance, Secretary of State John Foster Dulles emphasized that "all problems of local industry pale into insignificance in relation to the world crisis." In the case of Japan, the White House stated in 1954 that the "overriding interest of the United States is to strengthen our national security by taking the first step to bind Japan to the free world." In connection with talks with Britain, President

Eisenhower noted that "trade restrictions which tend to drive away an ally as dependable as Britain do more harm to our security than permitting a U.S. industry to suffer."

Of course, those leaders making these statements had supreme confidence in the dominance of U.S. producers. Dulles, for instance, advised the Japanese to concentrate on exporting to Southeast Asia and to forget about the U.S. market because "Japan could not make anything Americans would be interested in buying." The chief U.S. negotiator with Japan from 1954 to 1955, C. Thayer White, emphasized that it would be stupid for Japan to build an auto industry and that it should instead import cars from America.

Signs of Trouble Brewing

Despite America's confident dominance and its rapidly rising living standards, there were harbingers, even in this Golden Era, of a gathering storm—one that by 1971–72 would put America in such trade and balance of payments difficulty as to sweep away much of the Bretton Woods system and create an entirely new dynamic of globalization. As early as 1956, Japanese textile exports to the U.S. market had made such inroads that the Eisenhower administration pressured Tokyo to "voluntarily" restrain some of its textile exports (a voluntary restraint agreement, or VER). By 1960, this had been broadened to include nearly all Japanese textiles; by 1969, there was also a VER on Japanese steel exports, which was later broadened to include European steel exports as well. From 1955 until 1970, sales of Germany's Volkswagen Beetle grew to 7 percent of the U.S. auto market, but that was nothing compared to what Sony and other Japanese producers were doing in the television market, where by 1972 they had captured 62 percent of sales of black-and-white TV sets and by 1976 had 45 percent of color set sales too—all this, of course, on top of their total dominance of radio, stereo, and recorder sales.

The constant American trade surpluses of the 1950s and early 1960s vanished in 1968–72. In a 1959 National Security Council debate on international trade policy, CIA Director John McCone noted that "the problem of foreign competition was going to grow rapidly in the future. The costs of production abroad of competitive products were shockingly lower than in the United States, mostly as a result of cheaper labor costs." And Treasury Secretary Robert Anderson emphasized that the balance of payments was the "acid test" of a sound economy. Now America seemed to be failing that test, with the likely consequence that both its global role and its standard of living would eventually have to be reduced. Indeed, the Norwegian historian Geir Lundestad remarked that "the United States is organizing its own decline."

Part of what was happening was the natural recovery of competitive position by the industries of Europe and Japan. But other more fundamental factors were at work as well. Washington had been engaging in unregulated or unilateral free trade, not the reciprocal free trade of the GATT. Not only had the United States opened its markets more than other countries had, but its official policy of promoting imports and of acquiescing in foreign restrictions on U.S. exports as well as in arrangements that compelled transfer of U.S. technology as a condition of entry into foreign markets was having a significant negative impact on U.S. industry. Furthermore, by the late 1960s the exchange rates for the dollar fixed by the IMF in 1947 had still not been adjusted despite dramatic increases in relative productivity by Japan and most of the major European countries. As a result, the dollar was seriously overvalued, and U.S. producers were increasingly priced out of foreign markets and beginning to move factories abroad to supply foreign markets with products made abroad rather than in overpriced America.

The United States was losing its competitive advantage, a development that underlies the problems of globalization today. By 1958 the habitual U.S. trade surplus was in serious decline, having fallen to $3.5 billion from $6.3 billion in 1957. In 1959, it fell to only $1.3 billion. This meant that the United States was not earning enough through its trade to cover the large outflow of dollars then stemming from U.S. overseas military expenditures, economic aid payments, and corporate investment in Europe as U.S. companies got around high European tariffs by buying European companies or simply putting new factories in European markets.

Whereas the problem after the war had been that foreign countries had too few dollars, now they had too many. By 1960, foreign dollar holdings exceeded U.S. gold reserves and were actually becoming a cause of dangerous inflation in Europe as they added to the monetary reserve base on which the banks did their lending. More reserves meant more and easier lending and more inflation. In addition, the fact that America increasingly could not pay its way meant the dollar glut would increase, and that meant a likely devaluation of the dollar sometime in the future. As a hedge against that outcome and also as a way of reducing what they saw as the artificial buying power of the United States, the Europeans began to exchange their dollars for gold. From 1958 to 1968, America lost nearly half its monetary gold and faced the prospect of having to reduce spending of all kinds dramatically.

In the early 1970s, as the U.S. trade balance continued to deteriorate and job losses in manufacturing mounted, the AFL-CIO reversed labor's traditional support of free trade in favor of "fair trade." At the same time, the U.S. Commission on Trade and Investment Policy warned that Washington was overemphasizing geopolitical considerations at the expense of U.S. economic interests. It further warned that the U.S. manufacturing base was declining (as had that of Britain before it) as a result of the industry-targeting policies of other countries. Meanwhile, as gold continued to flow out of Fort Knox, President Nixon faced the Hobson's choice of either accepting the loss of all U.S. gold reserves or imposing an austerity policy of spending cuts and controls on overseas investment as a way of reversing the dollar flow. But on August 15, 1971, Nixon found a third way. He suspended the dollar's convertibility to gold. Henceforth, the dollar would be a purely fiat currency, meaning it was money only because the U.S. government said it was. Its value would be determined entirely by supply and demand in the currency markets and ultimately by the extent to which people all over the world trusted the promises and the competitiveness of the United States.

This step by Nixon amounted to an immediate devaluation of the dollar, which made American exports more affordable abroad and foreign imports less so in the United States. As Secretary of the Treasury John Connolly explained to foreign dignitaries, "The dollar is our currency, but now it's your problem," meaning that the foreign leaders would now have to figure out a way of dealing with the inflationary excess of dollars other than redeeming them for gold. The answer, they all knew, was obvious but painful: revalue their currencies and make themselves less competitive in the international marketplace.

This marked a watershed in American economic history. By cutting the dollar's tie to gold while the dollar remained the world's main money, Nixon had put the world on a pure dollar standard and placed the United States in a uniquely privileged but seductively dangerous economic position. As Keynes had warned years earlier, now America could print money with no fear of losing gold. The only constraint on its ability to borrow and buy would be the possible unwillingness of other countries to continue accepting dollars. But if not dollars, what else were they going to use—yen, pounds, deutsche marks? And if they did so, who was going to defend them and buy their exports? No. There might come a day when the world would desert the dollar, but it wasn't today. So now America was empowered to buy and borrow and keep running deficits in its trade, its balance of payments, and its national budget just as long as it liked. The only check on profligacy would be its own common sense, and the consequences of any folly would not be fully reckoned for many years.

The Oil Crises

Initially, the dollar's divorce from gold and its accompanying devaluation helped stimulate a surge in U.S. exports while dampening imports so that trade moved back toward balance. But this positive development was overshadowed by the shockwave of the 1973 Arab oil embargo, which triggered a global recession and brought on stagflation, a combination of recession and raging inflation that Americans had never before experienced.

The oil crisis was a profound shock. The American way of life had come to be premised on cheap energy. From the discovery of oil in Titusville, Pennsylvania, in 1859 until 1973, the United States was not only the world's biggest oil producer; it was the swing producer, meaning that it had the capacity to fill any gaps in supply and thereby maintain relative stability in prices. The Arab oil producers had tried to enforce embargos before, in 1956 and 1967, but had failed because the United States still had enough domestic production capacity to offset that loss of supply. In a short time, the embargos had been broken. But by 1973, due to a combination of rising demand and declining production, the United States was importing an ever-increasing amount of its oil and had insufficient reserve capacity to foil an embargo. As the price of gas at the pump relentlessly rose and waiting lines at gas stations extended for miles, the Golden Era abruptly ended.

By eventually raising oil prices more than 250 percent, the embargo effectively imposed a huge sales tax on the world. The U.S. economy, along with those of virtually all other non-oil-producing countries, went into reverse. Unemployment in the United States hit 8.5 percent in 1975 and inflation progressed to 6.2 percent in 1973, 11 percent in 1974, and 13 percent in 1975. In their efforts to stabilize the situation, presidents Nixon and then Ford tried everything from jaw-boning to price controls to lower speed limits to alternative energy programs to the beginnings of auto gas mileage requirements to pinning "Win Against Inflation" buttons on their jackets. By 1978, the gas lines were a bad memory, and progress seemed under way. But then the 1979 Iranian oil crisis again sent prices soaring.

The extreme fiscal measures required to break the back of the runaway inflation obviated the benefits of the decoupling of the dollar from the value of gold. Federal Reserve Chairman Paul Volcker pushed short-term interest rates up to 20 percent, with those for home mortgages running up to 17 percent. Inflation was finally tamed, but the high interest rates also made investing in the United States extremely attractive; the high returns they would bring led to a rush of foreign investment into the U.S. economy. That, in turn, dramatically strengthened the dollar, more than offsetting the devaluation that followed decoupling from gold. The resurgence of the dollar made the United States a very costly place to produce goods and services for trade, and many more U.S. companies moved production to offshore locations such as Singapore, Hong Kong, and Malaysia.

Japan Rocks the Boat

A third shock to the system was the further evolution of Japan's catch-up growth strategy. U.S. leaders had hoped that the dollar devaluation would facilitate negotiations to open Japan's market while also dampening the successive waves of U.S.-bound Japanese exports. But neither wish was fulfilled. The Japanese and American negotiators couldn't even agree on the meaning of the word *open* as it applied to markets, let alone on any method for achieving an open market. As for exports, rather than reconciling themselves to any diminution, Japan's authorities moved vigorously to ensure that exports would remain as strong as ever. Directives from the Ministry of International Trade and Industry instructed Japanese business leaders to buy Japanese. Capital was provided at preferential rates to key producers along with tax rebates and other incentives for exports. Myriad regulations and unique Japanese standards were created in part to inhibit market penetration by foreigners. Meanwhile, new laws and programs to promote the electronics industry were instituted, and even as the Japanese government agreed to allow Texas Instruments, IBM, and other foreign companies to begin doing business in Japan, it did so by insisting that they transfer technology to or conclude joint ventures with Japanese companies. Both of these steps entailed substantial transfer of proprietary technology to active or potential competitors.

Cartels were also routinely organized to coordinate the penetration of the U.S. market. One, known as the Okura Group (because the leaders of the companies met every Monday at the Okura Hotel), coordinated attacks by Japanese electronics companies, which engaged in systematic and illegal price discrimination as well as targeted dumping of television sets in the U.S. market. The U.S. Treasury Department, charged with enforcing trade laws, turned a blind eye for reasons both of diplomacy and of the entrenched ideology of unregulated free trade. The result was that the Japanese share of the U.S. market soared. Eventually, in 1980, Japan's own domestic antitrust authorities stopped the collusion; by then, however, only three of the twenty-seven American companies that had made television sets in 1960 were still in business, and employment in the industry had fallen by nearly 75 percent.

Starting in the mid-1970s, the television story was repeated in the auto, semiconductor, machine tool, steel, videotape recorder, and other industries. The U.S. machine tool industry lost more than 40 points of market share. While in 1976 Silicon Valley's semiconductor producers accounted for 65 percent of the market in memory chips, ten years later their share had fallen to 25 percent. Many companies moved into services or other industries not in the Asian line of fire. RCA bought Hertz Rent a Car, for example, while continually cutting R&D and investment in electronics as the competition from Japan steadily squeezed market share from its consumer electronics division. Nor was it only Japan. Lee Kuan Yew, Singapore's prime minister, famously told his planners to "look East" for their model, and the South Korean and Taiwanese authorities followed suit.

Partly in response to the consequent onslaught of Asian exports, America's trade deficit, especially in manufactured goods, began to swell again, and U.S. manufacturing as a percentage of GDP fell while manufacturing employment also declined. Other important statistics were also showing negative trends. Productivity growth was stagnating, and median family income had actually fallen. Savings and investment fell, too. Perhaps most significant of all, more families were finding that two incomes were now necessary to maintain the middle-class lifestyle formerly supported by one. To be fair, this development wasn't all due to trade or to Japan and its Asian imitators. The oil crises, the impact of the Vietnam War, and rising inflation all played a role. But trade globalization was a major element.

Under the pressure of the deteriorating economy, Washington tried desperately to correct the trade imbalances by pressuring Japan and other GATT members participating in the Tokyo Round of the GATT trade negotiations for really meaningful tariff rate and import quota reductions. The hope was that such reductions would open the markets and trigger big increases in U.S. exports which would, in turn, revitalize the U.S. economy. By the round's conclusion in 1979, Tokyo had agreed to remove most quotas and to cut its average tariff rate to less than 5 percent, a rate lower than that of the United States. From then on, the Japanese response to "closed market" complaints was that their market was completely open with lower tariffs and fewer quotas than the U.S. market. They emphasized that Americans just didn't "try hard enough." The truth was more complicated.

Tariffs are not the only means of limiting imports. An export-led economy is organized and managed so as to avoid any imports that might prevent the achievement of that country's trade surplus objective. Thus, the myriad regulations, inspections, standards, and distribution arrangements that in a laissez-faire economy are left to individual actors are, in an export-led economy, carefully managed and orchestrated to achieve policy goals. For example, when Japan agreed in the mid-1970s to reduce tariffs on imported semiconductors, the Japanese government quickly passed a law to subsidize domestic semiconductor research and production. At the same time, the Ministry of International Trade and Industry (MITI) actively urged Japanese electronics companies to buy Japanese. As a reinforcing measure, it also limited investment in Japan by foreign semiconductor companies. Meanwhile, at the macro level, the Ministry of Finance was managing the exchange rate of the yen to the dollar to ensure that exports remained competitively priced, and that the incentives for saving and investment as well as the disincentives for consumption remained strong. Thus, while the Japanese economy was relatively "open" in terms of having low tariffs and few import quotas, it was as a practical matter still nearly impenetrable.

For this reason, one striking aspect of the response in Japan to any concessions made in trade negotiations at this time was that after every round of tariff reduction negotiations, the Japanese press would loudly proclaim that the tariff cuts agreed to would result in no significant increase in imports.

Despite its loud objections to Japan's mercantilist protectionism, the United States took no significant counteraction. Because unregulated, pure unilateral free-trade doctrine remained beyond question, the emphasis was all on negotiations to open Japan's market, then the world's second largest. Thus, even as Japanese producers continued to conquer one American industry after another, and trade friction intensified into nearly continuous negotiations (in which I acted as one of the chief negotiators), the United States held back on filing complaints of unfair trade with the GATT and on any tit-for-tat measures.

In the case of some industries, such as autos, the United States pressed for and the Japanese government agreed to "voluntary" export restraints under which Tokyo and the Japanese industry worked together to self-limit its U.S.-bound shipments. While that did provide some relief to the U.S. industry, it did so in a very costly way. If tariffs had been applied, Washington would have benefited from a big increase in revenue and the profits and likely market share of the Japanese companies would have been reduced. With the voluntary restraints, there was no loss of sales volume, just a limited increase. So profits stayed high. More important, however, was the fact that none of the dynamics underlying the situation were changed. Nor was this only the case with autos. Other industries like steel, machine tools, and consumer electronics had similar experiences.

In contrast to Japan, the European countries had allowed their currencies to appreciate without taking countermeasures in the wake of the dollar's divorce from gold. Moreover, while they often supported so-called national champion companies, they neither pursued the same systematic kind of export-led growth strategy as Tokyo nor aimed as a matter of policy to accumulate trade surpluses. Of course, there were problems between the United States and Europe, particularly arising from the formation of the Common Market and its common external tariff, which resulted in some loss of U.S. export business in certain formerly low-tariff European countries. But this disadvantage was off-set to some extent by the rapid growth of the Common Market economies at the time.

The most important factor, however, was the very different European attitude toward foreign investors. Whereas the Japanese and some other Asians made it extremely difficult for foreigners to build factories, acquire Japanese companies, or otherwise invest in their country, the Europeans were more receptive. U.S. business was easily able to obtain footholds in European markets by acquiring European companies as well as by building its own green field sites. Moreover, the interlocking arrangements between banks, producers, and distributors that tended to seal foreigners out in Japan were looser in Europe. The result was fairly balanced trade between the United States and Europe with far less friction. Indeed, the Europeans had pretty much the same experience with Japan as the Americans had and often asked the Americans for advice on how to handle the Japanese.

As pressure mounted from business, labor, and especially the Congress for the White House to file unfair trade complaints with the GATT and to declare Japan an unfair trader under then existing U.S. law, debate raged between the national security agencies (departments of State and Defense and the National Security Council) and the economists at the Department of Treasury and the Council of Economic Advisers on the one hand and the trade negotiators at the Commerce Department and the Office of the U.S. Trade Representative on the other. In this struggle, the majority of academic, media, and economic analysts sided with the first group while labor and much, but not all, of the business community sided with the latter group.

The trade negotiators essentially wanted the White House to give them some leverage. There were no real protectionists among them, but they wanted to initiate antidumping, antisubsidy, and unfair trade cases as a way of forcing the Japanese, who were well aware of the divisions within the U.S. government, to negotiate seriously under a real threat of possible unpleasant consequences if they rejected reasonable requests for market opening and the halting of subsidies and currency manipulation. Meanwhile, the attitude of the diplomats and the military was essentially that U.S. trade and economic interests should continue to be subordinated to geopolitical considerations. A good example was the case of the Japan Trade Task Force of 1984 headed by then vice president George H. W. Bush, to whose service I was seconded for a while from my post as counselor to the secretary of commerce. In the midst of extreme trade tensions with Japan, President Reagan designated Bush to head a team that would once and for all resolve the long-running and debilitating trade frictions. The expectation was that a final agreement would be crowned by an official vice presidential trip to Japan announcing success and a new era of mutual comity between the two countries.

Accordingly, the task force determined at the outset that there would be no trip without a satisfactory resolution of several key issues. At a crucial meeting in the vice president's office in March 1984, the negotiating members of the task force, including Deputy U.S. Trade Representative Mike Smith and me, agreed that sufficient progress had not yet been made. In particular, the issue of trade in semiconductors, a critical defense industry, remained problematic. While access to the Japanese market continued to be limited and patent and copyright protection difficult to assure, Japanese producers were, with government backing, aggressively dumping chips in the U.S. market and had attained a more than 60 percent share. Yet when Smith and I argued for more progress before any trip was scheduled, Assistant National Security Advisor Gaston Sigur slapped the arm of his chair and said: "We must have those bases. Now that's the bottom line." Although there had been no indication of any risk of our losing access to the bases (indeed, if the United States had threatened to vacate the bases, the Japanese would have been mortified), that statement was decisive. The trip was on.

Although the negotiations were declared a great success, most of the issues were left unresolved. Eventually a number of U.S. chip makers closed up shop, and more than 100,000 Silicon Valley workers lost their jobs. Even more significant, the United States lost technological leadership in production of several important kinds of semiconductor.

As for the economists, rather than moderating their argument for unregulated unilateral free trade in light of the obvious market distortions and disruptions, they emphasized all the more the view that trade is always and under virtually all circumstances a winning proposition for an open-market country. Moreover, they also insisted that while corporations compete in the marketplace, countries do not. These experts were completely unconcerned about the structure of trade and of the domestic economy. Whether the United States produced semiconductors or water conductors or orchestra conductors was a matter of no consequence. America would always have a comparative advantage in some things, whether they were wheat, or airliners, or wood chips, or dung. It could always trade those to Japan for semiconductors. Thus, the particular bundle of goods a country made and traded didn't matter.

Often implicit in these discussions was the assumption that America was transforming itself from an industrial into a mainly service- and technology-driven economy and that its workers would be providing sophisticated, high-skill, high-wage services and discovering new technologies. There was no sense that maintaining an industrial sector might be important, or any acknowledgment of a possible linkage between industry and the ability to perform or develop certain services and technology. For example, in 1984, former Council of Economic Advisers member Herb Stein told me with regard to the Japanese: "They will sell us Toyotas and we'll sell them poetry." Similarly in a 1984 White House discussion on whether to act against illegal dumping of Japanese semiconductors in the U.S. market, assistant to the president Richard Darman asked: "Why do we want a semiconductor industry? If our guys can't hack it, let 'em go." It was this attitude that led then Ford Motor Chairman Don Peterson to lament in congressional testimony in 1985 that "I wish someone would tell me that manufacturing is not un-American."

Economists did acknowledge that there are some "adjustment costs" for U.S. workers displaced from their jobs by imports. But these were seen as small compared with the large benefits for the much larger group of consumers who could more than afford to contribute to covering the cost of worker adjustment from the savings they obtained by buying inexpensive imported goods. They discounted the possibility that the loss of employment might create downward pressure on all worker earnings because they believed the government could always create full employment through stimulatory fiscal and monetary policy. That this power might be limited is now becoming increasingly clear, but the arguments at the time assumed no limits.

The few exceptions to the laissez-faire orthodoxy were usually linked to national security or major unemployment/political considerations. In 1979–80 when Chrysler was in danger of going bankrupt and laying off scores of thousands of workers in the midst of a recession, the U.S. government bailed out the company. To address the U.S. semiconductor crisis, Sematech was formed in the mid-1980s as a 50–50 industry-government R&D joint venture. The National Science Foundation also took over from DARPA development of what would become the internet and guided it toward commercialization.

But for the most part, the government exercised benign neglect as one after another U.S. industry shriveled: machine tools, consumer electronics, batteries, optics, flat panel displays, printed circuit boards, and many others. The argument that "we don't want government picking winners and losers" became an article of faith, and there was resistance to anything smacking of industrial policy or of government intervention specifically to improve the competitiveness of any industry. In particular, as noted above, manufacturing was said to be passé; America was leading the world into a postindustrial age. The U.S. economy would be better off specializing in finance, sophisticated services, and high technology. As manufacturing moved to Asia, it was argued, the U.S. economy would move to "higher ground."

TURNING POINT IN THE REAGAN REVOLUTION

In 1980, Ronald Reagan campaigned on the slogan "government is the problem," and his election gave laissez-faire ideology a decisive boost. As president he championed deregulation, one consequence of which was that Salomon Brothers trader Lewis Ranieri took advantage of looser regulations on savings and loan mortgage lenders at this time to develop the market for the first mortgaged-backed collateralized debt obligations (CDOs), which, in later iterations, would lead to so much wreckage in 2008. To kill the "beast" of government, Reagan also called for big tax cuts and smaller government except in the area of defense, where he pushed for a 600-ship navy and dramatically increased the Pentagon's budget. As a result, despite Reagan's dedication to "small" government, federal spending rose substantially while revenue fell, leading to another turning point in American economic history. As the federal budget deficit soared, hitting nearly 6 percent of GDP in 1985, household debt was also rising sharply (credit card debt went to more than $500 billion in 1985) as strapped workers borrowed to maintain living standards. Because America did not have the savings to finance all this debt itself, we became dependent on borrowing from Japan and other countries to fund our operations.

By 1985, the United States—having been the world's leading creditor nation in 1980—had become its leading net debtor. As I noted earlier, this inflow of foreign capital sent the dollar soaring, which in turn sent the trade deficit to an eventual $140 billion, or more than 4 percent of GDP. The "twin deficits" fed each other and became a symbol of America's declining competitiveness. Much as Caterpillar Corporation's CEO Lee Morgan and other Business Roundtable executives begged the president and Treasury Secretary Don Regan to do something about the strong dollar, they got no sympathy. I was present at one White House session in which Regan shouted at the executives: "Who said the dollar is overvalued? It clears in the international markets every day. The strong dollar is a reflection of a strong America."

Only it wasn't. Indeed, in 1983, even as the economy began to recover from the recession of 1980–82, the Cabinet Council on Commerce and Trade under the secretary of commerce reported to the White House that America was losing competitiveness. That was followed by a similar presentation to the cabinet in 1984 from the President's Commission on Industrial Competitiveness, chaired by Hewlett-Packard Chairman John Young. The response is best captured in a note pushed across the cabinet table to Commerce Secretary Malcolm Baldrige: "If the U.S. is in such trouble, why are the Europeans so jealous?" Of course, they weren't. In any case, in 1985, with the trade deficit breaking records every month and Congress threatening protectionist legislation, the president did appoint a strike force to identify unfair foreign trade practices and take action against them. I was made the head of it, and we quickly identified European subsidies for the development and production of the Airbus as an excellent first target for a strike.

The subsidies were clearly in contradiction of any concept of free trade. Their overt purpose was to create a European company to compete against and displace the dominant U.S. aircraft makers, and they were in fact doing just that. The U.S. companies had lost a substantial part of the market, and thousands of American workers had lost their jobs not only because of the subsidies, but also because the European airlines were under pressure from their governments to buy the new airbuses. In terms of a valid complaint, this one was a slam-dunk. But none of that mattered. When the time came for a White House meeting to decide on whether or not to proceed, Secretary of State George Shultz torpedoed the move, arguing that attacking Airbus subsidies would shatter NATO.

In retrospect, this was a pivotal, if confused, moment. Although the economy was coming out of recession, few people were feeling good, because employment was slow to pick up and incomes were slow to rise. The dollar was heading for the stratosphere along with the trade and federal budget deficits. Fear was palpable in Silicon Valley, Detroit, Pittsburgh, Seattle, and other centers of key U.S. manufacturing industries that were targets of strategic Asian and European catch-up policies. Indeed, there was a depression in the San Jose area, where, as mentioned previously, the semiconductor industry laid off nearly 100,000 workers in 1983–84. Many voices were demanding many things, and Congress was responding with hundreds of proposed bills and amendments. But most of what was being demanded and proposed was poorly conceived, impossible, or just downright crazy. The volume and diversity of complaints signaled one thing for certain: the American people knew something was wrong, though they weren't sure quite what or how to fix it.

Eventually, four broad views of the situation emerged. Wall Street and the White House said that actually not much was wrong. The strong dollar and the trade deficit simply reflected the strength of the U.S. economy and the desire of foreigners to invest here. The federal budget deficit would fix itself as soon as growth stimulated by tax cuts kicked in. This group's recommendation was to do nothing and accuse those who did call for some kind of action of being Smoot-Hawley protectionists and Japan bashers.

The economists in academia and in think tanks like the Brookings Institution, the Institute for International Economics, and the American Enterprise Institute saw the problem as one of saving and investment imbalances. The Japanese and Germans saved, invested, and produced too much while consuming too little and thus accumulated chronic trade surpluses. The Americans did the opposite. The bogeyman was the federal budget deficit, which was a major and, in principle, relatively easily fixable cause of the low American savings rate and thus of the trade deficit. Excess American consumption was being exacerbated by the strong dollar. The economists' solution was to balance the federal budget (cut spending and raise taxes), negotiate another dollar devaluation, stand firm against any trade action or industry support, and also accuse anyone suggesting these things of being a Japan-bashing Smoot-Hawley protectionist. A third group comprising some members of Congress and people in hard-hit industries were, in fact, pretty close to being Japan-bashing Smoot-Hawley protectionists. Their solution was pretty much to raise tariffs and severely limit foreign access to the U.S. market.

The fourth group, in which I found myself, was known as the "revisionists" because it argued that the conventional view of Japan as more or less an American-style free-market, free-trade democratic capitalist economy needed to be "revised" to account for Japan's declared industrial and strategic export policies as well as for its uniquely homogeneous and tightly organized society. This group included the likes of University of California, Berkeley, professor and China and Japan expert Chalmers Johnson, *The Atlantic* magazine's editor James Fallows, the Dutch journalist and Japan expert Karel van Wolferen, and a number of what might loosely be called fellow travelers such as University of California, Berkeley, professor Laura Tyson, New Mexico Senator Jeff Bingaman, and *U.S. News and World Report* editor James Impoco. Also loosely tied to the revisionists were a number of industry figures like Intel founder and chairman Bob Noyce, Ford Motor chairman Don Peterson, FedEx founder and chairman Fred Smith, and Lockheed chairman and former undersecretary of defense Norm Augustine.

These people all saw themselves as internationalists and free traders. I myself had lived in Switzerland, the Netherlands, Belgium, and twice in Japan. All of us wanted to have closer trade ties with other countries and greater global economic integration. We saw ourselves as pioneers of globalization. At the same time, we did not hold the orthodox view that potato chips and computer chips have the same economic significance or that simply watching the subsidized European Airbus Industrie take big slices of the market away from the U.S. aircraft industry was a good thing for the U.S. economy. We also knew that the Japanese did not accept the orthodox view and that many of the top Japanese leaders knew that America's leaders were unaware that they didn't. While we believed in free trade and at one time had been disciples of orthodoxy ourselves, our views had been tempered by experience in the real world, and we had come to believe in a free trade based on broad reciprocity and regulated by the basic rules of fair play, including prohibition of purposeful market distortion. We also knew that this kind of free trade would, from time to time, involve conflict and necessitate a willingness to stand firm and even to play tit for tat in certain circumstances.

Our solution was in part that of the economists. We also proposed reducing the federal budget deficit and bringing savings and investment more into balance globally. But whereas the economists and much of the media saw the problem primarily as one of deficits, we saw it more as one of trade and industry structure. For example, balancing the budget and deficits would not open the Japanese market for air freight delivery by FedEx, but FedEx getting such access was nevertheless important. Nor would it stop the devastation of Silicon Valley by the overvalued dollar and the dumping of Japanese semiconductors. So in addition to the macroeconomic balancing measures, we proposed more industry-focused measures as well.

If Japan was targeting the U.S. semiconductor industry, we wanted to take various offsetting measures, such as creating an industry-government consortium to foster closer ties between American device makers and equipment makers or negotiating target amounts or percentages of markets for imports into Japan as a way of gaining concrete as opposed to theoretical market opening. We didn't have a one-size-fits-all solution but were proposing a sophisticated, multifaceted strategy that took into account the cultural and institutional differences between participants in globalization. Unlike many critics, we didn't call Japan "unfair." We simply said it was different from the norm anticipated by the GATT and by U.S. economists and needed to be treated in a somewhat nonnormal fashion to accommodate its valid and understandable cultural and institutional variations.

If the adherents of the conventional wisdom in academia and the media had been willing to sit down with us and have a real discussion, we might have been able to find common ground. But their tendency was much more to impugn us as Japan bashers and Smoot-Hawley protectionists than to talk with us. Having a Chinese wife and two adopted sons of Japanese and Filipino extraction, I found this attitude more than frustrating. This was a moment when a deeper, pragmatic analysis might have led to a more nuanced approach to globalization that would have avoided many of our present difficulties.

Alas, amidst the clamor and with the soaring trade deficit, which was making even the Treasury nervous, Treasury Secretary James Baker turned to an old solution—devaluation of the dollar and another GATT round of market-liberalizing negotiations. On September 22, 1985, in talks held at the Plaza Hotel in New York, he was able to strike a deal under which the United States, Japan, West Germany, France, and the UK agreed to engineer a gradual devaluation of the dollar against the Japanese yen and the German mark. The twofold objective was to reduce the U.S. trade deficit (and the political pressure Baker thought it was generating) by reducing the price of U.S. exports and increasing that of imports, thus fostering export growth and the consumption of U.S.-produced goods and services. A year later, the Uruguay Round of GATT negotiations was launched and aimed at further removal of overseas import barriers and market opening, measures that U.S. leaders hoped would reduce the American trade deficit or at least the complaints over unfair trade.

The Plaza Accords, as the currency deal came to be known, had mixed results. Over the next two years, the dollar declined by more than 50 percent against the yen and somewhat less against the mark. Although the U.S. trade deficit with Western Europe fell as intended and as predicted by conventional economic wisdom, the deficit with Japan actually grew for two reasons. First, Tokyo offset some of the deal's impact on its exports by reducing interest rates, thereby lowering the costs of investment and borrowing and increasing the competitiveness of Japanese exporters. Second, a number of American companies, like the consumer electronics producers and a number of semiconductor makers, simply went out of business or, like the VCR pioneer Ampex, outsourced their production to Japanese producers. For both reasons, Japanese exports to the U.S. market rose. As for the Uruguay Round, the talks dragged on without any indication that there would be any market opening that might stimulate U.S. exports.

Nevertheless, the mere announcement of the Plaza deal and the launch of the GATT talks helped to ease pressure a bit as people waited to see whether anything actually came of them. Other factors also contributed to an initial abatement of complaints. Ironically, the exit of many U.S. companies from the market meant there were fewer complainers. Also, in the wake of Fed Chairman Paul Volcker's conquest of inflation and President Reagan's tax cuts and rising defense expenditures, the economy was beginning to recover. Finally, a number of Reagan administration initiatives aimed at shoring up U.S. industries—the Sematech consortium and assistance for the revival of motorcycle maker Harley-Davidson, for example—began to have a positive impact.

But the honeymoon didn't last long. Not only didn't the trade deficit with Japan decline, but the Japanese continued to gnaw away at U.S. industry while their own market remained mostly closed. It became clear that Chrysler was destined to be replaced by Honda as number 3 in the U.S. auto market. Under its ambitious CEO Jack Welch, General Electric acquired RCA in 1986 and Welch promised that it would "be able to compete successfully with anyone, anywhere, in every market we serve." By 1988, however, Welch decided RCA couldn't compete with anybody and sold it to France's Thompson SA. (Woodrow Wilson must have twirled in his grave.) As a symbol of the decline of American competitiveness, this was powerful indeed. But it was soon topped by Mitsubishi Estate Corp.'s acquisition of New York's Rockefeller Center. And that was just the start. Soon the Japanese owned famed Pebble Beach and virtually all the hotels in Waikiki.

The reduction of Japanese interest rates in reaction to the Plaza deal had led to a buying spree in stocks and real estate that drove prices sky high. At one point, the value of the Imperial Palace in the center of Tokyo was estimated to be greater than that of the entire state of California. Japan seemed to be well on the way to becoming number 1, and that it seemed to be doing so unfairly caused resentment. While Japanese were free to buy these trophy properties in America, Americans would not have been allowed to make similar acquisitions in Japan. There was fear and anger in the United States, and Japanese cars were trashed in Detroit while members of Congress tore up Toshiba VCRs on the steps of the Capitol. Beyond this largely symbolic protest there was also real pain. In the early 1980s, the Reagan penchant for getting the government out of things had resulted in full deregulation of the nation's savings and loan banks (S&Ls) and the slashing of the Federal Home Loan Bank Board's supervisory staff but not in the abolition of their traditional government guarantees. This invitation to recklessness led to extremely risky lending that first engendered a real estate boom and then a bust in 1987, which caused the insolvency of the Federal Savings and Loan Insurance Fund and a subsequent costly bail-out. On October 19, 1987, the Dow Jones Industrial Average of stocks fell by a one-day record (larger than the crash of 1929) of 22.6 percent. The Federal Reserve responded quickly by easing short-term interest rates, and the market soon recovered. But the jolt had been serious.

Shortly thereafter, however, these gloomy developments were over-shadowed by the fall of the Berlin Wall in 1989; victory over Saddam Hussein's Iraq in the First Gulf War; the achievement of the first U.S. trade–current account surplus in ten years in 1991; and the fall of the Soviet Union on Christmas Day of the same year. The competitive challenge from Japan also seemed to evaporate as the bursting in 1992 of a massive financial bubble that had developed there left its banks in ruins and many of its major companies drowning in a sea of bad debt. On top of all that, it was clear by now that China had definitely chosen the "capitalist road," and then, in the wake of the collapse of the Soviets, India also swapped socialism for market capitalism. All this good news was a powerful elixir. It looked like America was back, more powerful and more successful than ever. Free-market, democratic capitalism had won. Indeed, professor and author Francis Fukuyama pronounced the triumph of the American model in the title of his book *The End of History*, which foresaw global adoption of the American model as the last stage of economic and political evolution. It was all over. Why had anyone worried about the Soviets or Red China or even bothered to mention the Japanese model? It was free-market, free-trade America that the world wanted to imitate, or so Americans gave themselves to understand at the time.

The underlying economic problems nonetheless kept flaring up. A spike in oil prices following Iraq's invasion of Kuwait in mid-1990 added to the economic drag created by Black Monday and the S&L

crisis, and triggered a recession that carried into 1992. The trade–current account surplus went back in the red by more than $50 billion in 1992, as it became clear that the surplus of a year earlier had been an artificial by-product of the war, the result of payments from Japan and other allies of over $50 billion to help share the war's costs. By the close of the Reagan-Bush era, the underlying economic trends were belying the Cold War victory. The national debt had more than doubled, and consumption had risen to 66 percent of GDP (from 56 percent in 1960) as savings had substantially fallen. Honda had accomplished its displacement of Chrysler as the third most successful car seller in the U.S. market, household liabilities had risen by more than 50 percent, average weekly earnings (1973 dollars) had fallen from $319 in 1973 to $272 in 1980 to $262 in 1990. The federal budget deficit was up to $171 billion from $111 billion in 1989, and unemployment was rising as U.S. companies shifted more production and jobs offshore. With the 1992 presidential election looming, it was clear that once more the problem was "the economy, stupid," as Arkansas governor Bill Clinton kept repeating on his way to the White House.

While this might have been a moment for serious reconsideration of the policies that had so undermined the foundations of the country's economic strength, the story of the era to follow was quite different. Pride and joy in a great triumph were tempered by fear and uncertainty about the future as people felt the tectonic plates of the global economy shifting beneath them.

4

Goldilocks and Bubbles:
The Faith in Efficient Markets

Why do we wish to inhibit the pollinating bees of Wall Street?

—ALAN GREENSPAN, 2007

lected largely on the basis of voters' economic discontents, Clinton was actually the luckiest of presidents in terms of the circumstances he inherited and the potential they offered for shaping the course of history at a moment of epic changes. By the time Clinton took the oath of office, the economy was already coming out of what was later seen to have been quite a mild downturn. Several factors were pushing the economy ahead: the fall in oil prices following the liberation of Kuwait in the First Gulf War, the Fed's maintenance of relatively low interest rates, the reduction of the federal budget deficit by dint of reduced defense spending in the wake of the Soviet collapse, and the natural turn of the business cycle. But the effect of these was not evident at the time. Moreover, Clinton faced an excruciating decision over taxes. Although he had campaigned for a middle-class tax cut, he had also promised that if elected he would balance the federal budget whose inexorably rising deficit, in the context of paucity of U.S. savings with which to finance it, augured higher interest rates and lower long-term growth.

His political advisors urged him to do the tax cuts first, but National Economic Council Director Robert Rubin pushed for a tax increase to balance the budget, arguing that a balanced budget would create confidence in financial markets and lead to low long-term interest rates that would spur steady long-term growth. In this he was seconded by Federal Reserve Chairman Alan Greenspan. Ultimately, and at substantial political cost at the time, Clinton opted for the tax increase. In retrospect it is not clear what the real impact of this step was, but coming on top of the other developments, it coincided with the start of what appeared to be the longest, most robust economic boom in U.S. history, finally ending in 2001. Based on the economic ideas of the Washington consensus, the boom strengthened American confidence in globalization as a kind of Americanization and in the geopolitical status quo. It also made harbingers of trouble easy to ignore and blinded our entire leadership elite to the reality of our rapidly eroding position.

THE WASHINGTON CONSENSUS

Although the boom would prove, as we will see later, to have a downside, its advent and long duration were not only very welcome but also coincided with a global boom that followed in the wake of the Soviet collapse, the bursting of the Japanese bubble, and the apparent worldwide adoption (especially in China and India) of the free-market capitalist system. This, in turn, gave wide credence to a formula for economic success that came to be called the Washington Consensus. Originally a set of policies and guidelines for enabling Latin America to overcome its 1980s economic and financial crises, the Washington Consensus eventually came to signify a broad set of market-oriented—even market-fundamentalist—policies deemed essential for economic success anywhere and everywhere. The formula was an amalgamation of free-market and free-trade theory and included the principles of deregulation, privatization, rule of law, transparency, primacy of market forces, free trade, fiscal discipline, promotion of education, health care, and infrastructure investment, moderate marginal tax rates, promotion of inward foreign direct investment, competitive exchange rates (preferably floating exchange rates), and democratization. Do these things, said much of the Western economic, business, media, government elite, and your country is sure to become rich.

From Trade to Globalization

As more and more countries did some or all of these things in the 1990s, international trade morphed into the far broader and more complex phenomenon of globalization. Heretofore, international economic negotiations had concerned themselves mostly with tariffs and barriers to trade at the border on the one hand and with currency exchange rates and regulation of financial flows on the other. Moreover, these negotiations and the expanded international trade they fostered really applied only to the half of the world that called itself the "free world." The establishment of the European Economic Community (EEC, or Common Market) in 1957 had actually been a harbinger of a more economically integrated future, but it wasn't until 1992–94 that a series of developments extended and deepened the Common Market concept and applied it on a global basis. We have already noted the addition of the former Soviet Union, China, and India to the free world's free market in 1992. At the same time, the EEC transformed itself into the European Union (EU) with a single market fully integrating—more or less—all aspects of the economy. Also in 1992, the United States, Mexico, and Canada essentially extended the 1988 U.S.-Canadian Free Trade Agreement into the North American Free Trade Agreement, or NAFTA. Despite the use of the words "free trade," the agreement was essentially for an economic union, looser than but similar to the EU arrangement. Then in 1993, President Clinton hosted the first meeting of the leaders of twenty-one nations of the Asia Pacific Economic Cooperation group (APEC), who committed to greater economic integration of their nations.

Finally in 1994, the Uruguay Round of GATT negotiations concluded by turning the GATT into the World Trade Organization (WTO), the final realization, after forty-odd years, of the International Trade Organization (ITO) that had been rejected in 1952 because of overwhelming opposition in the U.S. Senate. Institutionally, substantively, and structurally, the WTO revolutionized both the concept and the administration of the world economy. Of the two key new elements, the most important was compulsory dispute settlement—a term that sounds like bureaucratese, but is a requirement that essentially cut the United States off at the knees and made the WTO perhaps the most powerful international governing body. The contracting parties to the GATT had all committed to certain deals and to consult with each other in the event of disputes. While they had even gone so far as to create panels to investigate and report on disputes, the enforcement of the panel findings had been purely a matter of shaming a country and hoping for its voluntary cooperation. If a country, particularly a big important country like the United States, wanted to ignore the GATT and its panels, it could and did. Indeed, the United States had (and still formally has) section 301 of its trade law, which enabled it unilaterally to declare another country an unfair trader and to impose tariffs or other sanctions on imports from that country. The threat of 301 had given U.S. trade negotiators a great deal of leverage in attempting to ameliorate objectionable practices by its trading partners. Few Americans realized it at the time, and had the negotiations been over nuclear weapons few would have agreed to the deal, but the WTO arrangement essentially negated 301. It meant that a country could not ignore trade complaints and that, in principle at least, no country, not even the United States, could act as its own policeman on global economic issues. Of course, it also meant that other countries, again, in principle, couldn't ignore U.S. complaints. In short, it put teeth into WTO commitments. The second key new element of the WTO was its expansion of the concept of "trade" to include such things as patent and copyright law, industry development financing, health regulations, and procurement of supplies by government buyers. Things that previously had been of strictly domestic concern were suddenly now part of international trade and under the oversight of this new international institution. It really should have been called the World Globalization Organization.

So we have countries moving to integrate their economies more broadly and deeply, a brand-new institution to set and enforce the rules of the new game of globalization, and lots of new countries joining the game. Then, in the mid-1990s, the game was transformed by going first to supersonic and then to light speed.

In the 1970s and 1980s, FedEx had revolutionized package and cargo delivery in the United States with its air express overnight service. Then, in the early 1990s, it expanded service to Asia, and then to Europe and the rest of the world. By the latter half of the decade, FedEx and its rivals like UPS could pick up a cargo from any point in the world and deliver to any other point in the world in about thirty-six hours. But that was nothing compared to what the internet was about to do. Nurtured for years by the Defense Advanced Research Projects Agency (DARPA) and then by the National Science Foundation, the internet had long been a toy for geeks and a tool for really elite university researchers. But with the advent of the browser around

1995, the internet revolutionized communication, business organization, social life, and much more, including, most important of all, globalization. Suddenly, anything that could be done or sent digitally—back-office accounting, software design, radiological analysis of brain scans, to name only a few items—could be done anywhere in the world and sent anywhere else in the world in a maximum of two seconds, borne at the speed of light over optical fiber cables. Singapore, Shanghai, Bangalore, London, Rio, and anywhere else you like were now next door.

These developments both spurred and were spurred by the evolution of global production and supply chains. The policies of the Asian export-led growth economies aimed to make them the low-cost centers of production, and especially with the entrance of China into the global system, they did. The advent of global air express delivery and then of the internet greatly facilitated moving production and even the provision of what had previously been considered local services to these centers. As a result—in what came to be called "offshoring" and "outsourcing"—companies like General Electric, Motorola, and Citibank closed many of their U.S.-based operations and moved the work either to their own factories or to those of outside subcontractors in Guangzhou or Singapore or Bangalore.

To be sure some people at the time worried about the wisdom of moving U.S. jobs and key technologies overseas, but, initially at least, they were surprisingly few and were readily dismissed in light of the U.S. boom with its full employment and productivity gains. Indeed, our economic elite emphatically presented the outsourcing, offshoring, and rapid increase in U.S. imports as positive sources of strength for the American economy. They were said not only to hold down inflation by providing low-cost goods and services, but also actually to increase net U.S. employment by raising the productivity and profits of U.S. companies, thereby allowing them to expand and hire more Americans. In short, all things were working together for good for the American and global economies.

The Dot-com Boom

What made for such sanguinity was the extraordinary boom then taking hold in the U.S. economy. The rapid adoption of email and websites for every taste and purpose created enormous demand for massive expansion of the internet. The factories were humming day and night to turn out the optical fiber cables for filling in the trenches then being dug in the streets of every city across the nation. Orders for more switches, routers, and other high-tech gear soared as such "start-ups" as Cisco, Google, and Amazon.com sprouted like weeds after rain. Spurred by this demand, low inflation, and low interest rates, investment as a percentage of GDP in the U.S. economy rose to levels it hadn't seen in thirty years, and unemployment fell to under 4 percent, the level long considered equivalent to full employment and also a level not seen in thirty years. Very important was the fact that median wage and family income levels began to rise for the first time in a generation. Even more important, productivity growth, which had been stuck for years at about 1.5 percent, suddenly jumped to 2.5 percent. The stock market, especially the technology-laden NASDAQ index, seemed to be setting new record highs every day. *BusinessWeek* spoke of the Goldilocks economy—everything was just right. America appeared to be more competitive and more the fount of new technology, innovation, and wealth than ever before. Why, many commentators wondered, had anyone been concerned about the Japanese challenge of the 1980s? It was the American model of the Washington Consensus that was driving this win-win globalization and that everyone wanted to imitate. Or so, at least, America's elite believed.

The Three Apostles: Greenspan, Rubin, and Summers

In particular, the new prosperity and booming world growth were widely interpreted as confirmation of the validity of the twin pillars of the Washington Consensus–based American model—efficient-market theory and free-trade theory, in which the three most influential economic players during the Clinton era were staunch believers.

Alan Greenspan's management of the Federal Reserve (1987–2005) represented a doubling down on Reagan's bet on deregulation and the magic of markets. A longtime disciple of the extreme libertarian novelist Ayn Rand, Greenspan was among the most ardent devotees of the relatively new efficient-market theory, which by the 1980s had swept Wall Street and become the dominant explanation of how and why markets work. First postulated by French mathematician Louis

Bachelier in his 1900 dissertation on the theory of speculation, the
efficient-market concept was largely ignored until 1965 when the
University of Chicago's Gene Fama published his dissertation on
the "random walk" pricing model with which Wall Street became
greatly enamored. MIT's Paul Samuelson published some refinements
on this thinking, and then in 1970, Fama published a review both of
the theory and of the empirical evidence to support it, thereby cement-
ing his position as the father of the random walk efficient market hypothesis (EMH). The EMH ruled thinking about financial and other
markets until the great 2008–9 economic crisis.

Under EMH, market participants are assumed to be completely
rational actors always making decisions in their self-interest and ab-
sorbing and responding to new information immediately. The rational
expectations of any particular actor may be wrong or biased, but those
of the group of actors as a whole will not be. This is the "wisdom of
crowds." Thus, EMH considers that market prices always incorporate
all available information and are therefore always correct at any particular moment. The arrival of new information may alter expectations
and prices, but they will simply shift the system to a new, stable equilibrium awaiting further information. Thus, the next move in any price
is completely random, like flipping a coin, and professional investors
cannot beat the market over any extended period because they have no
information not already priced into the market. Wall Street found this
random nature of the market particularly attractive because mathematicians and physicists had long ago figured out how things move when
controlled by random processes. Indeed, Albert Einstein had received
his PhD for working out the math that explains such random walks
as the paths of particles—or asset prices—when stimulated by random
shocks. With a large enough number of movements, the pattern is that
of the normal bell curve. Once you have a bell curve and figure out the
width or standard deviation of the distribution of movements, you can
forecast the entire probability set of future asset returns, an obviously
very handy capability for a vast range of financial concerns.

But EMH was also handy in another way. Because the market is
always correct, it cannot have bubbles when left to its own devices.
Deregulation would remove such distortions and also spur innovation
that would increase efficiency while reducing risk by increasing the
number of market participants. This thinking logically led to the con-

clusion that deregulation would make markets both more efficient and safer. From there it was only a hop, skip, and a jump to deregulation of the trucking, railroad, and airline industries in the late 1970s and then to that of the S&Ls and other depository institutions in the early '80s along with the lifting of the last vestiges of oil price controls. Later, the 1988 Basel Accord exempted banks from maintaining significant reserves against the risk of losses on marketable securities. Then, in 1989 and 1993, in moves that would set the table for big events later, the U.S. Commodity Futures Trading Commission exempted swaps and derivatives from all regulation.

Greenspan passionately subscribed to the argument that deregulation would engender financial innovation that would reduce risk, increase the productivity of capital, and promote greater prosperity. He had an unshakable faith that markets police themselves. The assumption was that in order to protect their shareholders, their own profits—and their reputations—leading market participants monitor each other closely. Greenspan further argued that banks were "much better situated and staffed" to understand what other banks and hedge funds were doing as compared with "by the book" government regulation. He insisted that any restrictions on fund investment behavior would curtail risk taking that is integral to the economy of the United States—"Why do we wish to inhibit the pollinating bees of Wall Street?" In view of this attitude, he was pleased to find, as he wrote in his book *The Age of Turbulence*, that the Fed's supposed watchdog Division of Bank Supervision and Regulation had a very "free-market orientation" with "less emphasis on 'thou shalt not' and more on disclosure that would enable markets to function more effectively." In fact, Greenspan largely halted the Fed's active oversight of the banking industry.

In this passion for deregulation, he was joined by Treasury Secretary Bob Rubin and his deputy (and successor as treasury secretary), Larry Summers. Together, the three mounted an aggressive campaign to halt any efforts to regulate trading of new derivative instruments like CDOs (collateralized debt instruments) and CDSs (credit default swaps). Indeed, they even argued against margin rules on derivative positions and demanded that Congress stop Chairwoman of the Commodity Futures Trading Commission Brooksley Born from initiating oversight of derivative trading by stripping the commission of its jurisdiction over such trading. From there they went on to work closely with Senator Phil Gramm to achieve the 1999 abolition of the venerable Glass-Steagall Act that had been adopted in the wake of the Great Depression to reduce risk by ensuring separation between commercial and investment banking. But the three apostles thought financial supermarkets and nonbank banks would make for more efficient and safer markets in the future because they would be unregulated and wholly governed by market forces.

HARBINGERS OF TROUBLE

Between 1990 and the financial industry's collapse in 2008–9, several incidents occurred that should have alarmed believers in the efficacy of the efficient-market theory: the deflation of the CMO bubble, bubbles in Southeast Asia, the collapse of the Long-Term Capital Management (LTCM) hedge fund, and the bursting of the dot-com bubble. Of course, there were along the way some analysts who were skeptical about the theory, but, in a supreme irony, the relative rapidity with which the economy recovered from each incident, along with Greenspan's skill in directing the economy much as a "maestro" directs an orchestra, only further confirmed the theory in people's minds. If the new, unregulated global economy could take such blows and bounce quickly back at a flick of Greenspan's baton, something must be working right, and the Fed chairman's argument that it was easier to clean up after a bubble than to spot, prevent, or abort one must also be right. At least that was the consensus view.

The CMO Bubble

The first shock to the system came in the market for collateralized mortgage obligations (CMOs). These had been developed by First Boston Corporation in the early 1980s to help Freddie Mac finance mortgages. By buying their mortgages, Freddie enabled S&Ls to free up and redeploy their capital into new loans, thereby fostering more lending to meet the demand of the baby boomers for new homes. But Freddie needed to maintain its own liquidity by passing the mortgages it bought on to other investors. It did this in various ways, none entirely satisfactory. The CMO assembled a slug of mortgages in a trust and then sliced, or "tranched," them (initially) into three segments, each of which would issue a bond backed by the mortgages. The trick was that the top tranche of bonds, representing, say, 70 percent of the mortgages, had first claim on all cash flows. Since it was extremely unlikely that more than 30 percent of a normal mortgage portfolio could default, these bonds got triple-A ratings. They yielded a relatively low return. The second tranche, representing, say, 20 percent of the mortgages, got a lower rating but offered a high yield, while the third tranche of 10 percent of the mortgages, though the first to absorb all the losses, paid junk bond–type high yields. In this way, CMOs looked and felt just like bonds and greatly facilitated the pass-through of mortgages to investors. They also generated nice profits for First Boston and other early issuers.

So nice, in fact, that by the early 1990s nearly everyone on Wall Street had joined the game, and there had evolved a very large market of ultracomplex instruments, sometimes with more than one hundred tranches of payouts from the same pool of mortgages. The risk of a CMO was, of course, that a lot of mortgages might default, forcing a reduction or suspension of the regular payouts from the various tranches. The CMO originators had been confident of containing the risk with very conservative tranche segmentation so that even an abnormally high rate of defaults would not affect the payouts of the top tranches. But with one hundred tranches, there was much less room for abnormal rates of default. The problem became the so-called toxic waste in the bottom tranches. Few wanted to buy it, so the issuing firms tended to keep a fair amount of it on their own balance sheets. There were also hedge funds that specialized in investing in the toxic waste, often borrowing three times their own capital to maximize their position. As long as home prices kept rising (which seemed a safe bet at the time) and interest rates stayed reasonably low so that the carrying costs of their borrowing were not too high, the funds could be confident of few mortgage defaults, and the high rates of return on the toxic waste combined with the funds' leverage would enable them to make a killing.

But by 1994 the economic recovery that had been accelerating since 1992 was gaining a real head of steam. In order to prolong the recovery by preventing a short, unsustainable burst of growth, the Fed began raising interest rates for the first time in several years, sending the stock markets into reverse. That changed all the fancy CMO calculations, especially those for toxic waste, which suddenly could not be sold at any price. Instead of making a killing, the hedge funds got killed along with lots of other investors whose CMOs were not paying back as expected or, worse, had become worthless. Losses eventually amounted to about $55 billion as the CMO bubble deflated.

According to the efficient-market theory, this whole experience should not have happened. Indeed, by definition, bubbles could not occur under the theory because the market price is always correct and instantly adjusts correctly to new information. The sudden deflation suggested missed signals or irrational expectations. This was one of the first signs of possible flaws in the theory. But the losses were relatively small (less than 1 percent of GDP) and had little effect on the surging economy as the markets recovered quickly in light of the Fed's explanation that it was merely nipping inflation in the bud. So it was easy to ignore a few hiccups and even to interpret their mildness as a sign of the broader correctness of the theories.

Indeed, Greenspan argued at this time against margin rules on positions in derivatives like CMOs: he claimed that the absence of such rules would "promote the safety and soundness of broker-dealers by permitting more financing alternatives and, hence, more effective liquidity management." It was such management based on the innovative new instruments that stood behind the current low rates of inflation and interest, he emphasized.

The Greenspan magic seemed to work as the stock indexes resumed their climb. By the end of 1996, the NASDAQ had topped 1,000 (up from 500 in 1992), and the Dow Industrials had risen through 4,000 to over 6,000 in just over a year and a half. In a speech to the American Enterprise Institute Greenspan revealed a bit of uncertainty as he cautioned investors about "irrational exuberance." In speaking of that period in his memoirs, he admits that "stock prices were beginning to embody expectations so exorbitant that they could never be met." He debated with himself over the true situation, arguing on the one hand that a stock market boom is a plus, but, on the other hand, that it had turned into a disaster for Japan in the stock market and real estate collapse of 1990. But then he considered that the market prices are supposed always to be correct and there was no way to know for certain when a market is overvalued or undervalued. Still, he wondered, "How could you talk about the economy without mentioning the eight-hundred-pound gorilla?" In the end, of course, he took the route of speaking out, explicitly indicating that irrational expectations (exuberance) can lead the market to incorrect prices. Yet his actions did not match his rhetoric. Had he been truly worried, he could have dampened irrational exuberance by, for example, increasing margin requirements on high-tech stock trading. In fact, he did nothing and within four years the NASDAQ was over 5,000; exuberance was running wild.

Southeast Asia Bubbles Over

In January 1997, the world's economic movers and shakers gathered in Davos, Switzerland, as they do every year, for the World Economic Forum's annual meeting. As one of the academic panelists the forum invites to provide entertainment, I was particularly struck by two things. First, the uniformity of thought. Here were people from a wide variety of countries, cultures, and walks of life. Yet they overwhelmingly embraced the Washington Consensus as a kind of latter-day gospel. Of particular interest was the fact that all the central bankers were devotees of the efficient-market doctrine, a puzzle in view of the fact that central banks exist to deal with inefficiencies that cause financial instability. The second striking feature of the meeting was its emphasis on Southeast Asia as the Most Dynamic Part of the World Economy. To be sure, the countries of the Association of Southeast Asian Nations (ASEAN), along with Hong Kong and Taiwan, had been enjoying remarkable growth and become very popular with investors. But I had lived and worked in Asia for many years and knew something of the actual dynamics of these economies. Most of them were close to the antithesis of the efficient free market with hands-off government envisioned by the Davos crowd. All of them had adopted strategic export-led growth strategies that entailed explicit industrial policies, suppression of domestic demand, maintenance of undervalued currencies, and subsidization of exports and inward foreign direct investment. To be sure, they were not socialist, but they had introduced a high degree of state capitalism. They were among the most government-guided economies in the world. I couldn't help but think that something was wrong in Davos.

In February, shortly after the Davos meeting, George Soros published an article in *The Atlantic* arguing that the efficient-market dream would eventually lead to a nightmare. Sure enough, shortly thereafter, the much-admired Asian Tigers (Korea, Taiwan, Singapore) began to have trouble sleeping. These countries had opened themselves to a significant flow of international investment while also effectively pegging their currencies at fixed rates to the dollar. A real estate cum investment bubble developed and became particularly acute in Thailand. However, the bubble had been deflating since the beginning of 1997, and the deflation had sparked a flight of capital that triggered heavy selling of the Thai baht. In an attempt to maintain the dollar peg in the face of the selling, the Thai central bank had been using its dollar reserves to buy its own currency.

In the wee hours of the morning of July 2, 1997, officials of the Central Bank of Thailand called their minister of finance to announce that Thailand would soon run out of dollar reserves and was effectively bankrupt. Soon the crisis engulfed the rest of Southeast Asia along with Hong Kong and South Korea. Even Japan's prime minister felt compelled to issue a reassuring statement saying that Japan would be fine, meaning, of course, that it might not be. For a while it seemed that the Asian miracle might turn into a global disaster. In an attempt to halt the panic, Tokyo tried to organize an emergency fund based on its own reserves to provide special loans and financial support to affected countries.

I was in Japan at the time and met with Eisuke Sakakibara, finance vice minister, who emphasized to me the urgency of the situation and his hope that Washington would be supportive. But after I reported this conversation to then undersecretary of the treasury Larry Summers, the response turned out to be quite unsupportive. Washington did not want any new funds undermining its ability to control events through its domination of the IMF. Indeed, the United States not only stopped this proposal dead in its tracks, but also aggressively pushed the IMF into a harsh rescue effort. As a condition for emergency IMF loans, countries whose financial industries were quite immature were forced to float their currencies with the likelihood of substantial devaluation. They also had to open their capital markets as a way of attracting a return of foreign investment, raise interest rates in order both to attract foreign investment and to counteract inflationary pressures arising from the currency devaluation, and introduce austerity measures (such as abolition of fuel and food subsidies) in an effort to reduce budget deficits and to establish a fuller scope for market forces.

While the objective was to make these countries more competitive and attractive to foreign investors, these measures overlooked the peculiar social and institutional characteristics of these nations. The likelihood of sudden, substantial currency devaluation and the potential for social unrest resulting from the end of food subsidies led not only to greater capital flight, but also to personal flight. Overnight, as a result, large numbers of people in these countries, who had only recently emerged from subsistence living, were impoverished once more. For example, GDP per capita fell 42 percent in Indonesia, 21 percent in Thailand, 19 percent in Malaysia, and 18 percent in Korea. Then, in 1998, what had become known as the Asian Financial Crisis jumped oceans to hit Russia and Argentina, and there was real fear that the rest of the world was next.

Eventually, in response to howls of pain and anger from spiraling economies in Indonesia, Thailand, Malaysia, Hong Kong, and especially Korea, Rubin and Summers, as well as the IMF, realized that the textbook laissez-faire programs they had foisted on the Asian economies were counterproductive. Accordingly they switched their approach and began to bless various forms of capital controls, subsidies, and industrial policy that were being adopted as emergency measures by the hard-pressed Asian governments. For example, usually staunchly laissez-faire in its approach, the Hong Kong Monetary Authority suddenly intervened to buy up a large portion of the shares listed on the Hong Kong stock market as a way to halt speculation against the pegged Hong Kong dollar. Washington cheered and then, in an effort to help Korea prevent complete evaporation of its dollar reserves, more or less ordered U.S. banks not to withdraw further funds from Korea.

Through all of this, the U.S. economy remained the strong anchor of the global system. The American consumer never blinked and kept right on consuming and loving Asian imports, and the NASDAQ and Dow indexes kept right on heading for the stratosphere. This was significantly fueled by Greenspan's quick slashing of interest rates in 1997. Thanks to that and their own emergency measures, the crisis countries were able to get back on track by 2001–2 when Korea resumed its role as the world's fastest-growing economy, Thailand repaid its IMF loans four years early, and Hong Kong sold its shares at a big profit. The Indonesian economy, however, was still smaller in 2005 than it had been in 1997.

The Pros and Geniuses Screw Up:
Long-Term Capital Management

Although generally spared, the U.S. economy did receive one major jolt from the Asian financial earthquake: the spectacular collapse of what had become the hedge-fund poster boy for the triumph of the quants (math whizzes). Long-Term Capital Management (LTCM) was a hedge fund founded and run by the crème de la crème of Wall Street bond traders, and its partners included economics Nobel Prize winners Myron Scholes (of Black-Scholes fame) and Robert Merton along with former Fed vice chairman David Mullins. The math of the trading algorithms was, of course, complex, but the strategy was relatively simple. Over time, interest rates on similar kinds of bonds tend to be similar. In the short term, however, they may diverge for all sorts of reasons. So, if you sell short (sell bonds you don't own) the higher-yielding bond and buy the lower-yielding instrument, by the time the transaction closes out, prices should have converged and you make a small profit. If you leverage your position by borrowing big to increase the size of the investment, you can make a big profit. Of course, you can also lose a lot if the bet doesn't work. To reduce the possibility of unexpected losses, LTCM traded mostly in government bonds, confident that governments rarely, if ever, default on their bonds.

As the Asian/world financial crisis began to unsettle markets in mid-1998, the interest rate spread between safe U.S. Treasuries and more risky international instruments soared. Yields on Russian euro bonds, for example, hit 90 percent. The Nobel quants and high-powered traders at LTCM thought that rise was irrational and proceeded to inhale global bonds, including lots of Russian bonds. Now, remember that governments aren't supposed to default. But in October, the Russian government did. The markets went crazy and so did LTCM's fancy mathematical trading models. Instead of making a nice profit, LTCM was losing a fortune.

An investment fund suffering a loss normally should be no big deal, especially in an efficient market. Indeed, such losses are usually considered part of the salutary "creative destruction" process. But a fund that was about to lose the $1 trillion it had borrowed from the biggest banks on Wall Street in the midst of a financial crisis with the potential to go global was a very big deal. It threatened to freeze world money markets and precipitate a 1929-style crash and perhaps another depression. This was a particularly awkward development for Greenspan, Rubin, and Summers. Not only would any government intervention run counter to the dictates of efficient-market doctrine and their own instincts, but even as the crisis broke they were in the process of halting a measure that would have put some constraints on the very kind of risky derivatives trading that was bringing LTCM to its knees.

Despite the cautionary CMO crisis of 1994, derivatives trading since then had exploded, raising renewed demands for oversight and possible regulation. Among those making the strongest demands was Commodity Futures Trading Commission Chairwoman Brooksley Born, who began suggesting the need for oversight of derivatives and other instruments not traded on central exchanges—the so-called dark market. In 1997 Born warned that such unregulated trading "could threaten our regulated markets or, indeed, our economy without any federal agency even knowing about it" and called for transparency, disclosure of trades, and creation of a buffer against losses. Instead of concern, Born's warnings had elicited "fierce opposition" from Greenspan and Rubin, who argued that even discussing new rules threatened the derivatives market that they believed was so dramatically increasing global financial efficiency while reducing risk. Greenspan warned that too many rules and regulations would simply lead the banks and hedge funds to take their business overseas. (Rubin later claimed he was for regulation but thought that it was politically not achievable.) In the summer of 1998, Summers had even called Born and criticized her actions, saying that what she was doing would lead to a crisis, presumably because it might "spook" the markets and lead to a sell-off. Later in the summer, Greenspan, Rubin, and Securities and Exchange Commission Chairman Arthur Levitt had called on Congress to stop Born from acting, and Congress was now considering whether or not to strip the CFTC of its jurisdiction over derivative trading even as LTCM was collapsing.

The problems for LTCM were time and debt. It needed time for some of its positions to come good and to raise more money, but its bankers were demanding payment now and refusing to extend new credit. Theoretically all these players were rich pros who had known the risks ahead of time, exercised due diligence, and been prepared for whatever discipline the market saw fit to impose. In fact, none of them had done enough due diligence to know the total size of LTCM's debt and to be aware that it could take them all down. Nor had any of them been aware of the risky nature of its Russian positions. Greenspan's view, expressed in congressional testimony, that the derivatives players were pros who knew what they were doing and could afford to do it, was totally belied by the reality of LTCM. Consequently, Greenspan, Rubin, and Summers faced the possibility that if market forces were left to themselves, LTCM's failure might trigger a global economic collapse. Would they turn their backs on earlier orthodoxy and intervene in some way? Or would they stick to their efficient-market guns? That was the question. The answer was a hedge. Greenspan instructed the Federal Reserve Bank of New York to convene the leaders of the major Wall Street banks to persuade them of the necessity of their undertaking a "voluntary" rescue. The banks reluctantly agreed to provide financing to LTCM, which eventually managed to sell out its positions in an orderly fashion but at a loss of more than $4 billion.

This maneuver allowed Greenspan to intervene while publicly claiming that the Fed had not intervened. It was a very thin disguise, but the market was happy to buy into it. The whole incident quickly came to be held up as an example not of the inaccuracy of efficient-market theory, but of just how well the magic of the market worked. Private actors had acted in concert to police themselves and to assure market stability.

The proposal that had been pending in Congress to strip the CFTC permanently of all power regarding derivative trading came back onto the agenda in the winter of 2000. In hearings about the measure, Senator Tom Harkin asked the Fed chairman: "If you have this exclusion and something unforeseen happens, who does something about it?" Greenspan insisted that Wall Street could be trusted and emphasized that "there is a very fundamental trade-off of what type of economy you wish to have. You can have huge amounts of regulation, and I guarantee you that nothing will go wrong. But I guarantee you that nothing will go right either." Later, at another hearing, he stressed that "many of the larger risks are dramatically, I should say, fully hedged." With those assurances, Congress went ahead and stripped the CFTC of responsibility for derivatives, and President Clinton signed the bill into law in December 2000. Brooksley Born quietly left the government for private practice in the summer of 1999.

Collapse of the Dot-com Bubble

At this point, *New York Times* columnist Tom Friedman took the Washington Consensus and turned it into the received wisdom of most globalists under the much more colorful and memorable label—the "Golden Straitjacket." In his bestselling book *The Lexus and the Olive Tree*, Friedman explained that the only way for countries to get the gold was by rigidly adhering to (or putting on a straitjacket that forced adherence to) the precepts of privatization, deregulation, small government, balanced budgets, low inflation, export orientation (which entails high savings rates), free trade, free flows of capital and technology, convertible (freely traded) currencies, rule of law, transparency, and democratization. Countries that donned the jacket forcing them to adopt these measures were assured of economic success. Those that did not would be disciplined by the Electronic Herd, another felicitous Friedmanesque turn of phrase by which he meant the securities and currency traders who move billions of dollars from one country to another at the tap of a key and thereby determine which countries win and which lose. No one is in charge of the herd, and it knows only its own rules. It is not infallible in each instance, but if a country keeps the straitjacket on, the herd will eventually recognize that fact and always come back to graze, thus rewarding good government and economic management. If a country does not, however, the herd will stampede out of there, leaving devastation in its wake. This understanding was only strengthened by the appearance of *Washington Post* pundit Bob Woodward's *Maestro*, a paean to Greenspan and his efficient market libertarian views, on the bestseller lists along with Friedman's book.

The dominance of this formulation was greatly enhanced by the fact that despite all of the shocks to the system, the United States and global economies continued their record roll. GDP and productivity growth remained strong. Nearly 21 million jobs were created as unemployment fell to 4 percent while the stock market climbed to ever new peaks. For the first time in nearly thirty years real average wages and median household income were up and personal wealth was soaring. A key reason for this state of affairs was that real estate values were rising due in large part to the growth of the housing market caused by the low interest rates Greenspan had instituted. So strong was the income and wealth trend that government revenue rose beyond expectations and the federal budget went into surplus in 1998 for the first time since 1969. Indeed, there was concern that the government would pay off the entire national debt within a few years. By the turn of the century, the Goldilocks U.S. economy had racked up its longest expansion ever and the NASDAQ was heading for 5,000. Greenspan had warned of irrationality when it was at 1,500.

But to those who now asked if the economy was experiencing a financial bubble, Greenspan replied that it is very difficult to know if you are in a bubble. Furthermore, he advised that the best approach is not to worry about it too much and simply move quickly to mop things up afterward if it is a bubble and happens to burst. The boom and the ability of the economy to bounce back from the shocks it had so far sustained seemed to have convinced him that the markets really had become extremely efficient and self-regulating. He was no longer talking about irrationality. Indeed, he and most economic leaders and the media were trumpeting how fantastic things were, especially compared with the rest of the world. Story after story and paper after paper spoke of Japan's Lost Decade and of Europe's stagnating social welfare states in comparison to the dynamic, entrepreneurial, high-tech, high-productivity, services-oriented American economy. For some reason, perhaps their own insecurity, Americans seemed to find comfort in this schadenfreude.

The collapse of what has come to be known as the dot-com bubble in March 2002 thus came as a shock. On March 10, the NASDAQ closed at 5,048 after hitting an intraday all-time high of 5,132. Then the bottom fell out: within eighteen months, it was at 1,114. The value of many well-known shares fell by as much as 90 percent. Other markets followed (though not as dramatically); eventually the bursting of the dot-com bubble resulted in the destruction of about $5 trillion of value and the first U.S. recession since

1991. More important, it suddenly lent credence to some of the niggling doubts and suspicions about the real strength of the booming economy that had been ignored or denied during the earlier hiccups. This was one hiccup too many, especially given the accepted view that efficient markets don't have hiccups.

Talk of the New Economy, the term that had come to describe the record boom, suddenly halted as people began to perceive that beneath the frothy surface, old issues had not only not been resolved, but had actually gotten worse. Even as the federal budget had gone into surplus, the U.S. savings rate had been steadily dropping as a consequence of continually falling rates of household savings. By 2001, household savings that had been about 10 percent of income in 1982 had fallen to nearly zero, and household debt had increased dramatically. At roughly $400 billion, the trade deficit was back to the 3 percent of GDP level that most economists considered unsustainable, and the U.S. international debt was more than $1 trillion.

This poor record was astounding in view of the constant stream of academic and media commentary calling America the world's most competitive country and glorifying the American model. Even more astounding was the fact that even in high-technology products, the area in which America was supposed to excel, the higher ground to which its economy was supposed inexorably to be climbing, the United States now had a large and growing trade deficit. The dollar was once more overvalued, and American manufacturers continued to close domestic plants while opening new ones abroad, especially in China. Walmart alone now sourced $9 billion in China. On top of this, banks, insurance companies, airlines, and many other service and R&D companies were accelerating the offshoring of major operations. The percentage of American students taking science and engineering degrees continued to fall, and PhD programs at MIT and other leading technical universities became filled overwhelmingly by non-American students. American high school students continued to do poorly on the comparative international tests.

Also, there was a new realization about the much advertised productivity gains that had done so much to convince Alan Greenspan that the economy had entered a new era. Not only had they begun to fall as U.S. production dropped off, but it also became clearer that as a result of the shift to the so-called hedonic scoring method of calculating productivity growth that I noted in chapter 1, part of the gain had been overstated in comparison with gains in other countries. Beyond this, the increasing trend toward offshoring of certain business functions often showed a gain in U.S. value added (prices tended to stay high even as costs fell due to offshoring of production to India or China) that counted as a productivity gain when, in fact, the actual physical production might even have required more (but cheaper) workers.

Moreover, the productivity gains had not done a lot for U.S. household income. While median household income had risen in the 1990s for the first time in nearly a generation, it was also true that by 2001 it was barely above where it had been in 1975 as translated into 1975 dollars. Thus, despite all the euphoria, some observers began to suspect that the United States had actually become less rather than more competitive during the boom years.

ONE MORE TIME

So, like the Japanese challenge of the 1980s, the dot-com bust would have been a good opportunity for our economic elite to reflect and reconsider the assumptions of orthodoxy. But a new president had been elected who had called for tax cuts, less government regulation, and more free trade—in other words, more of the same. At the Fed, Greenspan had maintained all through the expansion of the dot-com bubble that—because of the impossibility of recognizing a bubble until it bursts—the job of the central bank was to clean up the mess after a bubble burst rather than try to prick it beforehand. In view of earlier statements he had made about investors developing completely impossible expectations, I wonder if sometimes Greenspan's own expectations weren't impossible. In any case, he now jumped in to clean up the mess by slashing interest rates. As he had expected, the real estate market, which had already been growing strongly in the preceding years, took off like a rocket due to the resulting low mortgage rates. So rather than going through a painful period of adjustment, the economy took off on a quick recovery in which home ownership rose to 69.2 percent of households, unemployment fell to 4.8 percent, and the Dow Jones and S&P stock indexes rose to record highs. It has been calculated that from the end of 2001 to 2006 housing accounted for a significant portion of GDP growth and 36 percent of new job creation. Moreover, since the United States was the great engine of demand driving the world economy, the U.S. housing boom was responsible for the bulk of global growth.

A DECADE OF WILLFUL BLINDNESS

Now Greenspan, who had been dubbed "the Maestro" a couple years before the dot-com collapse, achieved rock star status. He attributed the success of his policy to the textbook model of market perfection. He also emphasized how the newfangled, mathematically complex financial products that had been evolving since the 1970s played a key role in containing the damage and spurring a rapid market turn-around. Hedge funds and innovative financial instruments like CDSs, had been essential in reducing risk by spreading it widely and to those who were most able to bear it. Rubin, although more cautious in his endorsement, acted even more aggressively than Greenspan. He joined CitiGroup as vice chairman after stepping down as treasury secretary and emphasized to the bank's leaders that if they wanted to make more money they needed to take on more risk by dealing more heavily in derivatives. Summers followed suit and became a managing director of the D. E. Shaw hedge fund, where he was pulling down more than $1 million a year while also teaching at Harvard.

This dramatic recovery of the U.S. economy from the huge dot-com shock gave another powerful boost to the credibility of both the efficient-market theory and the Washington Consensus broadly de-fined. It also sent the doubters into retreat once more as America again appeared to be leading the world into a new era of eternal prosperity with its new efficient-market economy. Indeed, in an ironic twist, the bursting of the dot-com bubble seemed actually to have accelerated what was now being called globalization—a phenomenon far beyond mere trade, one that encompassed investment, technology transfer, enormous cross-border capital flows, regulatory convergence, and es-tablishment of truly global production based on global supply chains. The dot-com phenomenon had involved investment in an enormous excess of optical fiber cable, switching, and other advanced internet capacity. The bubble burst because there simply weren't enough users for all the installed capacity. But that meant that prices customers had to pay to use the capacity fell to basement levels, spurring a great expansion of internet use and of globalization.

The integration of the world's economies appeared to have become a juggernaut. Trade barriers, distance, political, and regulatory barriers, and barriers of economic philosophy were falling by the wayside of the "information superhighway" and creating what Tom Friedman was to dub a "flat world" in which the free flow of goods, services, money, technology, and people would lead to a single self-adjusting global economy.

If the era ushered in by the Bretton Woods agreements and subsequent steps to open the world's markets could be seen as Globalization 1.0, we were now in Globalization 2.0. In this era, rather than government policy makers driving the process, entrepreneurs, financiers, and consumers would make the important decisions in a self-regulating, self-adjusting efficient-market structure. And not only would this new flat world of globalization enrich all the countries that came on board, it would also make them democratic and peace loving and kind of like America. After all, globalization was America's strategy.

THE TRUTH WILL OUT

In fact, as demonstrated by the 2008 financial meltdown, the U.S. economy was a kind of Potemkin Village. Superficially, it looked great, but behind the façade was debt piled on debt and a false understanding of how the world was actually working. For one thing, it turned out that the flat world actually had a lot of rough spots that made it unstable. Key among the problems was that the low long-term interest rates which Greenspan thought had resulted from the efficiencies stemming from deregulation and innovative derivative instruments were actually caused by the ever-growing trade imbalances between the United States and the export-led economies of Asia and the Middle East oil producers.

Greenspan and many other economists had failed to appreciate the reality that the huge dollar surpluses of the exporters had been the true force behind the low rates. A tsunami of money had been flooding back into the U.S. Treasury, in the form of foreign purchases of Treasury bills and other assets. This flood pushed up the prices of those bonds and thus (since interest rates move inversely to bond prices) automatically reduced the rates of interest they paid. Indeed, so great was the flood of foreign investment that when Greenspan tried to raise long-term interest rates in 2007 in a belated effort to stem the housing bubble, he couldn't. Of course, he could raise short-term rates because he directly controlled them. Usually in the past, if he raised short-term rates, long-term rates would follow. But this time they didn't because there was too much foreign demand for long-term Treasury and government agency notes. Thus, America's long-term interest rates were effectively being set in Beijing, Tokyo, and Riyadh. Not only had Congress not taken a vote on this transfer abroad of U.S. sovereignty, but its members weren't even aware of the loss.

For Greenspan, the irony had to be bitter. The health of the U.S. economy, of which he had been so proud, had been nearly totally dependent on a housing bubble that, according to his passionately held efficient-market faith, could not exist. Unlike all the other economists who had preached and acted on this faith, he did have the decency to admit he had been wrong.

Miracles, Tigers, Dragons, and Elephants

The reality that the advocates of Globalization 2.0 had continually failed to acknowledge was that most of the rest of the world, and particularly Asia, had not truly bought into the Washington Consensus. As we have seen, not only had Japan decided to pursue the opposite path, but so also had the Asian Tigers, the Chinese Dragon, and the Indian Elephant. All copied Japan in one fashion or another, and propelled by export-led growth strategies, all were getting rich during the 1990s and early 2000s at an unprecedented pace.

The most important new development in this time was China's takeoff followed by that of India. Like Japan, China maintained strong incentives for saving, a currency managed to be undervalued versus the dollar, strong export incentives, and state-aided development of strategic industries. But unlike Japan, China welcomed and even subsidized foreign investment. Inducing global companies to build factories in and transfer technology to China, a tactic the Chinese learned from Singapore, became a major element of Beijing's growth strategy. By making China an export platform for multinational companies that already had distribution capabilities and brand-name recognition in overseas markets, China hoped greatly to accelerate its development. In 1992, Motorola, which was suffering from the Japanese semiconductor onslaught and looking for a means to reduce costs but also attracted by the vision of a billion-plus Chinese consumers, was one of the first U.S. companies to respond to the Chinese strategy; it did so by establishing a plant in Tianjin. It was a huge instant success and was therefore soon imitated by many other global companies. Soon, Chinese exports were flooding the world and China was racking up 10 percent plus annual growth rates on its way to becoming the world's fourth-largest economy by the late 1990s.

Although India did not adopt the targeted manufacturing strategy of East Asia, the nation's large reservoir of highly skilled, low-paid professionals married to the instant communication capabilities of the internet made Bangalore, New Delhi, Bombay, and other Indian cities ideal locations for the outsourcing of call centers, back-office operations, and any kind of business that could be done digitally. Thus, India became an export platform of an entirely new kind with growth rates approximating those of China. Whereas China was rapidly developing as the new workshop of the world by becoming the location of choice for global manufacturing, India was becoming the service center of the world by becoming the location of choice for the offshoring of services.

This development was unexpected and challenging. For years as manufacturing had migrated from the United States to Asia and Mexico, most economists had hailed a new international division of labor in which the U.S. economy would be concentrated on services and high technology to complement the manufacturing of Asia. Americans had been reassured over and over that their economy was moving to "higher ground," where there would be better jobs in sophisticated services, design, investment banking, high technology, and R&D. That comforting mantra now began to sound a bit hollow as GE, IBM, and a host of others outsourced more and more of this kind of higher-level work to Asia.

The result of these developments has been the current hybrid global economic structure in which the world is half free trade and half neomercantilist. This flat world is tilted so as to slide production and provision of tradable goods and services and the jobs attached to them away from the economies of economic orthodoxy to those of neomercantilism.

Blind Men Feel Good

In a fascinating display of denial, most U.S. economists have rejected the Asians' explanation of their own success. Just as the science of aerodynamics says bumblebees can't fly (the equations argue that a bumblebee's structure should keep it grounded), so conventional economic wisdom argues that Asian industrial policy and strategic trade can't work. Indeed, many analysts long insisted that these interventionary policies weren't even in evidence. In work for the Institute for International Economics (IIE), the University of Michigan's Gary Saxonhouse argued that Japan's import and export pattern was just what you would expect from a free-trading country in Japan's location with Japan's resource endowment. In other words, there was no unusual protection of the Japanese market. This was actually a topic of serious discussion for some time in Washington until a few trade negotiators pointed out that Japanese agricultural tariffs were often more than 100 percent and in no way compatible with the notion of an open market. But Saxonhouse was not alone. Nearly all trade economists at the time downplayed the significance of Japanese protection, arguing that even if Japan completely opened its markets, U.S. exports would increase by only $5 billion to $10 billion. This figure, usually calculated by assuming a certain level of tariff reduction and then relating tariff rates to import growth, ignored the fact that the big barriers in Japan were not tariffs or import quotas, but cartels and regulatory rules. Second, it ignored the point that even if Japan's imports from the United States did not increase, those from elsewhere might, and other countries might then buy more from America.

Korean national and Cambridge University economics professor Ha-Joon Chang explains that conventional economists have developed their own story to explain the success of Asia. In this tale, Asian countries got the fundamentals right. They adopted market principles, opened themselves to trade, kept government small, privatized, deregulated, welcomed foreign investment, maintained sound fiscal and monetary policy along with high rates of saving and investment, established a high-quality noncorrupt civil service, created advanced infrastructure, and emphasized education. The repetition of this formula so irritated the actual authors of the Asian success that some Asian countries requested the World Bank to evaluate the sources of Asian success and especially the effectiveness of industrial and strategic economic policies.

Under the guidance of its then chief economist Larry Summers, the bank reconfirmed the conventional conclusion that most of the credit was due to good execution of the Washington Consensus. This conclusion so discomfited the Asian sponsors that it was later revised to give a bit of credit to "market conforming" intervention by extraordinarily competent Asian bureaucrats who promoted exports and engaged in mild suppression of domestic demand. However, later work by the IIE's Marcus Noland and Howard Pack reaffirmed the conclusion that East Asian interventionist industrial policies had little, if any, effect. In particular, it is argued that Korea's Heavy and Chemical Industries (HCI) programs of the '70s and '80s were a failure.

Nothing, says Chang, could be further from the truth. Take the Korean textile industry, for example. According to the World Bank study, the industry's success happened without government support, thus demonstrating that market forces rather than industrial policy were the key to Korean success. But, emphasizes Chang, the textile industry was actually heavily promoted by the government. It was the object of special legislation and got subsidized export loans and access to rationed bank credit that was unavailable to other industries. The truth is the opposite of the World Bank's conclusions.

Chang further notes that far from being open to trade, the East Asians are strong exporters but weak importers, especially Japan, Korea, and Taiwan. Indeed, he says, as a child he remembers being taught to tattle on people who bought foreign goods. He says further: foreign investment was obstructed, not welcomed; Koreans could not take money out of the country or even travel abroad, the won was managed to be undervalued, consumption of luxury goods was tightly restricted, consumer credit was unavailable, and commercial credit was controlled. Indeed, every effort was made to defy comparative advantage specifically to create industries with economies of scale that are the main path to wealth. So, far from being a failure, the HCI program was a success that not only created a major industry but also developed skills, knowledge, networks, and technology that led to the development of many other industries and a much higher standard of living. In short, says Chang, American economists don't have a clue about Asia and its success.

Where We Are Now

American analysts often disparage Japan's Lost Decade, so I bet you'll be surprised to learn that during the 1990s Japan's 1.4 percent GDP per capita growth rate was only slightly less than America's 1.6 percent. You probably also don't realize that U.S. per-worker productivity growth of 0.9 percent was actually behind Japan's 1.2 percent. Of course, you know that Japanese auto companies continue to eat Detroit's lunch, and you know that all the computer games are Japanese, and you may know that without Japanese silicon, tools, and chemicals, many American production lines would shut down within weeks if not days. But all you have heard is how much trouble Japan is in—right?

This is even more the case with regard to Europe. How often have you read about Eurosclerosis and how those poor Europeans suffer from low growth and high unemployment in their high-tax, inflexible, anti-entrepreneur welfare states? It is true that U.S. GDP has in recent years grown faster than EU GDP, but (as noted earlier) so has U.S. debt. Moreover, if you look at growth of GDP per hour worked, Germany, France, and America are virtually tied. How come? Americans work a lot more hours. Time with family doesn't count in the GDP, but Europeans think it's important. Further, one reason more Americans are working longer is because over the past thirty years, the bottom 20 percent of earners have become poorer while the middle 40 percent have barely stayed even. In Europe, the distribution has been much more even. Take something fundamental—life expectancy. In France it's 80.98 while in the United States it's 78.11, despite spending of double the French level on health care. Indeed, France is an interesting comparison. If Americans know one thing for sure, it is that America is a lot more competitive than France. Except that in the wake of the crisis of 2008–9, the French economy has been outperforming the U.S. economy on virtually every measure.

This same willful blindness has applied to the question of financial services, software development, and similar work. For example, in 2004 Council of Economic Advisers Chairman Greg Mankiw stated in the annual economic report of the president that such offshoring was good for the U.S. economy and no different in its economic effect than similar activities done domestically (like having a lawn service cut your grass instead of doing it yourself). Though Mankiw's argument ignited a firestorm of debate, the economics establishment strenuously defended his conclusions. Particularly influential was a study by the McKinsey Global Institute that showed a benefit to the U.S. economy of $1.12 to $1.14 for every dollar of offshore spending. The main problem with this analysis was that, based on surveys from the late 1990s at the peak of the dot-com bubble, it presumed 69 percent of workers whose jobs were transferred abroad would find reemployment at 96.5 percent of their previous wage. But the U.S. Census Bureau reported that, on average, in normal years 52 percent of job losers who are eventually reemployed take a substantial pay cut. Indeed, McKinsey itself had done another study in 2003 which showed that only 36 percent of those displaced got new jobs at equal pay, while 25 percent took pay cuts of as much as 30 percent. So if McKinsey had applied the results of its own earlier study to its offshoring analysis, there would have been a big loss for the U.S. economy instead of a gain.

This willful blindness was never more glaring than in the conclusion of a deal by U.S. negotiators to bring China into the WTO in 2001, and granting China permanent most favored nation status in the U.S. market. This will surely come to rank as one of America's dumbest deals. It extended the treatment meant for truly free-trade, market-oriented countries to an authoritarian country that not only was a potential rival but also was clearly pursuing a neomercantilist, state-guided strategy fundamentally at odds with the key assumptions of the WTO and of free trade. This deal was done with only superficial analysis of its potential impact on the U.S. trade deficit and international indebtedness and with no assessment of the implications for U.S. world leadership of China's possible accumulation of immense dollar holdings. Amazingly, in light of the American experience with Japan and the Tigers, there was virtually no analysis of what it might mean for China's power if it followed in their footsteps.

We enabled China to keep its currency undervalued against the dollar. We made the U.S. market, with its huge economies of scale, completely available to China-based producers including U.S. companies that moved their factories to China. And we did this without gaining completely reciprocal access to the Chinese market and its potential economies of scale. We acquiesced in China's pressuring of global firms to produce in China as a condition of selling in China, and we did this without returning the favor. We acquiesced in massive patent and copyright infringement by Chinese firms. Sure, we protested, but we did not take decisive steps to stop the practice.

We did these things for several key reasons. The American big business lobby was panting to get into China and to profit hugely by marrying the immense demand and economies of scale of the U.S. market with the cheap labor, tax holidays, and financial investment incentives available in China. This was as if the English of Ricardo's time had put their textile mills in Portugal, a thing Ricardo believed could never happen. But American leaders didn't read Ricardo; they only parroted his win-win rhetoric.

Politics also played an important role. Bill Clinton wanted to make history by being the president who brought China into the community of nations and set it on the road to democracy. He strongly embraced the familiar syllogism that free trade would make countries rich, and that being rich they would become democratic, and being democratic they would become peace loving. He also embraced the notion that globalization and Americanization are more or less the same thing and saw globalization as the way to make the Chinese more like us. U.S. trade representatives Mickey Kantor and Charlene Barshefsky also saw themselves as leaving a footprint in history by actually negotiating the deal. National Security Advisor Sandy Berger shared Clinton's views, and NSC China expert Ken Lieberthal promised him that "over time the United States will shrink its [then $43 billion] deficit with China." Treasury Secretary Bob Rubin and his successor Larry Summers also shared these views, and saw the arrangement as good for Wall Street and good for inflation and interest rates. Finally, virtually everyone involved could see a potential path to personal profit from the deal.

Virtually all the think tanks and the media plugged the arrangement with China. The Peterson Institute led the way, arguing that full liberalization of trade and investment with China would reduce the U.S. bilateral deficit because U.S. exports to China would rise faster than Chinese imports to the United States. Peterson further emphasized that China's dollar reserves, while large, were not extraordinary and that China was not a chronic trade surplus country like Japan because "China's markets were more open than commonly thought." The

Peterson scholars dismissed as "absurd" the estimates by the labor-oriented Economic Policy Institute (EPI) of a major increase in the U.S. trade deficit with consequent big losses of jobs. In a sense the Peterson argument was right. While EPI estimated that the deficit would rise to $131 billion by 2010, in fact it hit $240 billion in 2008.

I know all these people. I have disagreed with all of them on various issues. But I respect them, and I don't think any of them would do or say something they did not believe was in the best interests of the United States. But they all recommended and made a bad deal that has reduced American influence and power and constrained its future wealth-creating ability. They did so because they believed in Ricardo and that globalization is always a win for the United States regardless of the circumstances. They were all loyal disciples of a false faith.

Not surprisingly, the offshoring of U.S.-based production accelerated greatly as a flood of American companies opened up shop in China, and U.S. manufacturing fell to about 11 percent of GDP. Consequently, the trade (current account) deficit ballooned to $696 billion, or nearly 7 percent of GDP. We are now trying to recover from the biggest economic crisis since the Great Depression and not only owe Beijing $2.5 trillion but also have an annual bilateral trade deficit of over $200 billion. And the U.S. industries that have moved production to China en masse are not just textiles and labor-intensive low-tech stuff. Intel just announced a major multibillion-dollar semiconductor fabrication facility for China. If you are an entrepreneur looking for venture capital, you better have an R&D in China strategy.

As I noted at the start of this book, China now holds power in its relations with the United States that no other country has had since Great Britain in the earliest days of the Republic. By selling dollars, China could force the U.S. military to withdraw from its far-flung deployments such as those in the Persian Gulf and Afghanistan. China can use its dollars to corner markets of key commodities like copper and molybdenum or soybeans. And, of course, military might cannot be ignored. China is using its wealth to build a blue-water navy with quiet subs that will be able to counter the U.S. Seventh Fleet, which would have to withdraw from the western Pacific anyhow if the Chinese were to begin dumping dollars.

No, I'm not suggesting that China will do this, nor am I trying to "bash" China. It's obvious that we could also inflict great damage on

China. So, as pointed out before, we have a kind of MAD (mutual assured destruction) relationship. But there is no question that American power will be constrained by the counterweight of China. I don't consider China a threat to America, but the present relationship is not ideal from the U.S. viewpoint and not what any astute American strategist would have planned ten years ago.

So how should the United States proceed? Answering that question will be my concern in the remainder of this book. The first step will be to break the mystique of the efficient market, Washington Consensus ideology so that we can reach a more sophisticated, realistic understanding of the working of markets, of the irrationality that can determine economic events, and of the limits of the laissez-faire free-trade gospel that has blinded our economists and leaders.

5

The Irrationality of the Rational

The market can remain irrational longer than you can remain
solvent.

—JOHN MAYNARD KEYNES

A Casino Rises in Place of a Fallen Steel Giant." That headline
in the *New York Times* caught my eye recently. Filing his story
from Bethlehem, Pennsylvania—the birthplace and longtime
headquarters of former number-2 U.S. steelmaker Bethlehem Steel
Corporation—correspondent Steve Friess explained that the Las Vegas
Sands had just opened a $743 million complex of slot machines and
gaming tables on the site of the old steel plant, which had gone bankrupt in 2001. Local citizens, whose jobs and property values had disappeared along with that factory closing and so many others, were
hoping against hope that poker, blackjack, and slots would save them.
This story, summarized in its headline, is an apt microcosm of what
has been happening to the United States economy in the course of the
past sixty years of globalization. From the mass production of real
goods and services, we have turned to reliance on financial games
and speculation. Reading the report, I was reminded of John Maynard Keynes's 1936 comment that "when the capital development of a
country becomes the by-product of the activities of a casino, the job is
likely to be ill done."

Underlying both this unfortunate metamorphosis and the broader
global crisis have been the two key doctrines on which the Washington
Consensus was based: the efficient market and Ricardian free trade. In
addition, a high priesthood of misguided prophets assiduously misap-
plied mathematics to these doctrines. Although considerable analysis
by dissenting economists over the past forty years—not to mention the

series of economic shocks covered in the last chapter—should have raised serious concern that both theories were substantially flawed, the disciples of the conventional wisdom enforced a tough discipline that stifled all potential opposition to their rigid orthodoxy. The dissenting voices were downplayed (sometimes by the speakers themselves) and often ignored altogether. Now, if we are seriously to contend with the challenges confronting us in the wake of the 2008 crisis, we need to unpack the mythology of efficiency, especially as it was promoted as rigid economic orthodoxy by the Chicago school of economists, and see how the theory operated to help undermine our economy.

UNPACKING THE MYTHOLOGY OF EFFICIENCY

Among the many causes of the death of Bethlehem Steel, a major one was the notion that markets are efficient, produce optimal welfare, and should therefore be left alone to work their magic. The argument for the market's natural efficiency has been the subject of long and often heated debate, starting with Adam Smith's eloquent injunction to replace the choking, distorting hand of government intervention with the unseen but most efficiently operating hand of the market. Joining Smith in this view was his contemporary, French businessman and economist Jean Baptiste Say, who argued that in a purely free-market economy, the total supply of goods and services will exactly equal the total demand because the supply essentially determines the demand. In other words, if I produce a red widget with a value of one dollar and sell it, I then have a dollar with which I can demand or buy the green widget that you just produced. Without the production, there could be no demand, and the amount of the demand is exactly the same as the amount of the production. In this way, production provides both the means and the ends of acquisition. Theorists concede that imbalances in supply and demand do in fact occur all the time at any given moment and in any given area of the economy, but they explain that ultimately, if the market is left to its own devices, prices adjust to correct those imbalances. So a vital aspect of a free-market economy is the constant adjustment of prices.

Thus, recessions can occur only as the result of some inflexibility in prices. For example, suppose I insist on getting two dollars for my red widget while you are selling your green ones for only a dollar. Then you won't be able to buy my reds and I won't have any money with which to buy your greens: the result will be a recession until my price becomes flexible and adjusts to the one-dollar level.

Of course, real-world recessions happened regularly, and a key point of contention in the early twentieth century concerned the cause of the inflexibility of prices. Free-market theory adherents maintained that government intervention is always the cause, and thus argued for minimal intervention to lessen job losses and other downturns. Such intervention, it was thought, would actually prolong a downturn by preventing or delaying adjustment of prices. This viewpoint was summed up succinctly by Hoover administration Treasury Secretary Andrew Mellon's infamous injunction during the Great Depression to "liquidate labor, liquidate stocks, liquidate the farmers, liquidate real estate. It will purge the rottenness out of the system. High costs of living and high living will come down. People will work harder, live a more moral life. Values will be adjusted, and enterprising people will pick up from less competent people." That attitude, which represented the conventional wisdom of the academic business, media, and policy elite of the time, shows you why late-nineteenth- and early-twentieth-century capitalism was so brutal.

John Maynard Keynes argued otherwise in the 1930s. Looking at the empirical record of price inflexibility, he concluded that capitalism has an inherent tendency toward recession because markets are not and cannot be perfectly free. The existence both of industries dominated by a few major corporations that can influence prices and total production and of labor unions with wage-bargaining power meant that prices are "sticky" and often slow to adjust if they adjust at all. Moreover, in addition to price inflexibility, Keynes emphasized the role of money hoarding (excessive saving), and the frequent inflexibility of interest rates as being other important causes of recession. Convinced that there must be a better way to cope with the problem, Keynes argued that pumping up demand through government spending and increasing the money supply would ensure a level of demand sufficient to maintain full employment. He conceded that such intervention carries a certain risk because too much government spending could result in inflation. So the trick for the government is to achieve just enough stimulus to reach full employment but not so much as to set off inflation.

The Keynesian approach won the day during the Depression, and its apparent contribution to ending that long nightmare and generating unprecedented economic prosperity during the 1950–73 Golden Era led economists like Kennedy administration Council of Economic Advisers Chairman Walter Heller to become confident of being able to "fine-tune" the economy and put an end to recessions. The shock of the stagflation of the 1970s, however, made "fine-tuning" sound like a bad joke, and paved the way for a new era of economics founded on a new and improved version of efficient-market theory.

The Chicago School

In the 1960s, University of Chicago economist Milton Friedman developed a new argument about the causes of the Great Depression: it had been triggered largely by mistaken Federal Reserve intervention that had severely reduced the money supply and restricted credit at just the wrong moment (note that Friedman did not even mention Smoot-Hawley). Friedman then applied this argument to the stagflation that was mystifying policy makers at the time. The government was actually causing the inflation, Friedman argued, by printing too much money, as the Fed periodically juiced the money supply in its fine-tuning efforts. So he called for Washington to change its policy and to increase the supply only at a constant, predetermined rate—in other words, to go on auto-pilot.

The stagnation part of the problem was also addressed by other University of Chicago scholars, especially Robert Lucas, who critiqued the interventionist Keynesian policies by articulating the theory of rational expectations in the 1970s. Until then, economic models dealing with, for example, the probable future returns on a major investment would take historical relationships between, say, costs and prices and automatically assume that those same relationships would hold in the future, without regarding the possibility that changes in policy or circumstances might change those relationships from their present ratios. Following some earlier analysts like John Muth, Lucas argued that, in fact, people are broadly aware of what is happening and alter their expectations about future relationships in the light of present events and policy operations. So the models were wrong unless they incorporated those "rational expectations."

Take the simple example of Fort Knox and its gold. The fort is heavily guarded by a large security force. It has never been robbed. Now suppose the security force is disbanded, but your economic model of Fort Knox is still predicting no robberies in the future based on the historical experience of none in the past. Chances are, your model would be wrong. Robbers who heretofore had avoided the fort would learn of the disbanding of the security forces and maybe launch a successful robbery. The robbers' rational expectations had changed in light of the policy change.

Applying that thinking to the stagflation problem, Lucas and his colleagues argued that the fine-tuning of Keynesian intervention policies was being anticipated by a public that then changed its behavior in ways that undercut the effect of the intervention. For example, intervention would typically be meant to stimulate the economy, but if people were to consider that this stimulus would lead to inflation and eventually to high interest rates and a recession, they might—instead of buying more in response to the stimulus—actually buy less. The same kind of discounting might be true of labor unions whose positions could exacerbate the economic malaise. If labor saw government stimulus policies coming, the theory went, they would naturally anticipate inflation following them. In this case, the rational thing would be to demand inflation-indexed wage agreements that were likely only to exacerbate the ultimate inflation far beyond the government's original plans.

Thus, the 1970s stagflation could be explained on the basis that consumers had learned "rationally" to discount the Keynesian fine-tuning measures of the government. The result was a revolution in macroeconomic modeling and policy thinking as well as in government action.

The Market as God

Lucas's rational expectations analysis seemed to confirm, strengthen, and broaden to markets in general the efficient-market hypothesis that Gene Fama had developed to explain stock market movements. I noted earlier how Fama, following the work of Louis Bachelier and Paul Samuelson, had concluded that stock price movements follow a "random walk," meaning that they are unpredictable, and because of

this, no investor can beat the market over any significant period. Further, Fama demonstrated that one could not reject his concept of market efficiency without also rejecting the model of market equilibrium that is the basic price-setting mechanism. This point gave the concept great credibility and influence.

Although both were derived in a different context, the key assumptions of Fama's theory are similar to Lucas's: that market participants have rational expectations, and their best guesses about the future of the market are based rationally on all available information; that, on average, the population is correct (even if no one participant is), and that whenever new relevant information appears, the participants update their expectations appropriately. It is important to understand that the participants themselves don't have to be rational. The theory anticipates that in response to new information some actors may overreact while others underreact. All that is necessary is that investor reactions be random and follow a normal, unbiased distribution pattern so that prices cannot be reliably anticipated for profit. Anyone and everyone can be wrong about the market, but the market as a whole is always right.

Thus, professional investors cannot beat the market, Fama contended, because it is perfectly efficient. The market price of any stock, or of any other investment, always incorporates all available information and, at any particular moment, is always correct. The arrival of new information from outside may change prices, but only in a way that rationally and accurately reflects changes in value and that establishes a new stable equilibrium, provided there is no outside policy intervention. In other words, the market is God, or God is the market.

Not only did the Fama concept argue that the next move of any stock price is as random as flipping a coin, it also held that the magnitudes of the random price movements are equal. In other words, over a large number of movements the upward movements will not be larger than the downward ones. As I noted earlier, physicists and mathematicians have figured out how to model the phenomenon of random movements of equal magnitude known as Brownian motion. A large number of movements make the well-known bell curve pattern—an important fact for Wall Street and financial managers because, as we discussed, once you know the width of the distribution of prices, you can establish a standard deviation and forecast the entire probability

set of future asset returns. Moreover, Fama made getting the width of the distribution easy because efficient-market theory says the magnitudes of movements are equal.

So by looking at past movements, you can readily estimate the size of future movements. From here it took only a bit of fancy modeling to get to options pricing, CMOs, CDSs, and all the sophisticated financial products with which we have become familiar. Of course, you could get there only if the market was God.

The Importance of Math

Think for a moment about all this. All investors have all available information about a stock. The market price always incorporates all available information. The reaction to new information is both rational and instant. Do you believe that? It is hard to imagine that anyone who has actually invested in the market and followed its movements for any period of time could actually accept those statements. We know there is herd behavior, that's what so-called momentum investing is all about. We know that all market participants don't necessarily have all available information at the same time. We know that new information may cause overreaction and even panic. We know that bubbles occur more frequently than the theory predicts. Yet not only did this theory gain wide acceptance in economic circles, it absolutely dominated investment analysis on Wall Street, the teaching of investment in the business schools, and the discussion of investment in the media. Moreover, combined with the rational expectations thinking of Lucas and applied beyond the stock market to markets in general, the efficient-market hypothesis dominated economic policy making at all levels for more than thirty years.

A major reason was that even if the market weren't God, the complexity and elegance of the mathematical formulation in which the theory was packaged made it appear to have been handed down by God.

Adam Smith needed not a single equation to write *The Wealth of Nations,* but as economics evolved, economists developed physics envy and sought to gain the same certitude of understanding and the same respect for their discipline as existed for physics. Indeed, they defined

the economy as a kind of Newtonian system in equilibrium and increasingly articulated it in mathematical terms. The arrival of computers greatly accelerated this trend, leading to the development of the field of econometrics, the application of mathematics and statistics to the study of economic and financial data. While in 1940, less than 3 percent of the pages of the profession's leading U.S. journal, the *American Economic Review*, contained mathematical expressions, by 1990, 40 percent did. In 1940, only 1 percent of the members of the thirteen leading economics faculties in the United States were members of the Econometric Society: by 1990, 50 percent were. This mathematization of economics resulted in ever more sophisticated econometric models that combined with ever more powerful computers to crunch ever more voluminous amounts of statistics to support the efficient-market theory. The math was complex, arcane, and highly persuasive. It seemed to provide such powerful tools that economists could analyze the workings of the human-driven economy with an accuracy that was indeed comparable to that of physics. Yet, as we have seen in the implosion of the derivatives bubble, the most powerful models may be disastrously wrong if they are based on false assumptions.

Through the years there were continuous doubts about whether the mathematical metamorphosis of economics was altogether healthy. Human minds are not, after all, comparable to particles of matter. Gravity always works. The apple always falls. The sun always rises. The speed of light is always 186,000 miles per second. On the other hand, consumer preferences change, and often do so apparently according to whim or utterly unforeseen influences. Those who keep money in banks may panic. The usual buyers of bonds can exit the market overnight. In truth, it is easier to model mathematically the operations of gravity than those of bank depositors, or at least it is easier to do so to a high degree of accuracy.

Many of the fundamental assumptions upon which the elaborate math used to support efficient-market theory was based were, in fact, highly questionable. For example, it can be argued that the future can't be predicted and that therefore no expectations about it are rational. More practically, since information about the future may be costly to obtain, the "optimal forecast" may not be the rational expectation but merely the one that is affordable. Moreover, people may be unable to act on their expectations due to lack of bargaining power. For example, people bound by contracts: even if they have rational expectations, they are constrained by the conditions of the old contracts from acting upon these expectations.

Consider also the questionable assertion that prices always accurately reflect demand. Textbooks always show that supply increases in response to higher prices while demand rises as prices fall. But is that really true? In the market for fine art, high prices stimulate demand. Or take oil. Demand for it often shoots up in response to higher prices as speculative buying offsets declining consumer purchases.

Perhaps the most glaring flaws in the fundamental logic of efficient-market theory were two intertwined assertions: that market participants always act rationally; and that they always have complete information because the market, by its mysterious aggregating processes, makes sure that information is available. These assumptions were increasingly brought into question by the new branch of the profession called behavioral economics, which began to come to the fore in the 1990s. Behavioral economists questioned the rationality of market actors, noting factors like cognitive bias (overconfidence or overreaction), information bias (distorted evaluation of information), and other predictable human errors in reasoning and the processing of information, such as the herd behavior that in the recent housing bubble led the vast majority of people to believe that house prices could only rise because for a very long time that is what they had done.

Psychological research by Daniel Kahneman, Richard Thaler, and other behavioral economists also showed that these errors lead most investors to avoid high-value stocks and to buy growth stocks at high prices, thereby creating an opportunity for profit for those who avoid the errors and reason correctly. In a landmark 1995 paper, *Forbes* magazine columnist and *Journal of Behavioral Finance* publisher David Dreman shook the foundations of efficient-market theory by showing that stocks with low price/earnings ratios consistently earn greater returns than those with high ratios—a finding that went entirely against efficient-market theory.

The assumption that market information is always available to all market participants at the same time has long been particularly troublesome. Take the recently much discussed practice of flash trading in which some specialists obtain information several milliseconds before the market and use high-speed computers to profit by trading on that advantage. Or take the recently reported Goldman Sachs "trading huddle." Clients in the huddle get access to Goldman's research and stock tips before non-huddle clients. Obviously some investors are getting information not readily available to others.

Perhaps the best analysis of the reality of the markets has been that of the master market player George Soros. In numerous writings over the years, he has emphasized that in financial markets "buy and sell decisions are based on expectations of future prices, and future prices, in turn, are contingent on present buy and sell decisions." What Soros is getting at is that your expectation of tomorrow's prices is conditioned by the prices produced in buy and sell decisions today. If the market is up today, there is a greater chance that you will buy tomorrow than if the market were down today. So your expectations of the future are to some extent conditioned by the activity of the market itself and not solely by the arrival of some new outside information.

The central fallacy, says Soros, is that, contrary to rational expectations thinking, market participants do not base their decisions on their self-interest. Rather, they base them on their *perception* of their self-interest, and these are not the same thing. For instance, I may think that investing in a particular stock at a $1 per share is intrinsically a good deal. But then I may ask myself, What will most other investors think? I might conclude that other investors will interpret the very low price as a sign of trouble and sell. If I then decide not to buy, I am basing my decision on my perception of my self-interest rather than on that self-interest itself. Keynes made the same point when he noted that in a beauty contest one should not bet on what one finds beautiful but rather on what one thinks others will find beautiful.

Soros insists that "anyone who trades in markets where prices are continuously changing knows that participants are very much influenced by market developments themselves. Rising prices often attract buyers and vice versa." Further, market prices can affect the fundamentals they are supposed to reflect. For example, high market prices can affect interest rates and consumer behavior as well as reflect these variables. In other words, "prices are not uniquely determined and instead of equilibrium we are left with fluctuating prices that negate the concepts of rational expectations and efficient markets."

This view is similar to that of Hyman Minsky, who formulated the financial instability hypothesis in 1975. Concerned with financial market fragility, he argued that "a fundamental characteristic of our economy is that the financial system swings between robustness and fragility, and these swings are an integral part of the process that generates business cycles." When prosperous times generate excess cash, speculative euphoria leads to overconsumption and overinvestment that result in rising debt and financial bubbles that eventually burst. Thus, Minsky argued, price movements may be generated internally by market dynamics as well as by external shocks. Indeed, in a free-market economy speculative investment bubbles are inevitably generated from within the financial system itself unless the government steps in to control them through regulation, central bank action, or some other policy mechanism. Such government action is required because far from being self-adjusting toward a stable equilibrium, as argued by the efficient-market hypothesis, the system is unstable and naturally trends toward bubbles and crises.

Finally, there were the findings of Benoit Mandelbrot, in his 2004 book, *The (Mis)behavior of Markets*. The highly admired inventor of fractal geometry, Mandelbrot turned his attention to economics late in his career and proceeded to blow gaping holes in the dominant capital asset pricing model, the efficient-market hypothesis, and the Black-Scholes option pricing model. Not bad for a latecomer. The key point was that all of these models are based on two key assumptions: that prices are normally distributed (bell curve) and that market prices are independent of each other, yesterday's prices having no effect on today's prices. Mandelbrot demonstrated that the distribution of stock prices is not normal. Rather, it has a much fatter tail than the normal distribution, meaning that catastrophic events happen more frequently than the normal distribution predicts. He further demonstrated that even if prices are not correlated directly, their volatility is correlated over time. Thus, big price swings tend to cluster. If a stock moved by 10 percent yesterday, it is likely to move by an above average amount today, even if we do not know the direction of change. In this way, the market has a kind of memory.

Because the key assumptions are flawed, all the models built upon them are flawed and tend to underestimate risk. They, in turn, overprice stocks, underprice options, and understate the amount of capital financial institutions should hold to withstand the risk. Not only did

Mandelbrot fatally wound the efficient-market hypothesis, he told us exactly what was wrong with our financial institutions and system at a time when they were being hailed as one of the wonders of the world.

As a practical matter, John Maynard Keynes had the right understanding nearly eighty years ago when he noted that "the market can remain irrational longer than you can remain solvent."

DUMB OR MISUSED?

Keynes's comment points to an important point we need to understand. These analyses and critiques as well as the recent economic crisis can make the efficient-market theory appear pretty dumb. You may even wonder how it was that so many of the men who developed various aspects of it won Nobel prizes. The answer is that they were and are really smart guys. They were aware of many of the flaws and weaknesses when they were developing the theory, and knew it wasn't a comprehensive theory of everything. As Robert Lucas said recently in *The Economist*, "What we are not going to have, now or ever, is a set of models that forecasts sudden falls in the value of assets like the declines that followed the failure of Lehman Brothers."

Nonetheless, neither the models nor the work of the efficient-market economists is without value. In fact, they are powerful and have contributed important new concepts and ways of analytical thinking. It is true, after all, that, per Lucas, people do discount repeated policy actions. The point is that the theory and the models are idealized, purposely, to isolate certain elements in order to test them. In that environment they work very well. It is when we try to apply them to the real, messy world that they do not work so well.

The theory, after all, argued that bubbles are not possible, and yet the long history of economic bubbles is well established, beginning with the tulip and South Sea bubbles in the seventeenth and eighteenth centuries and running through the Japanese financial bubble of the 1980s. Of course, one could say that bubbles had occurred in the past because the market was too regulated, but perhaps the biggest bubble of all—the joint housing and derivatives bubble that burst in 2008—occurred largely due to the relaxation of regulations. The theory argued that recessions should not happen; yet the U.S. economy went into recession several times between 1975 and the 2008 meltdown.

And yet, along the way, the economists who had formulated the theory argued in favor of it being applied to the actual world. That was the dumb, or perhaps more accurately, arrogant part.

YOUR MODEL IS ONLY AS GOOD (BAD) AS YOUR DATA—ESPECIALLY REGARDING REAL ESTATE

This attempt to apply elegant idealized theories and models to the real world of subprime mortgages and CDSs was a major cause of the U.S. real estate bubble and the crash of 2008. Recall that the mathematical whizzes who crafted the mortgage-based securities at the heart of the meltdown argued that they were virtually risk-free. The models on which this assertion was based were wonderfully sophisticated, and though this is a subject of much debate, the math in itself may even have been fundamentally right. The core problem was that this fantastically complex mathematical edifice was built upon fatally flawed assumptions about the real world: that housing prices were not going to fall in the foreseeable future; that mortgage defaults would not rise in the foreseeable future; and that in a downturn the securities could always be sold at some price. This was a glaring case of incomplete information, which was then turned into bad information.

All the models had used historical data for the value of houses, data showing that home prices had not fallen since the Great Depression of the 1930s. But the available data was inadequate for at least three reasons. First, the country had never before experienced a nationwide bubble in home values. Second, banks had never before offered subprime mortgages. Third, the mortgages had not been subject to securitization for very long. The historical data on which the assumptions of the models were based indicated that defaults would not spike nationally—there might be local spikes if the housing market had overheated in certain areas—but that disease would not spread all around the country. The problem was that never before had lenders made so many loans to people whose income and assets would not have qualified them for mortgages under the old standards. The terms *liar loans* (mortgages for which a borrower had to provide no proof of income or assets) and *ninja loans* (no income, no assets) became part of normal language. There was no reliable data with which to calculate how a downturn in house prices would affect defaults on those loans.

None of the models allowed for even the slightest downturn in home values or, therefore, for a significant uptick in defaults. For this reason, when home values did in fact begin to turn down in 2007, and defaults began to rise, a domino effect was triggered as the value of mortgage-based derivatives began to fall. Because investors had been assured that the securities could not fall in value, a massive sell-off was provoked when they actually did begin to fall. Here, deregulation further exacerbated the problem, since the banks had been allowed to breach the old requirement of a 12-to-1 ratio of loans to capital and move the ratio to as high as 30-to-1 for these kinds of securities. They now had very little cash in reserve to pay any investor who might want to cash in some of his securities—a move that was deemed safe because the securities were supposedly risk-free.

As events unfolded, more and more investors did start to cash in. As they did so, some funds and banks began to fail, and a panic ensued. Then the fallacy of the model assumption that in a downturn the securities could always be sold at some price became apparent. What might be true for one company in a normal downturn is not true for all companies in a panic. The securities couldn't be sold at any price.

The many ways in which the crisis directly contradicted efficient-market theory are staggering. In an unregulated efficient market, all participants are supposed to have all available information at the same time. Yet the bankers who sold these securities and the investors who bought them lacked any information on how fundamentally flawed the models behind them were. Nor did the modelers have any information on the probability of defaults for subprime mortgages. And for that matter, the people taking out the subprime mortgages frequently had false information about the payment terms, while the buyers of the mortgages had little or false information about the ability of the borrowers to pay the mortgages. The investment bankers selling the derivative instruments often had no idea what they were selling. The epitome of this was Robert Rubin, who told Citibank to sell more of the derivatives, even though, as he later admitted, he had no idea what was in them. Finally, the ultimate buyers in places like Narvik, Norway, had no clue about what they were actually buying. Rather than full or perfect information, this market was characterized by no information or fully wrong information. It was the antithesis of an efficient market, and far from being the result of policy intervention, the inefficiency was the result of the withdrawal of intervention through deregulation in an abortive attempt to achieve a more efficient market. It was a really bad joke.

REMORSE AND BLAME

In testimony before Congress on October 23, 2008, Alan Greenspan honorably admitted that the economic crisis had put him in "a state of shocked disbelief" and that it had revealed a flaw in a lifetime of economic thinking. But the flaw wasn't only in Greenspan's thinking. As Johann Hari noted in *The Independent*, underlying the financial bubble had been the ideological bubble of market fundamentalism and a rigid economic orthodoxy that enforced its doctrine across the political and social spectrum. Now, as the noted University of California economics professor Barry Eichengreen explains, the crash has undermined the doctrine and the credibility of economists. They thought monetary policy had tamed the business cycle and that central banks had tamed market volatility to produce the Great Moderation. They thought they had learned how to prevent another 1929, and that financial institutions had become self-regulatory when, in fact, they hadn't. Eichengreen blames the problems less on the theory than on a misreading and misapplication of it conditioned by the social milieu that encouraged both the bankers and the policy makers—including the Federal Reserve—to cherry-pick the parts they found congenial to the risks they wanted to take. Whistle-blowing and scholarship that warned of disaster, he says, were discouraged as "influential trend setters consorted with financial risk takers" and business schools contrived to give their corporate customers what the customers wanted.

Eichengreen emphasizes that economists were actually well aware of the weaknesses in the theory, but that many were intimidated by the fact that the convention in the discipline was to assume efficient markets, and that they were reluctant to be the ones to risk ridicule by bucking the trend.

One who did buck the trend by long forecasting disaster was Yale University's Robert Shiller. His view is that there has always been a hole in the theory of classical and neoclassical economics, a hole Keynes identified as the role of "animal spirits." Shiller put special emphasis in his critique of efficient-market theory on the importance of stories in human motivation, and emphasized that people's economic moods are based largely on stories people tell themselves and each other about the economy. Consider that in the past few years we have had the story of the dot-com bubble producing hordes of young millionaires followed by the stories of smart "flippers" of properties who also got rich and induced imitation by others who assumed that the flippers had done their research and knew what they were doing. The role of these appealing—and often inaccurate—stories is, of course, absent from classical and efficient-market theory.

Shiller points out that Adam Smith expected his proposed free economy to be stable because people pursuing their own interests in a free market would exhaust all opportunities to produce and to trade with one another—a situation that could only result in full employment. But Smith failed to explain (because he probably didn't know) that capitalism will not only produce what people want, but also what they *think* they want. It will produce snake oil as well as soap. Further, it may even produce the desire for snake oil. If marketed aggressively enough, subprime mortgages start to seem perfectly safe.

Shiller concludes that this is where the role of government comes in: to regulate so that people are not falsely lured into buying snake oil. Government must ensure a "wise laissez-faire." He writes: "This is not the free-for-all capitalism that has been recommended by the current economic theory, and seems to have been accepted as gospel by economic planners, since the Thatcher and Reagan governments. The idea that unfettered, unregulated capitalism would invariably produce the good outcomes was a wrong economic theory regarding how capitalist societies behave and what causes their crises. It was wrong because it fails to take into account the roles of confidence, stories, and snake oil in economic fluctuation."

I can't say it better.

6

Orthodox Free Trade: God's Diplomacy

While . . . free trade is not passé, it is an idea that has irretrievably lost its innocence.

—PAUL KRUGMAN, 1987

Britain's nineteenth-century free-trade advocate and *Economist* magazine founder Richard Cobden spoke of free trade as God's diplomacy. Early in the twentieth century, America's wartime secretary of state Cordell Hull shared a similar faith in the power of trade to engender peace and comity among nations. And now, over the past sixty years, this faith has evolved into a kind of quasi-religious free-trade fundamentalism that the vast bulk of our economic, media, academic, and business elite have embraced.

My first encounter with this sect's fervor came when I was serving as counselor to the Secretary of Commerce Malcolm Baldrige under President Reagan. Executives of Pittsburgh's hydro-generator maker Siemens-Allis visited me to discuss problems in the market for the big machines that turn water power into electricity. They explained that in the face of severe price cutting by Japanese manufacturers, GE had moved its hydro-generator operations to Canada and Westinghouse had simply gotten out of the business. Siemens-Allis was now the only remaining American-based maker, but, said the executives, unless something could be done to stop the collusion and predatory pricing of its Japanese competitors, their company would have to exit the market as well. They also presented convincing documentation to back up their argument.

Over a period of several years, three Japanese companies had bid on a number of tenders for hydro-generators in the U.S. market. There appeared to be a pattern to their bidding. On project A, there would be several bidders including the three Japanese companies, Siemens-Allis, and a few others from Canada and Europe. All the bids would be around a similar amount, say $10 million, except Japanese company X, which would make a bid far below that figure. Then on project B, the same companies would make the same kind of bids except this time Japanese company Y would make a dramatically low bid, and so forth. The variation in the prices bid on the same equipment within short periods of time could be as much as 200 percent. The Siemens-Allis executives said they could understand how one manufacturer might have a consistent cost advantage, but not how a company could be the lowest bidder one day and the highest the next on the same equipment.

It seemed to me not only that they had a point, but also that the Commerce Department might be justified in initiating an investigation of possible violation of international trade laws as well as of U.S. antitrust regulations. At a time of recession with unemployment at 10.8 percent, it seemed desirable to try to preserve American jobs. My proposal got nowhere, however, in the face of adamant opposition from key members of the Council of Economic Advisers who were adherents of the Chicago school. One council member told me he didn't see the problem. As far as he could tell, American electric companies and municipalities were getting inexpensive generators, and consumers were thus presumably benefiting from lower electric rates. Nor was he worried about the fate of the Siemens-Allis workers who would lose jobs if the company closed operations. They could easily find something else to do in the more robust services economy (never mind that services jobs paid a lot less than Siemens-Allis).

I noted that prices in Japan were quite high and asked what would happen when the Japanese makers came to control the market and raised prices to match those at home. In that case, he said, the American producers could come back into the business. He and the council truly did not seem to realize that no businessman in his right mind would consider going back into the business only to face a repetition of the old experience. In the event, no action was taken and Siemens-Allis did lay off its workforce and leave the business.

Over the ensuing quarter century this story was repeated again and again. Indeed, it is going on even as I write in the case of exactly the kind of high-tech "higher-ground" company economists always say will be the future of America.

GOD'S DOCTRINE OF FREE TRADE

Why, you may well ask, would a whole range of U.S. leaders stand by over a thirty-year period and do nothing while perfectly competitive U.S. producers either went out of business or out of the country? The answer is, the doctrine of simple or Ricardian "free trade," based on British banker David Ricardo's valid but limited 1817 insights regarding trade and comparative advantage that were later elaborated into today's ruling orthodoxy.

The Gospel According to Ricardo

In his original analysis of trade based on comparative advantage, Ricardo had demonstrated that it was better for both Portugal and England to specialize—Portugal in wine and England in cloth—even though Portugal could produce both at lower absolute cost than England could. Because Portugal's advantage was comparatively greater in wine and England's disadvantage was comparatively lesser in cloth, ultimately each would do better by focusing on the production it did best while trading for the rest.

What made this concept so attractive and powerful was the conclusion that countries could always gain from trade because every country would always have some product in which it had the comparative advantage. Moreover, the theory argued that free trade always and everywhere produces an equilibrium of supply and demand that is a win-win solution. That equilibrium provides for optimal benefits for all parties while increasing world output overall. Indeed, even if England were to bar imports of wine, Portugal would still be better off continuing to specialize in wine production and to import its cloth from England than to bar cloth imports in retaliation. Unilateral free trade is better than no trade under the circumstances Ricardo posited. It was this doctrine, which I refer to as "simple or unilateral free trade," that captured Britain in the later nineteenth century and to which, as I have discussed, Britain tried unsuccessfully to convert the rest of the world. In the twentieth century, enhancements of the argument captured the attention of economists and policy makers in the United States.

The New Revised Version

In the early twentieth century Swedish economists Eli Heckscher and Bertil Gotthard Ohlin developed a revised version of the theory that has guided the trade and globalization policy of the United States and many other countries over the past sixty years, and still dominates public debate and commentary. The new model kept Ricardo's argument about the benefits of countries specializing in the production of certain goods—in other words, the benefits of comparative advantage—but refined his analysis in several ways. While Ricardo had argued that labor is the only factor of production, and that who exports and imports which products is determined by differences in technology within countries—wine making versus cloth making—he did not account either for a country's ability to obtain the technology it hasn't started out with or for the important role of a country's capital and natural resources in what it produces. The new model granted that new technology would spread readily to all players, and also added land and capital to labor as factors of production. This analysis led to the conclusion that those factors of production, rather than technology, are key determinants of trade flows. Thus, a country rich in capital and with a high quotient of skilled versus unskilled labor is expected to produce capital-intensive, high-technology products—such as computer chips—and export them in exchange for commodities and low-skill, labor-intensive products—such as agriculture and textiles—from countries with a lot of land or unskilled labor. Economist Paul Samuelson then added to this analysis to show that over time, under open trade conditions, the costs of production, such as wages, would tend to even out and, thus, benefit all trading participants.

As with Ricardo, comparative advantage determines one unique combination or equilibrium of production and trade, which produces optimal benefits for each country and for the world economy as a whole. Granting the assumptions on which this argument is based, the mathematics of its conclusions are irrefutable. This certainty and the apparent power of the theory to increase both overall welfare and international comity automatically without the need for government intervention has made it an extremely popular concept.

Nevertheless, the theory's actual predictive performance has been spotty. It works well with regard to trade based on agricultural and natural resources. But as early as 1954, the Nobel Prize–winning economist Wassily Leontief noted a huge anomaly. While the theory argued that countries with lots of capital should export capital-intensive products and import labor-intensive goods, Leontief pointed out that the capital-abundant United States tended to export more labor-intensive products while importing more capital-intensive products—just the opposite of what the theory predicted. Economists subsequently tried to explain this anomaly with the argument that capital should include human capital. Since many U.S. exports tended to be made by high-skilled labor, the inclusion of human capital in the capital category tended to allow the theory to appear to be working.

Then, in 1961, Swedish economist Steffan Linder spotted another chink in the armor. He noted that countries at similar levels of economic development tend to consume similar things, and thus to develop similar domestic industries to provide for that consumption—a tendency in apparent violation of the notion of comparative advantage. Moreover, the more similar the patterns of demand of two countries, the more they would trade with each other in their different versions of the same products. The United States and Germany are both major auto-buying and auto-producing countries. And, as Linder argued, a large portion of the trade between the two countries is in autos. Subsequent empirical testing proved a definite Linder effect.

The flaw in the standard theory that this exposed was that the theory assumed trade would be dominated by exchanges between developed and developing countries, not between developed and developed countries. And, yet, while these contradictions between fact and theory sparked some academic discussion, over the next twenty years they had no serious impact on trade policy or on the teaching and public discussion of international trade theory—even while during that period, the variance between the model's predictions and the actual patterns of trade widened considerably. As intraindustry trade between the developed countries of Europe, North America, and Japan came to dominate global trade, developing countries—like South Korea—took to imitating the production of the developed countries rather than specializing in the labor-intensive products in which the theory said they had the comparative advantage. They were seeking to take market share from the developed-economy producers and to catapult their economies forward. None of this was as the theory said it should be.

CRITIQUES OF ORTHODOXY

Of course, the disjuncture between theory and reality increasingly gave rise to various critiques of simple free-trade theory. The first of these were aimed at the simplifying assumptions underlying the theory. But this criticism then led to analysis of possible new trade structures in which the trading partners might be as much adversaries as partners. Beyond this, some critics noted that the morphing of trade into the broader phenomenon of globalization had really obviated the conventional trade concepts and that none other than Ricardo himself had anticipated this possibility. Finally, analysts from the real world of economic development came to explain that the ultimate logic of conventional theory can actually lead to disastrous results.

Blindingly Bad Assumptions: Krugman

It was in the late 1970s and early 1980s that several young economists like Paul Krugman, Laura Tyson, James Brander, Barbara Spencer, and Joseph Stiglitz began to wonder whether the assumptions of simple free-trade theory were too much at odds with reality. Krugman, who later gained a Nobel Prize for his work, emphasized that much of world trade seemed to be operating outside the theory—a discrepancy he attributed to the fact that the theory rested upon a host of truly unrealistic assumptions.

That list is remarkable. First is the assumption of perfectly competitive markets. This means that all markets are assumed to be like those for commodities like wheat or soybeans, in which there are many producers, no one of whom has a significant impact on the final amount of total production or on market prices. To put this another way, the assumption is that no market is like those for steel, airplanes, or automobiles, in which there are only a few producers, each of whom can dramatically affect overall production levels as well as prices. Another key assumption is that of constant returns to scale: that is, whether I have a big steel plant or a small steel plant makes no difference to my costs and profits. But everyone knows that a big steel plant does not cost twice as much to build as a small one even though it may produce twice as much. So a big steel plant running at full capacity will have a lower cost per ton of steel than a small one. That is called economies of scale and is perhaps the most important fact of life in big manufacturing industries. But the assumption, in effect, is that such industries don't exist. It is also assumed that there are no technological innovations, no significant increases in productivity, and no spillovers of know-how from one industry to another. Other important assumptions include those of fixed exchange rates, full employment, operation of factories at full capacity, zero costs of entering or exiting a business, and zero transportation costs. Beyond all these are two final killer assumptions: that workers and machinery can switch immediately and without cost from making, say, steel in Pittsburgh to making computers in Silicon Valley; and that there is no movement across borders of technology, labor, or capital (i.e., there is no foreign investment).

As Krugman knew, merely to list the restrictive assumptions of the conventional wisdom was to explain why it no longer provided sensible answers. In his attempt to improve the theory, he altered the conventional trade model so that rather than assuming away economies of scale, it incorporated them as a major element of the equation. He also adopted Linder's analysis about the high volume of trade for similar but differentiated goods, such as Jaguars and BMWs. In Krugman's model Jaguars and BMWs are no longer incorporated as just generic cars. Rather, they are noninterchangeable brands, each with its own largely nonoverlapping markets of ardent fans (different dreams, you might say). So, rather than having a comparative advantage in the production of cars, Germany might be said to have a comparative advantage in the production of BMWs while the UK has a comparative advantage in the production of Jaguars. Because production of both brands requires a lot of capital and skilled labor, both these products are most likely to be produced in developed countries with lots of those so-called factors of production.

Now an obvious question is, Why not just produce BMWs and Jaguars in all countries where there is significant demand for them? Here's where economies of scale enter. If the cost of each unit of production (each car in this case) falls as the total amount of production in a factory or a network of factories rises, it is less costly to mass produce at a few large factories in one or a few locations—even considering shipping costs—than to produce relatively few units at a lot of factories scattered all over the globe. Thus, BMW, for example, will concentrate production of its autos at its factory in Germany. Eventually, of course, the company may develop enough unit sales in a very large market, like that of the United States, to enable it to obtain sufficient economies of scale to justify locating a factory there. (BMW has a U.S. factory in South Carolina.)

Along with the contributions of other critics I have mentioned, Krugman's formulation became known as new trade theory or the new international economics. Although it shook the foundations of orthodoxy and made the arguments for free trade less certain, Krugman maintained that free trade remained the best policy. This was so, he argued, because trade generates more demand and thus more large-scale production, which lowers unit costs. It also increases the variety of consumer choices—we in the United States can buy not only Fords, Chryslers, and Chevrolets, but also Saabs, Volvos, and Toyotas—and it sharpens competition by adding new competitors in key markets. Nevertheless, he, and especially many of his colleagues, recognized that, at a minimum, the incorporation of economies of scale into the model changed the theory from one of mathematical infallibility to one of mere probability or possibility. The reason is that once falling unit costs are allowed into the calculation, the notions of free entry into and exit out of an industry, of perfect mobility of labor and capital from one industry to another, and of perfect competition are no longer valid. If large-scale production yields lower costs, then newcomers in an industry will have to start to produce big right away in order to survive, even if their sales are small. Since this requirement will constitute a barrier to entry, such industries will be dominated by only a few firms in an imperfectly rather than a perfectly competitive market. Finally, the great difficulty of morphing large-scale specialized production capabilities into something entirely new in a short time makes it difficult not only to gain entry into industries, but to exit from them as well.

At the least, the point seemed clear that the ability of the theory to explain and predict trade patterns was substantially limited.

Krugman and his colleagues also pointed out that, contrary to the theory, government intervention in trade might, under some circumstances, be in the national interest after all. For instance, subsidizing and/or protecting an industry to enable it to achieve unchallengeable economies of scale in key areas might be sensible (remember Alexander Hamilton?). Think of computing, aerospace, and the production of solar panels. Or consider the case of U.S.-based Boeing versus European Airbus. Europe has substantially subsidized Airbus in its attempt to overtake Boeing, and most analysts agree that this subsidization has benefited not only the European aerospace industry, but also the European economies as a whole.

In view of all this, Krugman concluded that while "free trade is not passé, it is an idea that has irretrievably lost its innocence. There is still a case for free trade as a good policy ... but it can never again be asserted as the policy that economic theory tells us is always right."

Adversarial and Strategic Trade: Gomory and Baumol

In the early 1990s, Krugman's work was extended in important ways by the former IBM chief scientist and Sloan Foundation president Ralph Gomory and the eminent economist William Baumol. They developed a series of models that more nearly approximated the reality of international trade by incorporating the effects not only of economies of scale, but also of rapid technological changes and sudden shifts in productivity. Such a shift might arise, for example, when a company like, say Intel, places an advanced facility in, say, China, and the latter suddenly leaps to the forefront of chip manufacturing and development. In contrast to previous models, which incorporated only a few countries and products, Baumol and Gomory took a further step toward reality by including in theirs very large numbers of products and countries—a step that allowed them to demonstrate just how badly flawed the conventional notion of one win-win trade pattern uniquely optimal for all trading partners is. Instead, they found that there are many possible trading patterns, of which some are optimal for one party and others for other parties but none is optimal for all parties at all times at once. In other words, rather than always being win-win, trade is more frequently adversarial or zero sum—my gain is your loss.

Again, think of Boeing and Airbus. A Boeing sale tends to be a gain for the United States and a loss for Europe and vice versa. (I know this is a bit simplistic, but you get the point.) Depending on the relative economies of scale, levels of technology, rates of productivity, and industry or national strategy, any given country might actually produce amounts of a product that are not optimal for other trading partners. Take the classic case in which England produces all the cloth. Suppose, for example, that the Portuguese came to see cloth as a high-growth market and wine, their area of comparative advantage, as a low-growth one. To ensure full employment for their rapidly growing population, they decide to kick-start cloth production with a subsidy, a ploy that eventually leads to much larger scale production and lower costs (even without the subsidies that have now been discontinued) in Portugal than in England. As the Portuguese take most of the global cloth business, they need so many workers that they turn their wine pressers into cloth makers. With no wine coming from Portugal and no work in the cloth mills, the British workers turn to wine making, precisely their area of comparative disadvantage. Here the introduction of economies of scale has turned the areas of specialization upside down to the disadvantage of England and the global economy but possibly to the advantage of Portugal.

This example demonstrates another key Gomory-Baumol conclusion. Whether or not a country achieves large-scale production, innovation, or major jumps in productivity is largely unrelated to climate, geography, and national endowments like the amounts of capital, land, and labor. Sometimes the leap will be made by a strategic choice to subsidize large-scale production. It may also come by serendipity, for example, if a Portuguese entrepreneur were to innovate the latest cloth fashion. The key point is that, once achieved, economies of scale and technology innovations become barriers to entry for newcomers. Whether foreign or domestic, a new competitor will have to make an enormous investment to match the existing scale and technology of the dominant player. Making this even more difficult will be the fact that normal market dynamics will reinforce the existing market structure. Customers will favor the lower prices (based on the lower costs arising from economies of scale) of the dominant producer, thus creating more production that will lead to even greater economies of scale.

Consider the case of Intel. Before the advent of the PC, it was one of several fiercely competing Silicon Valley semiconductor companies. However, IBM adopted Intel's microprocessor chip to power the original PC, and IBM's dominance of corporate computer markets and of early PC sales ensured that the Intel chip would start as the microprocessor market leader. Motorola had a competing chip that many analysts thought was technically superior. It powered the Apple II and the Apple Macintosh. But since Apple didn't have the corporate sales muscle of IBM, the PC quickly outsold Apple by a wide margin. Intel gained economies of scale and also was able to tie its microprocessor intimately to the PC's Microsoft operating system in ways that made it difficult to imitate. When the PC clones came along, they could, in principle, have gone with a non-Intel chip, but that would have been chancy and expensive. So they went with Intel, thereby reinforcing Intel's scale and technological advantages. Intel even licensed its technology to Advanced Micro Devices (AMD) as a backup supplier. But AMD has never been able to gain a market share more than 10 percent to 15 percent. So Intel was able to freeze out the domestic competition.

Intel was also able to freeze out foreign competitors. In the beginning a number of Japanese chip producers challenged the company, but they could never get to the scale or the close relationship with Microsoft that Intel had. It is only by dint of Intel's market dominance and the fact that Intel is a U.S.-based company that America is considered the world's leading semiconductor producer today. If Intel had been a Japanese company at the time its chip was adopted by IBM, Japan would be today's leading semiconductor producer.

As Baumol and Gomory pointed out, once a dominant market position like Intel's is attained, it tends to generate extra high profits and is therefore defensible for a long time because those high profits allow the company to compete in ways that raise even more the barriers to entry. Under conventional trade theory assumptions, such barriers don't exist. But try telling that to Intel's marketing people, who have spent billions over the past twenty years on raising the barriers by developing Intel's "Intel Inside" marketing and corporate promotion campaign.

A final key point emphasized by Gomory and Baumol, and also one at odds with conventional theory, is that the attainment of the kind of large-scale production that yields economies of scale can be very much influenced by public policy if, for example, the government adopts a favorable regulatory policy, or constructs supporting infrastructure, or uses government procurement to provide an early market, or provides a special tax incentive, or takes several of hundreds of other steps to foster an industry. The same is true for the spurring of innovation. Governments can also do a great deal to help companies attain and maintain market dominance. Intel benefited greatly from the U.S. government's Minuteman missile program, from strong U.S. protection of patents and intellectual property, and from U.S. antidumping and market-opening measures toward Japan in the 1980s. Because countries with a large number of dominant producers tend to be more prosperous than other countries (such producers are more profitable and pay better wages), national leaders often pursue interventionist policies aimed at supporting producers in their countries in attaining and maintaining dominance. The European Airbus program, Japan's development of its shipbuilding, semiconductor, and other industries, Taiwan's semiconductor industry, China's ten key industries strategy, and the U.S. Sematech consortium are all examples.

Such national promotion programs are a key reason that, as Baumol and Gomory showed, the fundamental premise of free-trade theory that trade never hurts any trading partner is also wrong. I have already noted the classic Boeing-Airbus duopoly and its zero-sum trade characteristics. The ascendance of Korea's semiconductor and semiconductor equipment makers tends to make Korea more prosperous at the expense of the American semiconductor and semiconductor equipment industry and of the U.S. economy. Another example would be Asian printed-circuit-board producers displacing U.S.-based producers. The stark reality is that global trade can just as easily be adversarial as win-win. If a country cannot replace industries lost to a trading partner with similarly productive and profitable new industries, its relative income will be reduced and there will be an overall decline in its standard of living. This decline is evident in the current recession as displaced U.S. printed-circuit-board workers, for example, have had difficulty finding equivalent new jobs or even any jobs at all, and hiring of other people into other high-tech jobs is also not occurring. Indeed, unemployment in U.S. high-tech industries has been climbing for some time.

In fact, based on their analysis of the multitude of possible trade patterns for multiple trading partners, Gomory and Baumol found that a large share of trade appears to fit into the adversarial, zero-sum category. Thus, for example, China's subsidized and rapidly growing exports of solar panels to the United States are undercutting not only U.S. solar industry sales but also the ability of the U.S. industry to maintain a competitive technological capability in a field it invented and in which it should be competitive based on its capital, educational, and technological resources. That this kind of trade accounts for a major part of total trade is not surprising in view of the extent of intraindustry trade between developed countries and the drive of virtually every developing country to move into those industries now dominated by the developed countries. The wonder is not that there is conflict but that anyone could suppose there would not be. The final conclusion of this analysis is that countries practicing unilateral free trade in the face of trading partners with interventionist policies will suffer overall economic losses. This doesn't mean that those countries practicing interventionist policies necessarily achieve optimal results. They may actually do more harm than good to their own economies, as orthodox economists often argue. But, contrary to conventional wisdom, they often also will harm the economies of trading partners.

Bad Logic and Globalization

A second line of critique of conventional trade theory has been aimed at the very foundation of its logic. In Ricardo's day, the businessmen of one country typically neither established factories nor acquired businesses in other countries. Such foreign direct investment was rare, and, as I have noted, Ricardo's theory assumed that it would not occur. Indeed, in his original essay on trade, Ricardo noted that the English cloth makers and the consumers of both countries would be better off if the cloth makers moved their factories to Portugal, and if both wine and cloth were entirely supplied from Portugal. This was because, as I've explained, Portugal required fewer man hours to produce both wine and cloth. So Ricardo himself understood that his comparative advantage analysis would break down in the face of significant foreign direct investment. But, he emphasized, such investment would not occur owing both to the risks of operating in an unknown land and to the commitment of businesspeople to the welfare of their own countries. In this age of globalization and rampant foreign direct investment, however, Gomory and Baumol insisted that we must ask what would happen in Ricardo's classic example if the English cloth makers were in fact to offshore their operations to Portugal. They demonstrated that Portugal would still make all the wine but would also take over some of England's cloth production. As a consequence of this shift, Portugal would become relatively richer and England relatively poorer. Portugal's workers would be making a greater absolute share of world production—in those two goods—than English workers. In a world of offshoring and outsourcing abroad, the simple formulation at the heart of Ricardo's argument is grossly inadequate. Indeed, the cross-border flow of capital, technology, and labor—modern globalization, in other words—makes the concept of comparative advantage irrelevant. While the prescribed conditions for simple free trade may assure win-win results for all national participants, the same definitely does not happen when trade morphs to globalization. And in this case globalization means that Portugal wins and England loses, not that both are winners.

Of course, if England can find something else to produce that is of equal value and productivity to the lost cloth, there may in real life be no net loss. But there is no guarantee of such an evolution either in theory or in reality. Things could as easily go the other way.

University of Texas economist James Galbraith says flatly: "Ricardo was wrong. Comparative advantage has very little practical use for trade strategy." He strikes at the fundamental assertion that countries will always have a comparative advantage in something. What happens, he asks, when there are three countries and three commodities? Will each country automatically be the relatively most efficient producer of exactly one good? If not, does the country with no comparative advantage have no trade or refuse to trade? In the actual world, says Galbraith, there are more than two hundred countries and thousands of commodities, and the calculation of comparative advantage is intractable and tells us nothing about who should specialize in what.

In actual practice comparative advantage is based largely on hindsight; the conjecture of advantage comes after the fact of a country gaining a strong position. If a country has specialized in making a certain product, the assumption is that it must have a natural comparative advantage in doing so. Actual analysis of the relative costs underlying the world's myriad trade patterns is virtually never conducted.

Yet there are other perfectly possible explanations to explain why a country may be competing in a given market. One is that what countries produce tends to be what economists call path dependent, meaning that present areas of specialization are substantially determined by past production activities and by what a country is able to learn given what it already knows. For example, Finland dominates production of icebreaking ships based in large part on its history of dealing with ice and ships. A country might also be specializing due to government subsidies or other incentives put in place to encourage that specialization. A good example is Taiwan's leadership in semiconductor foundries stemming from the Taiwan government's establishment of the first such foundry.

Cambridge University professor and Korean economist Ha-Joon Chang points out that a nation may well decide that it will subsidize a given industry because it wants more advanced technology. In fact, Chang argues, economic development is largely about acquiring and mastering advanced technology; countries need manufacturing, and new technology, because it is in advanced manufacturing that the greatest gains in productivity are made. And because unfettered market dynamics tend to favor the early developers of a technology, it is necessary for countries that wish to develop the same capability at a later date sometimes to defy the market and provide government support for the development of that technology even if that entails short- to medium-term losses. Says Chang, it's like going to school. You sacrifice present cost efficiency and income for huge future productivity and wealth. He points to Tom Friedman's golden straitjacket in *The Lexus and the Olive Tree* and notes that if Japan had worn that straitjacket in the 1960s, there would be no Lexus today.

Specialization Can Kill

Not only is the assumption that countries will have a comparative advantage flawed, argues Galbraith, but the conclusion Ricardo drew from this assumption—that countries should specialize in a narrow bundle of products, or that agriculturally based economies should stick to agriculture rather than trying to industrialize—leads to very unwise and even dangerously risky policy. Countries fated by climate, geography, and history to specialize in agricultural (bananas, coffee) or certain mineral commodities (like potash) are usually poor because the demand for their products is relatively inelastic; people consume about the same amounts of them even as their prices fluctuate. In addition, the costs of making these products tend to rise as production increases because poorer and poorer land or mineral deposits have to be brought into production as the better land and deposits are used up, thus diminishing profitability. In this regard, economist Eric Reinert cites the example of Mongolia, which became the World Bank's star pupil after the collapse of the Soviet Union. Overnight, it adopted free-trade policies and opened its industries to international competition while moving to specialize in its area of certain comparative advantage: the traditional raising of livestock on its vast expanses of grazing land. The result was the collapse of the country's relatively new industrial production, a halving of per capita income, and an ecological disaster as too many animals began chewing too little grass.

Diversification and industrialization have more often been the path to riches than has narrow specialization. Diversifiers are not only less vulnerable to shocks, but also are more capable of taking advantage of new technical opportunities because by diversification they will have more skills, be familiar with more processes, and see more potential new combinations than their specialized brethren do. Reinert emphasizes that with a few exceptions, such as the oil-producing countries with small populations, the only way for a poor country to gain a modicum of prosperity is by establishing industries with economies of scale that simultaneously generate rising income and falling costs. The way to acquire such industries, he asserts, is by emulation of others, not by relying hopefully on the evolution of some later to be assumed comparative advantage.

He uses the example of the Russian Sputnik, the first man-made satellite to orbit the earth. Because Russia was then, in 1957, the leader in rocket and satellite production, comparative advantage would have argued for America's forgoing development of rockets and satellites and saving money by using the Russian rockets instead. Presidents Eisenhower and Kennedy, however, neglected to read Ricardo and chose the way of emulation. They said that anything the Russians could do, Americans could do better, and proved it by beating the Russians to the moon and grabbing back the so-called comparative advantage.

None of this is to say that nations shouldn't trade. Clearly, countries like China, Japan, Korea, and, indeed, the United States, have benefited enormously from trade. Rather, it is to say that trade is highly desirable but only under the correct conditions.

OTHER PROBLEMS WITH CONVENTIONAL FREE TRADE

In addition to the problems with the theory and logic of conventional free trade, a number of practical, real-world issues have also increasingly come to the fore in recent years. One is the question of who really wins even if trade is being conducted under win-win conditions. Is something that appears to be a plus at the national level really a plus at the human level? Are there costs attached to free trade, and, if so, what is their true magnitude? Another major question has been that of the role of exchange rates and especially of the systematic manipulation of the dollar's exchange rate by countries with export-led economies. What does "free trade" really mean in the face of these practices? In the same vein is the issue of the impact of industrial policies that involve the targeted development of specific industries and the response to such policies under free-trade rules. Finally, there is the question of whether trade globalization involves competition among only corporations and individuals or whether the competition is also between countries.

Winning Countries, Losing People

One negative result of simple free trade that is indisputable but that its advocates often ignore or downplay is the fact that win-win applies only to countries, not to individual people. In the comparative advantage models, the gains from trade are net gains for countries as a whole, but these net gains may well be the result of huge gains for a few citizens of a country outweighing losses for the bulk of the population. Ricardian free trade assumes that workers can instantly switch from a declining industry to the favored area of specialization. Thus, the hypothetical English wine makers who would lose their jobs when Portugal took over all production could instantly switch to the expanding English cloth-making industry. In the real world, however, jobs are not so easily exchanged; workers may not have the necessary skills and may need training that they may not have the funds to pay for; the jobs may require moving to another part of the country, which imposes its own high costs. The fact that English consumers would surely stand to gain by getting cheaper and better wine from Portugal would be cold comfort to the unemployed wine makers, unless they were compensated with lifetime pensions. As much analysis by the Department of Labor and the Economic Policy Institute has shown, in the real world it's rare for displaced workers to find new jobs that match the income of the ones they lost. So there are almost always some losers from trade.

The statistics for national income may not reflect this fact, because it is quite possible for the gains of a very few people to be so large that they yield a statistical net national gain even though many citizens— even the vast majority—have ended up losing. This raises the very real question of what we mean when we talk about the gains of trade. It is in acknowledgment of this problem that in recent years many advocates of simple comparative advantage trade have urged better unemployment and worker retraining schemes.

Strong Dollar, Weak Economy

A further problem with conventional trade theory is its handling, or perhaps I should say nonhandling, of exchange rates. Most analyses assume exchange rates are fixed, as that was historically the situation and in any case that assumption simplifies development of the models. It also, of course, means that exchange rates play no part in comparative advantage and are thus not a determinant of trade patterns. But even when the current floating exchange rate system is incorporated into the analysis, exchange rates are typically not seen as an important element of trade policy and trade negotiation. They are conventionally seen as significant in terms of investment and of overall current account balances and financial flows, but not as an important trade issue. Indeed, in the U.S. government, trade negotiations never deal with exchange rates, and the U.S. Trade Representative and other negotiators are strictly forbidden even to mention exchange rates, which are seen as the exclusive province of the Treasury and the White House. This view is consistent with the conventional notion that trade is not only always win-win but also that all types of trade are equally beneficial and that the nature of a country's comparative advantages is unimportant or in any case, can't be altered very easily by policy initiatives or currency manipulation. But this understanding is, of course, based on the familiar assumptions that exclude economies of scale and rapid shifts in technology and productivity.

Once scale economies and technological innovation are admitted, as in the Gomory-Baumol analysis, win-win trade is significantly replaced by adversarial trade, and here exchange rates become nuclear weapons. An undervalued exchange rate is like a subsidy to exports just as an overvalued exchange rate is like a tax on exports. Such subsidies and taxes can dramatically change trade patterns and the structures and fortunes of whole economies. Recall, for example, how in the 1960s and 1970s we saw the U.S. consumer electronics industry replaced by the Japanese industry. The export-led growth strategies of many countries have as a fundamental element the use of the tool of intervention in currency markets to maintain a "competitive" exchange rate.

The result of this has been a succession of situations in which trade negotiators haggle endlessly to achieve tariff reductions of 5 percent or 10 percent or even 20 percent that are quickly negated by exchange rate movements of 50 percent to even 100 percent. I recall wondering in the 1980s why we were bothering to try to open the Japanese market when the then soaring dollar wiped out every little opening we managed to achieve. Yet that fact was never discussed in the negotiations, and the apostles of simple free trade, with a few exceptions like the Peterson Institute's Fred Bergsten, rarely called for it to be discussed or at least to be discussed in the context of trade negotiations. Indeed, the WTO has virtually nothing to say about exchange rates.

Over the years, this disconnect between simple free-trade policy and exchange-rate policy has contributed to huge distortions of international trade and to dramatic erosion of important U.S. industries and wealth-producing capabilities.

To Intervene or Not to Intervene

In view of all these difficulties, some economists in the 1980s, such as David Brander of the University of British Columbia, began arguing that governments might be wise to judiciously intervene in support of their industries in situations where there was an adversarial trade pattern and the actuality or likelihood of intervention by other governments. As an example, he chose the competition between Boeing and Airbus in which he supposed that the two companies were competing for an order of 100 big jets from Japan. Not only would the winner stand to gain significant profits on the fulfillment of those orders, but the winner would also create 1,000 new, high-paying jobs in its home market. Clearly a little boost for Boeing from the U.S. government could bring a big payoff for America and avoid a big loss that might materialize as a result of the subsidies the EU was paying to Airbus.

Other economists noted the phenomenon of "externalities" or benefits that accrue to the overall economy as a result of work done by a particular company. For instance, the fact that R&D spending on developing a new Boeing jet may also result in new materials and processes that can be used broadly throughout the economy also argued for possible policy intervention. However, the majority of economists continued to promote conventional free trade. In an article in the fall of 1987, Krugman himself summarized their view. In the first place, he said, the admission of economies of scale into the analysis often strengthens the traditional case for free trade. Scale economies mean potentially lower costs for consumers and the intraindustry trade that tends to occur when scale economies are present can increase both the diversity of goods available and the degree of competition in the market. Second, according to research by several economists, including Larry Summers, there are very few industries in which the extranormal profits that are the objective of strategic market intervention are actually available—the reason being that, once available, they are usually quickly competed away.

Then there was the point that spillover benefits "don't leave a paper trail" and are difficult to quantify and to forecast. Maybe an engineer will learn something on one project that he transfers into a major contribution on another completely unrelated project. But how does anyone know for sure, and how does anyone predict that this will happen? And if you can't predict what the payoffs of particular interventions will be, how can sensible policy choices be made? Further, in cases where there might be several domestic firms (e.g., steel), any subsidy would tend to be competed away and passed on in the form of lower prices to foreign consumers even if the intervention succeeded in deterring foreign competition. Then there was the problem of fostering one industry (e.g., semiconductors) only to see limited resources (e.g., electrical engineers) artificially diverted from another (e.g., telecommunications).

The clinching argument, though, had nothing to do with economics itself. Krugman noted that all of these objections to interventions did not actually negate the argument for doing them. Rather they dictated only that such action be taken with caution after hard study. The killer objection was political. Special interests would likely capture and distort any strategic trade policy activity; moreover, foreign governments would retaliate to nullify any action. Hence, the conclusion was that while the traditional free-trade policy was no longer theoretically best, it was still best as a practical matter of policy.

But that was no killer argument at all. Rather it was a bit of sleight of hand and even an admission of defeat. If the issue is practical politics, why should we pay special attention to economists? When economists speak of the politics of trade as justification for their recommendations, they deserve no more respect than any other ordinary citizen. Their job is to tell us the economics and let us decide the politics and policies.

As Berkeley economist (later Clinton's national economic adviser) Laura Tyson insisted, the politics weren't actually that difficult. It was relatively easy to figure out which industries had extra profits (unlike Summers, she could identify a number of such industries) and beneficial spillovers and to control lobbying on that basis. She noted that high-tech industries support a hugely disproportionate share of national R&D and that the extra rate of financial return to R&D is 35 percent to 60 percent above normal returns. Further, such industries employed one-third of all scientists, and their value added was a third higher than the average for manufacturing industries, which was higher than the national average for all industries. Moreover, Tyson explained that sacrificing an industry meant losing a myriad of special skill sets and networks and even the ability to teach those skills in the future, all unquantifiable elements but oh so important. Finally, Tyson emphasized that the U.S. share of world technology exports and of world high-tech production was falling dramatically with very bad implications for the U.S. economy in a world of increasing returns and imperfect competition. Labeling herself a "cautious activist," she called for judicious but strategic trade and industrial policy intervention.

Boston College economist Barbara Spencer concurred and established several criteria to guide policy makers around the objections of Krugman and other traditionalists. These included the conditions that a target industry earn additional returns sufficient to exceed the cost of the subsidy, that the domestic industry be subject to serious foreign competition, that the domestic industry be equally as or more concentrated than its foreign rival, and that the domestic industry have a fundamental cost advantage vis-à-vis the foreign competition.

Both Tyson and Spencer, along with others, were concerned that without some kind of strategic trade policy, the fears of Columbia University economist Richard Nelson would materialize. He noted that with the world's largest market, U.S. producers would naturally tend to enjoy the greatest economies of scale and thus the highest productivity and lowest costs. However, as a result of asymmetric market opening and currency and other distortions, trade liberalization agreements were neutralizing the U.S. scale advantages and could lead to loss of U.S. technology leadership.

Countries and Competition

This concern, of course, raised another traditional objection, which was that while companies compete when it comes to trade, countries don't. For them, trade was said always to be cooperative and mutually beneficial. This argument has always seemed so obviously misguided to me that I wonder why serious analysts aren't embarrassed to articulate it. Countries most definitely compete for power, and power does not accrue to nations of taxi drivers. China had comparative advantages under its old regime, but it was poor and weak. China is powerful today because it changed the composition and structure of its economy, and did so expressly in order to compete. In fact, the whole notion that we should not be concerned when certain countries gain an edge in the production of certain products and in the development of certain new technologies is romantic in the extreme. Do we not care if China, or Russia, or Iran has leading-edge rocket technology? Such technology involves leading-edge semiconductor, materials, and processing technology. Do we not care if we lose those technologies, which is exactly what happens when U.S.-based production and R&D close and move to China or Singapore for better tax breaks or better engineers? Of course we care. Probably even some economists care.

As for the concern about special interests hijacking trade policy, while justified, it overlooks the fact that foreign interests also have powerful lobbies in Washington, including sometimes leading U.S.-headquartered companies. So Washington can as easily be captured by lobbies for foreign economic strategies as by lobbies for U.S. strategies.

THE REAL DEAL ON U.S. TRADE POLICY

As important and telling as all this debate was, however, it largely overlooked the central reality of the actual operation of U.S. trade policy making. All the emphasis that those pushing the simple free-trade view placed on the potentially damaging results of an activist U.S. trade policy was largely irrelevant. The question U.S. policy makers constantly faced was not which industry to choose for promotional subsidy, as they never had any intent to be proactive. The issue was always how to respond to the subsidies, protectionist market barriers, currency manipulation, and aggressive dumping of our trading partners. Should the United States respond with its own measures or practice benign neglect? Economists almost always argued against any kind of response, citing fear of foreign counterretaliation. But this was kind of a joke, since the foreign governments were already acting strategically. It was like saying don't call the police when your house is robbed because the robbers might take more if you do. The fact was that the economists weren't terribly concerned about foreign strategic trade policies because they believed in unilateral free trade and thought our trading partners were only hurting themselves with their export-led policies. They didn't believe that those policies might be hurting us as well.

There are two other major reasons why U.S. administrations hesitated to respond to the strategic policies of our trading partners. One was a very real concern about the possible outbreak of a trade war—a concern rooted so deeply in the mythology of Smoot-Hawley that every little deviation from pure unilateral free trade was presented as the likely cause of another Depression, not to mention of World War III. Although the mythology of Smoot-Hawley is, as I have discussed, largely at odds with the reality, it has nonetheless exerted an enormous restrictive influence on U.S. trade policy. The second major restraining factor was concern about national security. Washington has always been afraid of losing a vote in the UN or a basing right in some critical country. The Pentagon has also played a role. It desperately wants the air forces of our allies to fly U.S. warplanes, for reasons both of better defense coordination and of cost sharing. Countries like Japan, Korea, Italy, Belgium, and many others routinely make the production of all or part of the planes and the transfer of key technologies a condition of buying U.S. So even as we were running enormous trade deficits with Japan, the Pentagon was literally forcing U.S. aircraft makers to transfer production and technology to Japan. A succession of trade officials and economic policy makers of both parties never objected because, as believers in simple free trade, they didn't think what we made mattered very much. After all, we would always have a comparative advantage in something—dung, for instance. Geopolitics trumped the insights of economic argumentation and analysis.

Orthodoxy Keeps Its Grip

Though the debate over trade theory and its policy implications became heated in the late 1980s and early 1990s, it ultimately ended with a whimper. Laura Tyson joined the Clinton administration, which embraced simple free-trade-based globalization as America's strategy and concluded a series of Asian trade arrangements culminating in China's entry into the WTO. As we have seen, these arrangements were based on traditional trade and globalization theories and have facilitated the movement of the production of tradable goods and the provision of tradable services out of the United States to Asia. In 1996, Krugman argued in a new book, *Pop Internationalism*, that it shouldn't be a priority to teach undergraduate economics students the innovative new trade theory arguments and wrote: "The essential things to teach students are still the insights of Hume and Ricardo. That is, we need to teach them that trade deficits are self-correcting and that the benefits of trade do not depend on a country having an absolute advantage over its rivals. If we can teach undergraduates to wince when they hear someone talk about 'competitiveness,' we will have done our nation a great service." And that is what they have been teaching. Most economics textbooks focus on the conventional theory and make little if any mention of economies of scale, imperfect competition, and adversarial trade, let alone of the fact that cross-border flows of capital, technology, and people tend to negate the concept of comparative advantage altogether.

The orthodox view also continues to dominate press commentary on trade and globalization. Just take the recent case of President Obama's decision to impose temporary tariffs on imports of Chinese tires. The decision was taken under the terms of a deal by which China agreed that such tariffs could be imposed in the event that surges of its exports were to disrupt U.S. markets and cause significant losses to American workers. The International Trade Commission investigated and duly found such surges and recommended that the president act. His action was entirely consonant with WTO rules, U.S. trade law, and all U.S. agreements with China. The surges were the result of China's systematic undervaluation of its currency, subsidization of its exports, and requirements that American companies establishing factories in China agree to export all or part of their production, all measures inconsistent with free trade and several WTO rules. The tariffs affect only a tiny amount of trade and will be lifted in 2012. The United States has a $600 billion trade deficit and nearly 10 percent unemployment, while China enjoys the world's largest trade surplus. Yet the major U.S. media unanimously condemned the president as a Smoot-Hawley protectionist who was threatening to cause a trade war and possibly worse. As I noted earlier, David Rockefeller invoked the specter of another world war in a *New York Times* op ed. No one bothered to mention the costly market distortions and damage to America being caused by China's mercantilism.

Globalization: Gains and Costs

The strong feeling underlying this support for orthodox simple free trade is that it is really good for America and has few if any downsides. Now certainly it is true that America has gained some benefits from increased access to foreign markets, from investment by foreign companies in U.S.-based production, from inflows of technology from abroad, and from the inflow of smart people who come here to study and stay to found companies. But again the conventional analysis tends to be flawed in that it overstates the gains and understates the costs of globalization.

For example, in a widely cited (e.g., by Fed Chairman Ben Bernanke) paper in 2006, the Peterson Institute estimated total U.S. gains from trade liberalization since 1947 at more than $1 trillion, or about 10 percent of 2003 GDP. The analysis on which these numbers was based set off a firestorm of criticism and countercriticism over methodology, data, and data use. I won't bore you with the details of the debate, but there was one particularly glaring weakness that has bedeviled analysis of trade forever, and that was the estimation of the costs of trade and globalization.

The paper put these costs at a paltry $54 billion—a sum calculated by estimating the number of workers displaced by imports and then figuring how long they were out of work and what the wages were at their new jobs. So the $54 billion represents the lifetime loss of earnings of workers directly displaced by imports. In arriving at this estimate the Peterson Institute exaggerated the number of workers and the amount of lost wages, in an attempt to be more than fair by producing numbers the institute actually thought were way over the reality. Yet this analysis, like those of most orthodox economists, ignores the major costs. The impact on wages is not just that of the directly lost jobs. Other workers in the same or related industries may still have their jobs, but they are certainly not getting the old annual wage and benefits increase. The downward pressure on wages is enormously more pervasive and costly to workers than the direct loss of jobs.

Of course, it's impossible to measure the exact amounts involved, but you have to be completely theoretical not to recognize this reality. A second point is the impact on families, neighborhoods, schools, crime, substance addiction, and so forth. Think of what happens to property values in depressed neighborhoods and regions. Decent houses in Detroit these days are selling for $10,000. A displaced worker may be forced to sell her house at a huge loss in order to move to another region to find a job. That loss may never be recouped even in the unlikely event that she makes higher wages at the new job. What about the costs of relocating? Then there are the losses of institutional knowledge and knowledge spillovers. When the Japanese semiconductor industry knocked out half of Silicon Valley in the 1980s, much knowledge evaporated, and some of the displaced engineers took their knowledge to Taiwan, where the government subsidized them to create the now world-leading Taiwanese semiconductor industry.

All of these things are big. They reduce U.S. income, savings, and consumption. But the biggest things are economies of scale and relative worker productivity. Major import penetration of the U.S. market means foreign producers are gaining economies of scale and the worker productivity that goes with them while U.S.-based producers are losing both. Since relative productivity largely determines wages, this kind of shift means downward pressure on wages. And this is true not just for the workers in the affected industry, but for all workers. Take your doctor. She probably makes well over $100,000 annually. Doctors in India make a quarter to a third of that even though many of them trained in the same schools as your doctor. The Indian doctors aren't less skilled or caring than your doctor, but they live in a low-productivity society where their income is determined by the productivity of the workers in Indian steel mills and auto plants.

So if a U.S. industry loses relative economies of scale and productivity and is not replaced by an equally productive new industry, not only do its workers suffer, but so also do U.S. doctors and all other Americans. In the Peterson Institute analysis, the U.S.-Canada Auto Pact of 1965 was undoubtedly counted as a plus for the U.S. economy. The deal abolished both U.S. and Canadian tariffs on auto imports, thereby integrating the two auto markets and enabling producers in each country to obtain greater economies of scale. It may have lowered the cost of autos to American consumers a tad (questionable, but maybe) and certainly lowered prices to Canadians, whose smaller industry had higher costs. Now, if tariff removal and full reciprocal free trade had been the whole deal, it is likely that the Canadian market would have been supplied mainly from U.S. factories and that the U.S. trade surplus with Canada would have grown. But the deal called for 60 percent of cars sold in Canada to be made in Canada and for those cars to have 60 percent Canadian content.

Without that requirement, it would have been advantageous to make most of the cars in the big U.S. factories and export them to

Canada. America had the biggest economies of scale and the established comparative advantage in auto production. With the requirement, the logic was that since you had to have a factory in Canada, it might as well be a big one to supply both the Canadian and the U.S. markets. That effectively shifted the comparative advantage to a significant degree and turned Canada into a big supplier of the American market, transferred enormous economies of scale and hundreds of thousands of potential new jobs from the United States to Canada, and transformed the U.S. trade surplus with Canada into a chronic deficit. Far from optimizing U.S. welfare, the deal minimized and may even have subtracted from U.S. welfare, although it was good for the Big Three Detroit automakers.

Of course, conventional theory holds that if the United States doesn't have or loses a comparative advantage in auto production or any other area, it will inevitably find another area of production in which it does have an advantage and where its workers can find jobs. While that is true within the terms of the theory, there are two problems. First, the theory in no way guarantees that the new industry will be as productive and pay wages as high as the old one did. The theory values all industries pretty much the same. So right now a major U.S. export is waste paper. Okay, we have a comparative advantage in waste paper, so the theory says the auto workers can become paper collectors. The theory assumes they get paid the same wages, but in real life, of course, they don't. The second problem is that while the theory assumes full employment, real life doesn't provide it. In fact, there may be no new jobs for workers whose industries move.

No one knows, in fact, what the full impact of globalization has been on the United States over the past sixty years, as there has been no truly comprehensive analysis. But a good case can be made that the gains have not been great and that there may well have been a net loss. The Economic Policy Institute reckons that the annual earnings of all workers without a college degree (the vast bulk of the workforce) are $1,400 less than they would have been without globalization. University of Maryland economist Peter Morici argues that globalization has cost the United States $1.5 trillion over the past ten years. The recent FormFactor case provides a telling example of the justification for such estimates contradicting the conventional view of globalization's overwhelming benefits.

FORMFACTOR

Igor Khandros grew up and studied materials engineering in Ukraine under the old Soviet Union. In 1978, the Soviets loosened emigration rules and Khandros managed to get to New York, where, like millions before him, he arrived penniless but optimistic. Working by day, he got his PhD in materials engineering at night at Stephens Institute of Technology. From there he went to work for IBM in its semiconductor operations. In those days, each circuit etched on a semiconductor wafer was painstakingly tested by hand before the wafer was sliced and diced into the "chips" that run your computer. Khandros figured there had to be a better way and dreamed up the idea of the Probe Card, a device that mirrors the wafer and tests all the circuits at once when placed over it. Literally retiring to his garage, Khandros developed the concept and developed prototypes with which he obtained venture funding from Mohr Davidow Venture Partners. From there he established a new company, FormFactor, Inc., in Livermore, California, in 1993. The company quickly established its leadership in the field of wafer testing and became an instant success. Today, it has sales of $210 million and employs about one thousand workers. Although the average worker has not completed high school, the starting wage is $40,000 annually with full benefits and stock options. The company exports more than 80 percent of its production to markets in Asia. When you hear American leaders or commentators speak of the future of the U.S. economy and of the necessity for it to move to "higher ground" in order to remain competitive, FormFactor is a great example of what they are talking about.

The problem is that the company is less and less likely to be in America's future. A few years ago, Korean semiconductor maker Hynix, with the support of Korea's Ministry of Industry, instigated the creation of Phicom, and Phicom essentially cloned Igor's product and started competing with FormFactor. The reason was simply that the Koreans believed that they could make this kind of product competitively once they got past the learning stage, and that this was precisely the kind of industry their country should have in its future. Korea, despite its market-based capitalist economy, believes the market occasionally needs government help in getting to the main objective, which is a dominant position in a number of high-technology, high-value-added industries. As Ha-Joon Chang told us earlier, Korea does not accept either the Washington Consensus or the Ricardian simple free-trade theory.

Of course, Phicom's cloning infringed several of FormFactor's Korean patents. But when FormFactor filed legal complaints requesting injunctions to compel Phicom to pay at least a royalty for use of the proprietary technology, Phicom countered by calling for annulment of the patents. At the first round, the Korean Patent Office (PTO) reaffirmed the validity of all the patents. But upon appeal, higher courts reversed the patent office and annulled three of four key patents. Still, that left one patent in force. So FormFactor requested the Seoul District Court issue an injunction enforcing that patent. The court refused, hinting that enforcement might put Korean workers out of work and arguing that the remaining patent should have been annulled along with the others. Eventually the Korean Supreme Court upheld this ruling, and FormFactor found itself threatened with the loss of its proprietary technology and eventually of its business if the Korean government continued both to support Phicom and to maintain its longtime policy of intervening in currency markets to keep the Korean won undervalued (versus the dollar) as a way of subsidizing exports. I should add here that in this regard FormFactor was equally threatened by the U.S. policy of maintaining a strong dollar as a way both of artificially enhancing American buying power and of facilitating the sale of the trillions of dollars of U.S. Treasury bonds necessary to finance the gargantuan U.S. trade deficit.

As this situation developed, the Economic Development Board of Singapore became aware of the squeeze tightening around FormFactor and began to visit Livermore, offering tax holidays, free land, and capital grants if the company would relocate all or part of its production to Singapore. Some Korean leaders suggested that locating a factory in their country would solve FormFactor's problems. Khandros thus faced a dilemma. Without adequate intellectual property protection, he would need to increase R&D spending in order to innovate faster to stay ahead of Phicom's cloning operations. But doing so would reduce his profitability and share price and thus increase his cost of capital unless he could find a way to cut costs dramatically. The Singapore proposal offered him exactly this opportunity by essentially providing a government subsidy in exchange for the move to Singapore. But

Khandros felt an obligation to the United States and hoped to keep production in America. He therefore came to Washington, where I worked with him to try to arouse some U.S. government interest in cracking down on the Phicom cloning operation. It was the time (2006–7) of the negotiation of the U.S.-Korea Free Trade Agreement, and we thought some U.S. officials might be interested in obtaining better protection of intellectual property in Korea as part of the deal. In addition, knowing that any agreement would have to be ratified by the Senate, we thought some senators would be interested in protecting U.S. intellectual property and that such interest might encourage U.S. negotiators to make a strong effort to retain FormFactor in the United States.

On Capitol Hill, we got a mixed reception from several senators. California Senator Dianne Feinstein, along with New Mexico Senator Jeff Bingaman and Nebraska Senator Chuck Hagel, wrote letters to the Korean ambassador and to the White House. California's Barbara Boxer showed little interest, and several other senators said FormFactor was not their concern because it wasn't in their state. The staff of the Senate Finance Committee chairman and Montana senator Max Baucus told us that his main objective with Korea was to get it to import more American beef, which I guess makes sense if you are from Montana, but not much if you are from the United States.

But this mixed reception was good compared with what we ran into in the executive branch. In fairness, the State Department, under the influence of old Asia hand and deputy assistant secretary of state Jim Foster, fired off a letter to the Korean ambassador in Washington while U.S. Ambassador to Korea Sandy Vershbow made representation to the Korean Foreign and Trade ministries. But the real responsibility for the deal and for our problem lay with the U.S. Trade Representative (USTR) and the Department of Commerce. The USTR and the White House very much wanted to conclude the Korean agreement in order to demonstrate accomplishment and also as a way of shoring up our political-military alliance with Korea. They did not want to hear about any problems that might slow things down, and anyhow they had negotiated new and better language on intellectual property protection. They didn't care much that the language was irrelevant if the courts wouldn't enforce it. The USTR could not find time to see us, and her deputies pedantically explained to me (an experienced trade negotiator who knew better) that the issue was a legal matter in which the USTR could not intervene.

But even that was a positive reaction compared with the one we were about to get at the Commerce Department. There we met with the undersecretary of commerce for international trade, who was a former businessman, a Republican fund-raiser, and a former ambassador to Singapore. If there was one person in the U.S. government responsible for promoting American exports and the interests of American business abroad, he was the guy. Imagine our surprise then when he responded to our request for help by asking: "Have you considered moving your operations to Korea or maybe Singapore?" Igor nearly fell out of his chair. We didn't bother to tell Lavin that we were talking to him in an effort to avoid moving the company, jobs, and technology out of the United States. He prided himself on being in the market and being a real "free trader." He wouldn't have understood our values and intentions.

We made one more effort. Of course, the U.S. federal government does not provide financial investment incentives, but some states do. We checked to see whether the State of California might be able to provide an offset to the financial incentives Singapore was offering. But the state could not. In the end, Igor felt he had no alternative but to plan on moving at least part of his production to Singapore.

As a result, several hundred highly desirable jobs that should have been created in Livermore may be created in Singapore. Nor is it likely that equivalent replacement jobs will be created in California, although, of course, waste paper collection jobs may be available. Singapore's technological base will expand and become richer while that of California and the United States will shrink. Singapore's exports will increase in value and its trade surplus will grow while U.S. exports will likely decline in relative value and the U.S. trade deficit will also grow. U.S. wages are likely to be less than they could have been, meaning that taxes paid, national savings, and national investment will also be less. The opposite will be true of Singapore. In discussing trade and current account deficits, economists often talk of imbalances of savings and investment as being the main cause. But here the savings and investment are being shifted by the impact of strategic trade and industrial policies. The tail is wagging the dog. These are the dynamics that are driving Americans to build casinos on the remains of their steel mills. But even in the gambling industry, America may not be competitive. The world's most modern casino is slated to open in Singapore in 2010.

Second Thoughts

In view of the persistence over three decades of the orthodox thinking that drove companies like Siemens-Allis and FormFactor either out of business or out of the country, it is heartening to see that some key actors in these policies are shifting their views. Larry Summers is now "picking winners and losers" in the White House as the U.S. government tries to revitalize General Motors, CitiGroup, and Bank of America while also promoting growth of clean industries and green jobs. Even before entering the White House, Summers seemed to have had an epiphany. In a *Financial Times* article in August 2008, he acknowledged that globalization might not lead to democratization and lamented that authoritarian governments are following economic strategies aimed at accumulating government wealth and geopolitical power rather than consumer welfare. He expressed deep concern that, contrary to all theory and his own expectations, capital flows were moving from developing to developed countries and that these had been a cause of the financial crisis. Finally, he lamented the fact that the old notion that companies compete but countries don't had become passé.

Another key figure who seems to be shifting directions is Krugman. Indeed, on some matters he has gone into reverse. In *Pop Internationalism*, Krugman stated flatly that developing countries like China would never be exporters of capital to developed countries like the United States. Not only has he acknowledged that error, but he has gone further to revise his earlier view that trade with developing countries would have little impact on American jobs and wages. Now he says that the effects of trade on income distribution in developed countries like the United States are "big and getting bigger." Krugman insists that he is not pushing protectionism but also that "free traders need better answers to the anxieties of globalization's losers."

Exactly so. And part of those better answers must be not only a more strategic view of trade and globalization, but also a far more sophisticated and realistic understanding of the motivations, allegiances, power, and modes of operation of the new global corporation.

7

Companies Without a Country

A corporation must consider the impact of its actions on all, from the shareholders to the society at large.

—BUSINESS ROUNDTABLE, 1981

Few trends could so much undermine our free society as the acceptance by corporate executives of social responsibility.

—MILTON FRIEDMAN

On December 8, 1981, at New York's Pierre Hotel, newly minted General Electric CEO Jack Welch gave a speech that was to have enormous consequences for U.S. business and the U.S. economy over the next three decades. Speaking on "Growing Fast in a Slow-Growth Economy," Welch emphasized his beliefs in selling underperforming businesses and aggressively cutting costs in order to deliver consistent increases in profit that would surpass global economic growth. In closing, he told the gathered analysts that "GE would be the locomotive pulling the GDP and not the caboose following it." From there he proceeded to put his money where his mouth was and took GE's market capitalization from $13 billion in 1981 to $400 billion in 2007 as profits rose tenfold to $14 billion. In compiling this record, Welch became iconic for his ruthless insistence on getting rid of any business in which GE was not either number 1 or number 2 and for his relentless cost cutting, including substantial workforce reductions.

When he took over in 1981, GE had 411,000 workers. By 1985 that number was down to 299,000. As a matter of policy, he fired the bottom-ranked 10 percent of the GE executive team each year, earning the moniker "Neutron Jack." The chart of the increase in quarterly earnings during the 80 quarters Welch was CEO is virtually a straight line up.

A good deal of this growth was due to good strategy, good acquisitions, globalization of the business, development of good products, and achievement of production efficiencies—to good business, in other words. But Welch and his team also employed a more questionable set of tactics for making the business look good. GE accounting became so creative in assuring steadily rising quarterly earnings that one commentator noted it could have been a candidate for the Museum of Modern Art. Frequent use was made of the same kind of off-balance-sheet vehicles that Enron used to doctor its earnings except on an even grander scale. These are separate legal corporations in which the parent company owns less than 100 percent of the equity, and they do not encumber a company's balance sheet and corporate investment potential. At GE, the company's huge finance arm, GE Capital, was also used as a kind of top-up fund whose earnings could be somewhat manipulated to enhance the corporate total whenever the industrial side of the business wasn't yielding the forecasted earnings. All of these techniques were legal, but they had little to do with making better products and providing better services. What they did have a lot to do with was providing increasing value to shareholders in the form of a steadily rising share price.

Indeed, Welch's Pierre speech heralded a radically new philosophy or perhaps a return to an old one for American business. Under the new doctrine, the central concern of CEOs became the steady accumulation of strong quarterly results in order to increase the value of a company's stock. This notion that a CEO's core responsibility is to the shareholders has by now become such widely accepted wisdom that it may seem always to have been the American business creed. But that is not the case. The view that had prevailed in America since the Great Depression was that a CEO is responsible to the many people, businesses, and services that have a stake in his or her corporation's welfare—to the society, that is, in which the corporation is embedded.

At about the same time as Welch's speech, in a manifesto on corporate governance, the Business Roundtable, a group of CEOs of America's major corporations, perfectly expressed what has become known as the stakeholder theory: "A corporation's responsibilities include how the whole business is conducted every day. It must be a thoughtful institution which rises above the bottom line to consider the impact of its actions on all, from the shareholders to the society at large. Its business activities must make social sense." According to this theory the stakeholders in a company are defined broadly as its employees, customers, and suppliers along with the community in which it operates and the larger society. But the Roundtable's statement was a lagging indicator. Welch had caught the new wave. And the fealty to that new creed of shareholder value above all else has by now been taken to such lengths that a host of the most powerful American companies—the companies most crucial to our economic well-being—increasingly do not consider that they have obligations to America or even that they are American. Nor is this attitude limited to American CEOs. The same could be said, although to a lesser degree, of many European CEOs, and to a much lesser degree of some Asian CEOs. The problem with this creed, as we have seen in the recent crisis, is that when a company gets in trouble, it turns to its domestic stakeholders, and especially to the U.S. government, to bail it out.

I was a witness to one particularly glaring changing of the guard in this great transformation of American business. As a young man, I attended Swarthmore College courtesy of the McCabe Scholarship, established under a grant from Thomas B. McCabe of the Swarthmore class of 1915. Those of us lucky enough to receive the scholarship had not only the good fortune of having our room, books, and tuition paid for, but also the great privilege of becoming friends of Mr. McCabe. The college president called him Tom, but I never heard anyone else use that name, for good reason. Mr. McCabe was a great man.

McCabe was made CEO of Scott Paper in 1927, at age thirty-four, at which time the company had a single paper mill in Chester, Pennsylvania, and a payroll of 500 employees. By 1980, when he stepped down from his dollar-a-year position as chairman, Scott Paper was a global giant employing over 40,000 people at about 60 locations around the world. Along the way, he worked as Deputy Director of the Priorities Division in the Office of Price Administration during World War II, served as chairman of the Federal Reserve Board from 1948 to 1951, and donated prodigiously to Swarthmore College and many charities, including especially the University of Pennsylvania Hospital in Philadelphia.

As it happened, I became a salesman for Scott Paper Company in the spring of 1968. McCabe had just stepped down as CEO but was continuing as chairman. His values suffused the company. On the wall of his office was a statement of the company's mission: to produce the highest-quality products for the customers, without whom there would be no company; to create the best possible environment for the workers, without whom there would be no company; and to earn a fair long-term return for the shareholders, without whom there would be no company; while also supporting to the greatest extent possible the citizens of the local community, without whose goodwill there would be no company. McCabe was a super salesman and an extremely competitive person who once stopped me from considering a banking position with the argument that banking was only for wimps who couldn't make it in real business. But he deeply believed that being competitive involved a lot more than just making his numbers; he would have said that that was making things too easy.

After helping to establish Scott's European operations, I left the company to work as a consultant in Japan. By 1978, however, I was back in the United States as head of global marketing for the consumer operations of American Can Company. By coincidence, one of my colleagues there was Al Dunlap, who years later came to be called "Chainsaw" Al. He wasn't known as such at American Can. He was manager of some of the plastics operations and then left to go to work for paper cup maker Lily-Tulip, where he began making the bold management moves that earned him the moniker. Apparently his first move at the company was to fire all but two of the executive team. Had you told me or anyone else at American Can that Al was going to become CEO of a major company, let alone, a celebrity CEO, we would all have been incredulous. But the gods of business are truly unpredictable. One day I opened my morning newspaper and found that Al had been made CEO of Scott Paper.

Scott was dogged in the late '80s and early '90s by the declining fortunes of one of its divisions, and its stock price had languished in the $30-to-$40 range. In an effort to turn its fortunes around, the board established a search committee to find a new CEO who could deliver quick results. The committee's own quick result was Dunlap, who, according to some former board members, was presented without the benefit of a thorough vetting process. Nevertheless, the board quickly voted Al Dunlap in as the chairman and CEO of Scott Paper Company.

With his beloved German shepherd at his heels even in his office, Dunlap proceeded quickly to meet with the key Scott executives. Former Scott senior vice president Paul Schregel noted that upon being introduced by outgoing chairman Phil Lippincott, Dunlap looked at his shoes while extending his arm for the formal handshake. Schregel sensed that he, Schregel, might not be long for the Scott world. At the Monday morning executive committee meeting, Dunlap went around the room alternately listening to the views of some executives and tearing into those of others. At moments, he could become extremely agitated. In this meeting, he particularly singled out, in addition to Schregel, Senior Vice President John Butler, Vice President and General Counsel Ellis Horwitz, and Vice President Barbara Rice as targets of his agitation. Sure enough, three weeks later Schregel was summoned to Dunlap's office (now known as the Dog House) at 3:00 p.m. on a Friday and told: "We're changing direction. You're done." So, in short order, were the other three of the Gang of Four old-time Scott executives. That was just the beginning.

Dunlap quickly axed all R&D activities while throwing into the market anything that could be called new or improved. In one case he ordered a go-ahead without testing for a line of tissue containing talcum powder. Unfortunately, the abrasive powder burned out the bearings of heavy paper-making equipment and caused havoc in the mills. Dunlap also sold off Scott's enormously valuable woodlands in Alabama and other southern states along with the division that had been struggling and eventually fired over 11,000 employees. Needless to say, Scott's extensive charitable giving evaporated. Managers were directed to develop plans to double earnings for the second half of 1993 and to double them again in 1994.

The company was obviously being structured to be sold off, and its share price rose dramatically from $37 to $84 as market players (risk arbitrage traders, for example) anticipated an acquisition by one of Scott's competitors. The deal came in the summer of 1995 when long-time Scott rival Kimberly-Clark negotiated a tax-free merger of the two companies that effectively valued Scott at $45 per share after a share split, making the comparable price before the split about $90 per share. Many shareholders rejoiced, as the deal made them rich overnight. Others, like me, lamented the passing of a once great company. Of course, those who lost their jobs and the communities and institutions that lost the source of much of their well-being were saddened if not devastated.

The vital question about the deal is whether it was a net benefit to the U.S. economy or a net loss. Certainly the shareholders came out ahead, at least in the short run. No one knows what might have been in the long run, although the company was certainly a potentially powerful competitor with great resilience. Scott was the low-cost tissue producer at the time, and Kimberly-Clark's later restructuring of manufacturing and distribution appears to some analysts actually to have raised costs. There is also the fact that the closing of pulp mills by Kimberly-Clark resulted in a surge in imported pulp and a rise of the U.S. trade deficit. On the other hand, Kimberly-Clark had a lot of good technology that improved many of Scott's brands, providing additional value to the consumer. This added value came at a heavy cost, however, as the consolidation of the industry reduced competition and burdened consumers with substantial price increases. On balance it looks as if shareholders (especially short-term speculators) benefited enormously while consumers and workers incurred losses, and the U.S. trade deficit and international debt burden increased a bit as a result of the deal.

SHAREHOLDER PRIMACY

This kind of outcome and the transformation in the underlying purpose of a corporation from which it derived, was another legacy of Milton Friedman and his Chicago school's rational expectations/ efficient market hypothesis theories that were in sharp contrast to previous business school teachings. Moreover, this legacy had profound implications not only for business, but also for American competitiveness—especially since countries like Japan and Germany were not persuaded by the new theories.

THE HARVARD BUSINESS SCHOOL CREED

At the founding of Harvard Business School in 1908, Dean Edwin Gay said the purpose of the school was to teach business leaders how to "make a decent profit by doing decent business." That was McCabe's creed and what thousands of future business leaders learned at Harvard for many years. But in 1970, the University of Chicago's Milton Friedman sounded a different note. Said he, "Few trends could so much undermine our free society as the acceptance by corporate executives of social responsibility other than to make as much money for shareholders as possible." This tune was quickly picked up and elaborated upon by Harvard's professors and especially by professor Michael Jensen, who became the dominant American voice on corporate architecture and the proper role of a board of directors and a CEO.

In a hugely influential 1976 paper and subsequently, Jensen propagated Friedman's doctrine of shareholder sovereignty and of increased returns to shareholders as the sole purpose of the CEO. His argument was grounded in the view that the shareholder is the corporation's final risk bearer and therefore also its final claimant. He added the notion that, as agents of the shareholders, the corporation's managers do not necessarily share the interests of the shareholders. Indeed, the managers and the shareholders may be at war because the way for the CEO to maximize his/her private gain may be at odds with maximizing shareholder gains. For instance, a CEO may like corporate jets or want to be part of the society scene, but the costs of such indulgence may be a burden to shareholders. Thus, the central problem is how to align the interests of managers and shareholders and to establish a monitoring mechanism that easily indicates whether the managers are acting properly on behalf of the shareholders.

Jensen's solution was to grant gobs of stock options to CEOs and to evaluate their job performance by focusing on the progression of quarterly earnings. This is a single, readily available, objective number upon which a CEO can concentrate all her attention and which the shareholder can readily use to determine whether a CEO is working for him. Jensen emphatically rejected stakeholder theories on the grounds that giving a CEO multiple objectives would be confusing, distracting, and make it impossible in the end to measure performance.

Of course, there were many counterarguments. Is it true that shareholders are the residual risk bearers and claimants? The shareholder does not own a corporation in the same way he owns his house. He owns only a right to the residual cash flow. He doesn't own the actual assets or business of a corporation, which is itself a legal person. Indeed, owning it would not be compatible with the limited liability concept on which a corporation is founded. Further, the value produced by a corporation is produced by a combination of resources. In addition to those of the shareholders, there are also the workers, suppliers, customers, public infrastructure and services, the legal system, and the society at large represented by the government. So why should the distribution of value favor only shareholders? Moreover, it is not clear that the shareholder bears more risk than do other stakeholders.

Indeed, simply by selling shares the shareholder can divest himself of risk more easily than can any stakeholder. Workers, suppliers, and communities cannot so easily extract themselves from failing corporations. Take the case of the recent bankruptcy of General Motors. Many shareholders were able to sell out with relatively small losses when they realized the company was in deep trouble. But GM's independent dealers, for example, weren't so lucky. With employees and cars in their showrooms, suddenly they were told they were being cut off. Or take the communities where plants are being closed. Maybe the GM workers will get some kind of reasonable severance and even a pension, but the people who work in the coffee shops, machine shops, and other shops that depended on that now closed plant are all pretty much just out of luck. Further, several empirical studies and examples have indicated that stakeholder-oriented companies do better in crises and over the long term than do those narrowly and intensely focused on shareholder returns. In a 1992 study, John Knox and James Heskelt showed that stakeholder companies had grown four times faster than shareholder-driven firms.

But none of the objections stopped the momentum that quickly developed behind the shareholder value theory. The popularity of the new thinking was probably due in large part to the fact that the focus on short-term earnings made it so easy to quantify performance. It also rationalized a lot more Wall Street merger and acquisition activity and facilitated the quantification of business management theory and the building of models so that business professors could, like their economist colleagues, present their discipline as a science. The emphasis on the primacy of the CEO was also, for obvious reasons, quite popular with CEOs, and led eventually to the apotheosis of the CEO as a godlike figure in American business, credited with achieving near miraculous feats singlehandedly. For example, the April 14, 1997, issue of *Fortune* magazine stated that "in four years CEO Lew Gerstner had added $40 billion to IBM's market value." Really? Did Lew do that all by himself?

In 1997, the Business Roundtable reversed its earlier views and pronounced: "In the Business Roundtable's view, the paramount duty of management and of boards of directors is to the corporation's stockholders...The notion that the board must somehow balance the interests of stockholders against the interests of other stakeholders fundamentally misconstrues the role of directors. It is moreover, an unworkable notion because it would leave the board with no criterion for resolving conflicts between interests of stockholders and other stakeholders or among different groups of stakeholders." So fixed did this view become that eleven years later, despite the intervening debacles of Enron, WorldCom, Tyco, and Long-Term Capital Management, Jack Welch could still threaten his handpicked successor, Jeffrey Immelt, with mayhem for missing his quarterly earnings target. Said Welch in April 2008: "Here's the screw-up. He promised he would deliver and now he misses three weeks later. Jeff has a credibility issue. He's getting his ass kicked. If it happens again, I will get a gun and shoot him."

What Welch may not have realized is that his shareholder value/quarterly earnings fetish had become a big gun shooting a large hole in the competitiveness both of corporations and of the United States. The focus on short-term profits led to the slashing of R&D and of investment in longer-term, more risky projects. In short, companies were increasingly showing good short-term results while eating their seed corn.

Losing Our Edge

Ironically, the shift to the shareholder value philosophy came just as corporate America was about to be challenged as never before. As CEOs scrambled to defend themselves from each other's raids and to redefine their mission, they and their companies found themselves in increasingly hostile circumstances and losing badly in competition with foreign competitors in Japan and Germany (where the stakeholder doctrine was dominant). One study noted that whereas in 1960 the United States accounted for two-thirds of the global production in ten of fifteen major industries, by 1980 it did so in only three industries. Further, between 1970 and 1986, U.S. productivity growth averaged 2.9 percent annually compared with 3.4 percent for the UK, 3.8 percent for Germany, 4.2 percent for France, and 6 percent for Japan. Or to look at it another way, using an index of 100, from 1950 to 1988, U.S. productivity had doubled to 200 while Germany's had climbed to 650 and Japan's had skyrocketed to 2,000. From 1973 to 1989, output per hour in the United States grew less than half as rapidly as in Japan, and while Japan's investment ranged from 15 percent to 20 percent of GDP, that of the United States ranged only from 7.5 percent to 9 percent. Indeed, in 1989, Japan spent $4.6 billion more on plant and equipment in absolute dollars than the United States.

The story was the same in R&D. From 1972 to 1988, Japan's expenditures on nondefense R&D rose from just under 2 percent of GDP to nearly 3 percent while U.S. expenditures fell from 1.5 percent of GDP to about 1 percent before eventually rising to about 2 percent. More dramatically, U.S. market share fell by about half in such industries as fiber optics, semiconductors, and supercomputers. This was also the period when Chrysler received its first government bailout as Detroit's Big Three were battered by imports from Japan; Intel needed a capital infusion from IBM; and roughly 100,000 people lost their jobs in Silicon Valley due to the inroads of the Japanese electronics companies. Harvard professor Ezra Vogel's book, *Japan as Number One,* became an international bestseller and the big question facing both U.S. industry and the U.S. government was, "Can America compete anymore?"

This question, which aroused concern in both the government and the business community, led to several studies and recommendations. Most of these, however, were ignored by our leaders who were blinded either by economic orthodoxy or by arrogance or by both.

In 1983, as the 1984 presidential election began to loom large amidst the worst recession since the Great Depression, the competitiveness question was increasingly pressed by a Democratic party that saw America's apparently declining economic vitality as a possibly winning issue for the upcoming campaign. Contenders like former vice president Walter Mondale began talking about the need for an American industrial policy similar to those of Japan and Germany. As one congressional staffer of the time noted: "Only God can make a tree, but any government can create a comparative advantage." This idea, which reached back to the earlier "catch-up—can do" America, resonated with many political insiders and with many ordinary voters. It also resonated with my then boss, Commerce Secretary Malcolm Baldrige, whose Cabinet Council on Commerce and Technology had already reported a sharp decline in American leadership in high-technology industries. With the loss of twenty-four Republican House seats in the recent congressional elections fresh in mind and at Baldrige's urging, President Reagan appointed Hewlett-Packard Chairman John Young to chair a presidential commission on industrial competitiveness that would report by the end of 1984. A majority of the members of the new commission were CEOs of major corporations, but they were joined by key representatives of organized labor and of academia.

The first task was to decide exactly what this thing everyone called "competitiveness" really was. The commission's answer has become the standard definition. "Competitiveness is the degree to which a nation can, under free and fair market conditions, produce goods and services that meet the test of international markets while simultaneously maintaining or expanding the real incomes of its citizens." The commission added that "it is in the national interest to maintain a broad and diverse industrial base in which many industries achieve high levels of productivity." In other words, while it wasn't choosing a set of industries to target, the commission was emphasizing the need for a large, diversified industrial base rather than embracing the then increasingly popular view of many economists that America should abandon manufacturing in favor of a pure service economy.

In judging America's performance by these standards, the commission concluded the country was not doing very well as demonstrated by its loss of leadership in a broad range of industries and its large and growing trade deficits. It called for major new steps, including the establishment of a cabinet-level Department of Science and Technology to devise and execute a national technology policy; measures to increase the supply and reduce the cost of capital to U.S. industry; dramatic improvements in education; greatly improved and enhanced life-long learning and flexible work training and up-skilling programs; and a cabinet-level Department of Trade to put trade issues on a par with domestic and geopolitical policy issues. In particular the commission called both on business schools to "prepare managers for this new era of competition" and on the government to "respond to foreign government policies aimed at fostering specific industries."

The report was notable for some things it didn't say. For example, there was no mention either of the role and the then very large overvaluation of the dollar or of the need to respond to foreign currency manipulation that was driving this overvaluation. Nor was there any focus on the financial incentives that many other countries were using to entice investment in industries such as semiconductors in which they could realize the benefits of big economies of scale and knowledge spillovers. While the report called for promoting exports and enforcing trade laws, it did not question any of the flawed elements of the reigning trade orthodoxy. Nevertheless, it was a significant break with the myth of inherent and effortless American superiority, and made serious, important recommendations.

In December 1984, Young presented his findings to the president and his cabinet in the Cabinet Room of the White House. A sophisticated, immensely experienced, and classy executive of the stakeholder school, Young made a crisp thirty-minute presentation and then turned to the assembled officials for questions. Silence. Young waited. More silence. Finally, seeming more to want to relieve embarrassment than to really gain information, Secretary of State George Shultz made a few rambling remarks and asked a couple of desultory questions. The president remained mute next to his bowl of jellybeans, and when no one else had a question, the session was over.

Pause for a moment. This was the same Cabinet Room in which decisions were made to enter wars whose favorable outcome depended on American industrial and technological superiority. This was the same Cabinet Room in which the decision was made to protect against a possible Soviet missile attack by building a Star Wars space shield whose ultimate success also depended on maintaining American industrial and technological leadership. This was the same Cabinet Room from which the president sometimes spoke of "Morning in America." Here were the country's top business, labor, and academic leaders telling some of their most important stakeholders that the whole foundation of national security and morning in America was increasingly shaky. And no questions. A lot of CEOs would have walked away never to return.

The Council on Competitiveness

But not John Young. He had been mentored by Hewlett-Packard (HP) founders William Hewlett and David Packard. Starting in a garage in Palo Alto, they had built HP into a world-class giant by following a no-layoffs policy and managing "by walking around" and talking to a continuing cross-section of ordinary employees. The notion of "giving something back" was strong at HP and with Young. Maybe the president didn't have any questions, but Young had answers and intended to make them known. So in 1986, with the assistance of National Association of Manufacturers President Sandy Trowbridge, he founded the Council on Competitiveness as a nonprofit organization headed by top CEOs, labor leaders, and university presidents. The council would be dedicated to promoting policies to recover American competitiveness. At about the same time, I founded the Economic Strategy Institute (ESI) as a nonprofit think tank to develop the rationale and the concepts for the competitiveness policies that the council and its allies would want to promote. The original strong backers of my effort included Ford Motor CEO Don Peterson, Chrysler CEO Lee Iacocca, United Steel Workers President Lynn Williams, Intel CEO Andy Grove, Motorola CEO Robert Galvin, Corning Glass CEO Jamie Houghton, TRW CEO Ruben Mettler, Communications Workers President Morty Bahr, National Semiconductor CEO Charlie Sporck, U.S. Steel CEO David Roderick, United Auto Workers President Owen Bieber, and FedEx CEO Fred Smith. Thus, between the council and ESI, the top corporate, labor, and academic leaders of America, most of whom still lived by the stakeholder creed, had united behind the idea of an economic strategy to maintain and revitalize U.S. industrial, technological, and service industry leadership.

The council issued a series of reports calling for new policy directions and a new emphasis on competitiveness. Its initial recommendations called for an American Technology Policy (I know it seems mundane, but in the "government can't pick winners and losers" environment of the time it was revolutionary) and detailed a plan to reduce the federal budget deficit and raise savings and investment to international levels. It was unfortunate that this latter recommendation coincided with the "read my lips—no new taxes" comments of then vice president and presidential candidate George H. W. Bush.

More unfortunate, however, was the council's drift toward an almost exclusive focus on technology and innovation and its failure to recognize the fundamental, systemic nature of the challenge. Of course, we needed to innovate more and to do better in technology. But the council members—mostly believers in the win-win free-trade doctrine—were largely unaware of the dangers posed by the role of the dollar. Not understanding that the same dynamics that had sapped the competitiveness of traditional U.S. industries would sap the competitiveness of the high-tech industries, they tended to address symptoms rather than causes.

Motorola chairman and CEO George Fisher replaced Young as chairman of the council in 1990. Under his guidance in 1991 it issued "Gaining New Ground," a report that called for making technological leadership a national priority; for developing a world-class technology infrastructure; for establishing more effective technology networks among industry, government, and academia; and for implementing best practices for the commercialization of new technology. It was all good stuff, but even if all of it could have been accomplished it would not have changed the disadvantages U.S. industry faced in competition with Japan and the Asian Tigers, nor would it have halted the broader erosion of American industrial and economic leadership. It did not mention exchange rates, the overvalued dollar, or most of the other fundamental issues. Implicit in its recommendations was the notion that with just enough of that good old American ingenuity and entrepreneurial spirit we could invent our way out of difficulty. Not that there was anything wrong with innovation; clearly, the more the better. But in terms of the competitive challenge, this was not a game-changing strategy.

Fisher was the perfect chairman for the council at this time. A brilliant young mathematician, he had spent his early career at AT&T's Bell Labs before switching to corporate management at Motorola in 1976. There he led the Chicago semiconductor and telecommunications maker to dominance in the emerging cell phone business and climbed quickly up the corporate ladder to become chairman and CEO in 1988. In both the cell phone and the semiconductor businesses he had had difficult skirmishes with Japanese competitors and was determined to meet that challenge and to crack the Japanese market. At the same time, he was steeped in traditional internationalist thinking and was also leading Motorola into a more global deployment of its assets. Further, he felt that the Japanese were playing the globalization game unfairly rather than that they were playing a completely different game. He was prepared to be energetic in helping to improve the U.S. performance, but he was not prepared to lead a revolution. When I asked him why he had focused so much on technology and downplayed the bigger, structural economic issues, he told me he had gone for what he thought was politically doable. Fair enough. Certainly at that time most of the Washington elite were not at all receptive to a more comprehensive strategy. But the utilitarian rationale ignored any potential for changing the politics.

U.S. BUSINESS GOES GLOBAL

As quickly as it had arisen in the 1980s, the competitiveness problem seemed to fade in the 1990s—for several reasons. One was that the U.S. government actually did adopt a lot of competitiveness policies. At this time the $1 billion 50–50 government-industry consortium Sematech helped to shore up the semiconductor and semiconductor equipment industries. Increased funds for the National Science Foundation sped development of what became the internet. The Plaza Agreement to revalue the Japanese yen, the German deutsche mark, and several other currencies pushed the dollar down and made U.S.-based production more competitive. Washington also negotiated some results-oriented trade agreements like the U.S.-Japan Semiconductor Agreement which actually boosted American exports. Another factor was the apparent collapse of the Japanese challenge in the wake of the bursting of the Japanese real estate and stock market bubble in 1992.

But this vanishing of Japanese competition was actually more apparent than real. While Japan surely had huge fiscal, banking, and financial problems that caused a dramatic decline in its growth, the likes of Toyota, Nikon, Honda, Matsushita, and Fuji Film did not falter. Nor, with a few notable exceptions, did American industries recover in areas of lost leadership. Indeed, one reason the fuss about declining U.S. competitiveness died down was that many of the companies making the fuss (Cincinnati Milacron, Zenith TV, Perkin Elmer, et cetera) had gone out of business. There was no one left to make a fuss. Many companies did, however, make substantial strides in improving the fundamentals of manufacturing and distribution by applying a set of business improvement methods pioneered by both Japan and the United States between the 1960s and 1980s. These included Six Sigma (very high quality) manufacturing, just-in-time delivery, and total quality control. They not only lifted the fortunes of many companies, they also contributed to the lessening of concern about competitiveness. It also helped that the rise of the personal computer established a kind of monopoly for Intel and Microsoft on the global market for microprocessors and operating systems respectively. As I noted earlier, the 1991 collapse of the Soviet Union and the subsequent peace dividend coupled with the takeoff of the long U.S. consumption boom and the dot-com bubble also boosted American confidence that the economy was strong.

The biggest factor in the diminishing concern was that U.S. business responded to the global challenge by going global itself. Of course, so-called multinational companies (MNCs) had been around for a long time. But that was just stage one in which a major mother company, like Scott Paper, established small replicas of itself around the globe in a kind of colonial network. Though these "colonies" operated with a large degree of autonomy, they were dependent on the mother company for capital and critical technology. Neither the markets nor the companies were integrated. Indeed, the toilet tissue sold by Scott's Italian affiliate was an entirely different size from that sold by the Spanish affiliate, which was different again from that sold in France and Benelux. Now, in stage two, the companies moved to integrate the markets and create global supply chains.

The U.S. electronics makers had actually initiated this trend in the 1960s as they tried to offset Japan's labor cost advantage by moving assembly and other labor-intensive parts of the production process to Singapore, Malaysia, and Taiwan, which had even lower labor costs than Japan. These countries and others like Ireland and Thailand accelerated this movement and pushed it into the capital- and technology-intensive parts of the production process as well by offering capital grants, tax holidays, free infrastructure, and other financial incentives to entice the transfer of production from the United States to their shores.

The China Factor

The entry of China—with 20 percent of the world's population—into the global economic system greatly magnified these dynamics. China's production potential was immense and so also was its potential for consumption. Had China, like Japan and Korea before it, kept domestic markets largely for domestic producers and prevented foreign investment while dumping its growing production on world markets, the response would have been a coalescence of U.S. and other industries to meet the challenge by becoming more competitive in their domestic production and also by seeking changes in the laissez-faire international trade rules. But, as I have said earlier, instead of adopting the Japanese model, China leaned toward the Singapore model—not all the way, mind you, but enough to preempt a strategic response. It allowed foreign companies to do real sales in many Chinese markets and used financial investment incentives such as tax abatements and capital grants to entice foreign companies to move their production to China.

For U.S. companies with their increasing emphasis on shareholder returns, here was a thrilling prospect. On the one hand, they could get in on the ground floor of what, in time, would very likely become the world's biggest market. On the other hand, by switching production to supply their global markets from a China base, they could quickly and dramatically increase profits by more than halving much of their production cost. Further, they could get away from pesky unions, rigid environmental controls, and the bulk of U.S. taxes. Forget about that comparative advantage nonsense, here was an opportunity to achieve absolute global advantage and thereby to strike back at the Japanese and the Koreans. What was not to like? Nothing, and American CEOs clamored to get into China and to get China fully into the global system.

They were led by Motorola. As early as 1985, then chairman, CEO, and founder's son Bob Galvin had had a heart-to-heart talk with Commerce Secretary Baldrige. Galvin, an American of the Greatest Generation, had led the charge for an economic strategy to make his country more competitive. But he was frustrated by Washington's failure to understand and react to the realities of the international market, and also foresaw the great economic potential of China. He asked Baldrige whether the Reagan administration might seriously respond to the competitive challenges facing the country and explained that if it did not, he would have to start offshoring more of Motorola's production capacity. Baldrige, who was tremendously frustrated by his own administration, responded by saying frankly that an effective administration strategy was unlikely. "I understand," he said, "that you have to do what you have to do." With that, Galvin was off to Asia, and especially to China. Motorola proceeded to expand greatly and to raise the level of sophistication and value added in its operations in Malaysia and Singapore. But it was in Beijing that the most critical steps were taken.

Galvin met with the top leaders, Deng Xiaoping and Jiang Zemin, who began by telling him that he would need a 50–50 Chinese partner whom they would assign as a condition for any investment in China. This kind of condition had, of course, long been part of the Japanese-Korean model, and Galvin was only too familiar with its enormous disadvantages. He countered by saying that he understood China's desire to advance industrially and technologically as fast as possible, and that he and Motorola could and were prepared to accelerate China's advance by transferring technology to production facilities and labs in China. He explained how Motorola and others had been burned in Japan and did not want to repeat the experience. Thus he set as a condition that a Motorola operation in China had to be wholly owned by Motorola.

The circumstances of the establishment of a Motorola facility in Tianjin are instructive from the perspective of the economic theories I've discussed. Former Motorola CEO Gary Tooker told me that at first the Chinese were so inept that even the factory's Motorola sign had to be brought in from the United States. So here was a high-technology factory that required skilled labor coming from a country with plentiful capital, technology, and skilled labor to a location that had only plentiful unskilled labor—in other words, the opposite of how orthodox theories said things should work. Of course, Motorola was going to supply the capital and the technology, but where did it think it was going to get the requisite skilled labor? By training it, of course. The factors of production are not immutable. They all, and especially labor, can be changed. And it is critical to note in this regard that the change was not going to be the result of better Chinese K–12 education and universities, but rather of corporate training and technology transfer in the factory. A huge spillover was going to occur because, once trained, the workers in that factory were going to have skills that could be useful in other factories and that could be taught to other workers. Indeed, that factory wasn't going to be so much a factory as a university.

Where Motorola and a few other pioneers led, the rest of American and, to a lesser extent, global industry followed. A relative trickle of foreign direct investment in China and Southeast Asia became a tsunami. In just the five years from 1984 to 1989, the percentage of U.S. company assets held abroad rose from 14.4 percent to 17 percent. By 1990, the capital spending abroad of American corporations was rising at a 14 percent annual rate compared with 6 percent domestically, and a quarter of the U.S. annual trade deficit was arising from imports of the foreign production of American corporations. On top of that, companies like Hewlett-Packard and General Electric were moving R&D to science parks in places like Grenoble, France, and Bangalore, India. Many large U.S. companies have more employees and sales outside the United States than inside.

The Sovereign Corporation

Offshoring was appealing not only due to the promise of lower production costs and increased sales in those markets, but also because it allowed companies to slip the leash of national governments and national identity. They could increasingly ignore stakeholders and even play off one government and society against another to get financial and regulatory advantages.

This power shift to the global corporation was particularly borne in on me several years ago when I was organizing a high-level conference in Washington and invited the then AIG CEO and Chairman Hank Greenberg to participate. When his Washington vice president asked me what was in it for Hank, I mentioned that it would give him the opportunity to meet with some important prime ministers and high-ranking officials from around the world. "Clyde," he said, "Hank doesn't need to come to a conference to do that. Those guys line up to beg for a chance to go to New York for a meeting with him."

The head of a major company like Intel, IBM, Google, or Goldman Sachs has more resources at his or her disposal and more power than all but a handful of prime ministers and presidents. He can decide to transfer highly desirable technology, to invest to create thousands of jobs, and to educate to raise a country's whole level of potential output. Just before the onset of his illness, Israeli Prime Minister Ariel Sharon preannounced that Intel would build a new advanced fabrication facility in Israel. His jumping the gun embarrassed Intel, but for Sharon, that announcement was more important than dealing with the Palestinians or his own settlers or almost anything else. Intel Chairman Craig Barrett and other top executives never had a problem in seeing Sharon.

At the same time, the perspective of the CEO inevitably broadens to encompass the interests of the various nationalities touched by the total enterprise. For instance, John Grant, former Ford Motor corporate strategy executive director, once noted that "in any country where Ford operates, the manufacturing value added in that country should be the maximum possible." Motorola's Galvin has emphasized that "we must treat our employees all over the world equally." To which former Colgate-Palmolive CFO Cyrill Siewert added that "there is no mind-set here that puts this country [the U.S.] first. Our goals could be at odds with those of the nation." I saw an element of this myself a few years ago when I addressed an audience of Intel's executives. Andy Grove, legendary Intel chairman, has been outspoken in voicing concern about America's declining competitiveness and in calling for a coherent economic strategy. During the Q&A period, some of the non-Americans in the audience turned from questioning me to raising the issue of whether Grove was intent on putting their countries at a disadvantage and whether he was calling for America to go protectionist.

Thus, because they have a multinational constituency, global CEOs have to be very careful about how they articulate their own national identities and those of their companies lest they offend important constituencies. Beyond this is the fact that with their private air fleets, offices, and staff assistants in cities around the globe, along with high-profile media attention, CEOs can find it easy to think of themselves as statesmen in charge of their own sovereign domains with their own quasi-national interests. Indeed, a prominent U.S. CEO once commented to me that his company was not really an American company. Rather, he said, it was an international company that just happened to be headquartered in the United States. He added, it could just as easily have its headquarters in a Boeing 747 and be run from there while constantly circling the globe.

Similarly, in 1995, Ford Motor Company CEO Alex Trotman said: "Ford isn't even an American company, strictly speaking. We're global. We're investing all over the world. Our managers are multinational. We teach them to think and act globally." In 2006, Cisco CEO John Chambers went even further in saying: "What we are trying to do is outline an entire strategy of becoming a Chinese company."

We may think of these as iconic American companies, but they do not see themselves in that way at all. Maybe we should change our views.

Global Corporations and Democracy

Now, it is important to realize that what may be in the interest of these corporate domains may not be completely in the interest of their home country. Take, for instance, the question of currency exchange rates. In recent years, the U.S. National Association of Manufacturers (NAM) has been experiencing a bitter civil war between its large global manufacturing members and the smaller companies in its membership who are manufacturing only or mainly in the United States. There is a broad consensus among economists and business analysts that the dollar is chronically overvalued against the Chinese RMB and several other Asian currencies and that this discrepancy puts U.S.-based manufacturers at a disadvantage. Nevertheless, the global NAM members have blocked all efforts by the domestically oriented producers to pass resolutions calling on the U.S. government to redress the currency distortions. Why? Because, of course, the overvalued dollar sends money straight to the bottom lines (remember, shareholder value and CEO stock options) of manufacturers with operations in Asia.

A significant aspect of the situation is the asymmetry in the relations between global companies and democratic governments on the one hand and relations between such companies and authoritarian governments on the other. In Washington, for instance, a global CEO is not only a business leader; he or she is also an important political player who makes big political action committee (PAC) donations, maintains legions of lawyers and lobbyists, writes or helps to write legislation, and influences regulatory decisions. Global companies can take the

U.S. government to court and win injunctions that stop the government dead in its tracks. And keep in mind that any U.S. incorporated subsidiary of a foreign company is legally considered a U.S. citizen and has the full rights of any other American. Further, global companies can join all of the industry associations and shape their agendas as illustrated in the example of the NAM.

In Beijing, Riyadh, or Moscow, or even in Singapore, however, the global CEO is not a political player. He or she is more in the position of a supplicant—a powerful supplicant, to be sure, since he or she will have access to the top leaders and may have the technology and investment they want. But a CEO does not file lawsuits against these governments or make political donations to their campaigns or pressure them through their docile or nonexistent parliaments. Since there is limited or no rule of law in many of these countries, a CEO has to maintain favor and keep the bureaucrats and party operatives happy. As a former advisor to several leading companies, I saw the subtly powerful way in which this works. Chinese officials and a company's own China executives constantly talk about the need for the company to be a good citizen and demonstrate its commitment to China's development in order to maintain the confidence of the people and the leadership. What this means in straight talk is that the company better put an advanced manufacturing facility in China as soon as possible. And that is exactly what most of them do. Of course, this kind of pressure is not the only or even the main reason why a company might decide to put a facility in China. There are lots of good business reasons for doing so. But the pressure is a constant element in the mix, and it is an element that is not present in the United States.

It is also true that many CEOs prefer doing business in authoritarian countries. The attitude toward business in many democratic countries is, at best, one of benign neglect and often one of outright hostility. In the United States, major global companies frequently find themselves the objects of political attack and of regulatory restriction or even dismemberment. In a China or a Singapore, on the other hand, the welcome mat is out for the CEOs. Decisions are made quickly. The incentives to induce investment are attractive, and the implementation of agreements is sure. For the emerging-market countries, as for the United States of the nineteenth century, the business of the countries is business. The leaders are often engineers and always think like CEOs. This means that global company CEOs are very comfortable with them and anxious to help them both within their own countries and in Washington, if necessary.

More troubling is the use of the global corporation as a mechanism to reverse the dynamics of the popular notion that by making nations rich globalization will also make them democratic and peaceful. In fact, authoritarian regimes like those of China and Russia are intimidating and sometimes even guiding global corporations. Until recently Google accepted Chinese government censorship on its Chinese websites. How Google's new defiance of censorship will work is a highly important issue to watch. Microsoft and global corporations sell the Chinese government the equipment and processes necessary to monitor and censor the internet. Yahoo has even turned one of its employees over to the Chinese police for alleged violation of censorship rules. Yet Washington has raised little fuss about any of this. (It did recently protest Chinese plans to install censoring devices on all PCs.) One reason is that all of these global corporations are big political players with significant lobbying operations in Washington, and they don't want Washington to act or speak in any way that might cause trouble for them in the authoritarian countries. Thus, while global corporations may sometimes transmit democratic values into authoritarian societies, they can also do the opposite by dampening what would otherwise be articulated as major concerns. In addition, the economic success that the global corporations largely make possible may be an important element propping up the authoritarian regime. Thus can authoritarian regimes be fostered rather than undermined by globalization.

Who's Advising Whom

Of perhaps even more immediate significance is the fact that these corporations are the primary advisors to the U.S. government on the setting of its international economic agendas and the conduct of international trade and investment negotiations. I noted earlier the progress of the negotiations to bring China into the WTO and to grant it most favored nation (MFN) status. Particularly I noted the lack of careful, comprehensive analysis of the implications for the U.S. trade deficit and long-term competitiveness of these deals. Yet the chief negotia-tor, then U.S. trade representative Charlene Barshefsky, once told me that "we got more than they asked for," "they" being U.S. industry, which was asking for conditions that would enable it not only to sell in China, but above all, to optimize production in China for export to America. While that was certainly in the interests of the companies and of China, whether it was entirely in the U.S. interest is another question.

As I write, the U.S. Commerce Department and the Office of the U.S. Trade Representative have batteries of industry advisory groups that are supposed to counsel them on what would be good for the United States to get or to avoid giving up in international negotia-tions like those for the U.S.-Korea Free Trade Agreement and the Doha Round of WTO negotiations. Most of the members of these advisory groups represent companies that have large interests in China and, given the prevailing shareholder value doctrine, no primary reason to be concerned about what is best for the United States. This was made clear to me a couple of years ago when I was interviewing Silicon Val-ley CEOs about outsourcing and offshoring. At the end of each inter-view I would say to the CEO I was interviewing: "You are moving a lot of production and jobs to Asia, and I understand that that looks like the best thing for your company. But you are also an American citizen. How do you feel about it as a citizen?" Almost invariably, the answer went something like this: "Yeah, sometimes it bothers me. But, hey, I have a fiduciary responsibility to my shareholders to maximize profits. My job is not to worry about American competitiveness. That's what those guys in Washington are supposed to do."

Indeed, except that many of those guys in Washington are with global corporations that are anxious to please China and are, at the same time, advising the U.S. trade negotiators. So, in effect, the U.S. negotiators are being advised, indirectly through the global corpora-tions, by the negotiators for Beijing and other key countries. Is it any wonder our trade deals never deliver the promised results?

I am not trying to knock American CEOs. Having spent many years as an international businessman and advisor to CEOs and global com-panies, I understand how complex the environment is in which they have to work and how the incentives in and structure of the global economy force them to offshore production and jobs. If I were in their position, I probably would be doing many of the same things. Former secretary of commerce and Blackstone cofounder Pete Peterson made a recent plea for American business leaders to rally to the flag à la their predecessors of forty or fifty years ago, which is touching and beautifully nostalgic, and I hope that some may respond in the same spirit. But such a response cannot be expected. The world has changed since then, and we must recognize that American interests are, at the moment, different from those of "American companies" and organize ourselves accordingly.

Winners and Losers

Not surprisingly, the unlinking of the corporation from its national roots has proved extremely profitable, both for the corporation and for its top executives. Over the past thirty years, the returns to capital have risen steadily as have the profits of U.S. corporations as a percent of GDP. At the same time, compensation for CEOs and other top executives has skyrocketed. In 1974, the compensation of the top 10 percent of the income distribution was 20 times that of the bottom 90 percent. In 2006, it was 77 times. In 1979, the top 1 percent of earners garnered 34.2 percent of all capital gains. In 2005, that number was 65.3 percent. This dramatic shift, of course, reflected the fact that globalization has diminished the regulatory and social constraints on the corporation and its leaders and given it much more leverage and flexibility to reduce costs via the global supply chain.

Consumers also did reasonably well as the flood of imports into the U.S. market helped to keep prices down and inflation under control. Walmart, for example, came all by itself to account for 9 percent of the U.S. trade deficit.

On the other hand, the vast bulk of working people (who, of course, are also consumers) lost ground. Between 1980 and 2005, U.S. productivity rose 71 percent. Yet real compensation (including benefits) of nonsupervisory workers (80 percent of all workers) rose only 4 percent. In the tradable manufacturing sector, productivity rose 131 percent while compensation climbed only 7 percent. This was in stark contrast to the period from 1950 to 1975 when worker compensation rose 88 percent while productivity doubled. Over the past thirty years, median real income has stagnated. The median male 2007 income of

$45,113 is actually less than the $45,879 (in 2007 dollars) of 1978. The stagnation was masked somewhat by the fact that Americans increased their borrowing (helped by rising house values) and that more women and children entered the labor force. But the hard fact was that in the year 2000, a new worker with a high school education had beginning earnings that were $5,000 less than in 1970. For a beginning worker with some college courses, the shortfall was $3,500.

Apostles of the conventional wisdom often dismiss such comparisons as a problem mainly of unskilled workers and of education. While there is some truth in their opinion, it is far from the whole truth. This stagnation occurred while those in the workforce with college degrees doubled from 15 percent to 30 percent and the share of high school dropouts fell from 29 percent to 10 percent. Moreover, the offshoring of jobs has now ratcheted up to jobs in R&D that Americans had always assumed would be theirs. The U.S. trade deficit in advanced-technology products will reach about $56 billion this year. As former Federal Reserve vice chairman and Princeton economist Alan Blinder has warned, "Tens of millions of additional workers will start to experience an element of job insecurity that has heretofore been reserved for manufacturing workers. It is predictable that they will not like it."

When I interviewed Silicon Valley CEOs about their views of offshoring, there was one CEO who had a nuanced answer, and that was Intel's Craig Barrett, with his worry about how his grandchildren will earn a living, as I quoted earlier. The biggest loser for the United States has been our productive base, not just the factories and equipment, but the skills and the ability for them to be passed on to the next generation and to evolve. We may still have universities on our campuses, but we no longer have the "universities" that were embedded in our factories and industrial laboratories.

In an important recent article, Harvard Business School professors Gary Pisano and Willy Shih emphasize that with the bubble years behind us, the United States will have to get serious about paying its way and restoring the high-technology manufacturing base to do so. Their concern is that in the quest for short-term earnings gains, the shareholder-value-oriented, increasingly stateless global companies have cut back so much on basic and applied research and outsourced to offshore locations so many of the critical production processes and their related skills, that the United States has lost much of its ability not only to produce current products and services but to migrate from there to new products and processes. These professors point out that developing or producing the next generation of energy-efficient illumination will be difficult or impossible in the United States because not only are the critical light-emitting diode components not made here, but the skills to make them here have largely evaporated. This is true also for such things as advanced displays for mobile phones, flat panel displays for computers, TVs, and handheld devices, and for the carbon fiber components of the Boeing 787 Dreamliner. Indeed, they enumerate a long list of items—electrophoretic displays, lithium-ion and NiMH batteries, crystalline and polycrystalline silicon, advanced ceramics, advanced composites, hard disk drives, and integrated circuit packaging—that are no longer makeable in America.

Nor is it just a matter of hardware and manufacturing. Pisano and Shih explain that the capacity to *create* new high-tech products and services is fundamentally affected. For example, with the exception of Apple, every brand of U.S. notebook computer is now not only manufactured and assembled in Asia. It is also *designed* in Asia. And the same is true of cell phones and many other devices. Or to look at things from another angle, although the United States invented the internet, it ranks fifteenth among nations in high-speed internet deployment. Worse, high-speed in the United States seems very slow and expensive compared to Japan and Korea. For example, with Verizon's FiOS fiber-optic service you can get 50 Mbps for $50 to $145 per month. In Japan, you get 100 Mbps (twice the speed) for $25 to $56 per month (half the price). None of this is actually a new story. Some of the names of the items have changed, but this story was told in 1989 by the National Advisory Committee on Semiconductors. It was told at about the same time in my book, *Trading Places: How We Are Giving Our Future to Japan*. It was told yet again in 2004 by the President's Council of Advisors on Science and Technology, which warned against the erosion of the U.S. innovation ecosystem. It was told once more by the National Academy of Science in its "Rising Above the Gathering Storm" report of 2005. And now to have the *Harvard Business Review*, the citadel of Jensen and shareholder value, also say it is an important step toward possible action.

ADDRESSING THE PROBLEM

Doesn't this seem to be the perfect time for the Council on Competitiveness to come forward with a comprehensive strategy to revitalize America's productive base? What is the council now proposing?
Well, one thing it is not proposing is anything that would deal with
the U.S. trade deficit or the unsustainable asymmetries of the global
economic structure. Indeed, at a council meeting I attended last year
I actually heard some council members argue that the United States
really doesn't have a trade deficit because the overseas production of
U.S.-headquartered companies should count as U.S. exports—never
mind that they are made by non-U.S. labor in non-U.S. factories using
non-U.S. components and raw materials and usually wind up being
imported into the American market. At its twentieth-anniversary dinner in 2006, Michael Porter, a council member (and author of some
of its reports) and Harvard Business School business strategy guru,
gave such a glowing account of U.S. competitiveness and of the success of the council that one member wondered privately to me if there
was any longer a need for the council since everything seemed to be so
peachy. In 2006, Porter, of course, never imagined the possibility of the
worst crisis since the Great Depression.

In fact, the council's main thrust at the moment is something it calls
Five for the Future. The introduction to this document states the following: "Any perception that the country is standing at the edge of an
economic cliff with one foot dangling in thin air is just not borne out
by the economic data." It does note, however, that the game is changing and that "the policies and approaches that ensured U.S. economic
preeminence for the past twenty years will not sustain our competitive
edge in the decades ahead." To maintain that, the council has the following five major recommendations: challenging the frontiers of science and technology by promoting innovation and high-performance
computing; renewing access to secure and sustainable energy by creating conditions that foster investment in energy innovation and infrastructure; achieving advantage with creative and cutting-edge talent by
promoting better education and promoting innovation; transforming
risk intelligence into enterprise resilience (I honestly can't figure out
what this means); and engaging in the global economy by preventing

protectionism and achieving a new balance between competing and cooperating internationally.

Well, as I said before, all good stuff (okay, some of it is gobbledy-gook), but none of this is going to change the game to get us out of the hole we've been digging.

But there have been some interesting new thoughts from none other than GE. In the aftermath of the crisis Jack Welch was interviewed by the *Financial Times* about his 1981 speech and his view of the shareholder value philosophy. Welch, who clearly believes with Ralph Waldo Emerson that "a foolish consistency is the hobgoblin of small minds" and that he does not have a small mind, said: "On the face of it, a focus on shareholder value is the dumbest idea in the world."

Jeff Immelt had a fuller and more sincere epiphany. In the GE 2008 annual report, he wrote: "I have learned something about my country. I run a global company. But I am a U.S. citizen, and I believe a popular thirty-year notion that the United States can evolve from a technology and manufacturing leader into a services industry leader is wrong. In the end, this philosophy transformed the financial services industry from one that supported commerce to a complex trading market that acted outside the economy. Real engineering was traded for financial engineering. In the end, our business, our government, and many local leaders lost sight of what makes a nation great—a passion for innovation. To this end, we need an educational system that inspires hard work, discipline, and creative thinking. The ability to innovate must be valued again. We must develop new technologies and a productive manufacturing base. Our trade deficit is a sign of real weakness, and we must reduce our debt to the world. GE will continue to invest globally, but that should include a preeminent position for the United States."

It will be interesting to see if Immelt can make this stick. But in the wake of the recent crisis maybe he has a chance. Indeed, maybe he can even lead the Council on Competitiveness to respond seriously to Pete Peterson's entreaty for the business community to recover its patriotic spirit of yore.

The reason is that in the crisis it wasn't the shareholders to whom corporate management turned. Indeed, most of them had exited, demonstrating that they are not the residual risk takers. No, it was the unions, the government, and the local communities—the stakeholders—to whom they turned and who bailed them out.

So perhaps we will come full circle back to the values of McCabe and a prominent place for stakeholders. But in that case we must ask the stakeholders also to be responsible, especially in regard to such important things as energy and the environment.

8

Cheap Energy: The Great American Habit

It would be absolutely insane to become dependent upon such
a volatile area [Middle East] for energy supplies.
—STATE DEPARTMENT COMMENT, 1970

Two stories in the *Washington Post* of March 10, 2002, said it
all about America's most dangerous habit. The lead, front-page
story was all about Operation Anaconda, the ultimately abortive effort to capture Osama bin Laden in Afghanistan's rugged Tora
Bora Mountains. About half the front page was taken up by a photo
showing massive bombing of mountain redoubts, and the accompanying story detailed the progress of the operation, which it noted had
already resulted in fifty-eight U.S. casualties.

Less prominent was the article buried on page A12 about that
week's Senate debate on whether to apply to SUVs the normal gas
mileage requirements for cars. Known as CAFE (Corporate Average
Fuel Economy), the standards had been introduced in the wake of the
oil shocks of 1973–74 with the objective of raising the average U.S. car
mileage from 13 miles per gallon to 27.5 by 1985. The standards also
called for light trucks to average 17.2 mpg by 1979. Initially, CAFE's
impact had been dramatic, with the average mileage of new American
cars climbing to 26.2 mpg by 1987. Since then, however, SUVs and
pickup trucks had become so popular as everyday family vehicles that
by 2002 they made up more than half the total number of vehicles
sold and were playing havoc with fuel economy. As the Senate began
its debate, the average gas mileage of new vehicles had slid to 24 mpg
and U.S. gas consumption and oil imports were soaring out of sight.
To help correct this, the Senate bill called for extending the auto stan-

dards to SUVs, with the objective of getting the average vehicle's gas mileage back to where it had been in 1987.

Leading the opposition in the Senate was minority leader Trent Lott of Mississippi, who said that raising the standard would be unacceptable because "this is still America," and if the new standard were adopted he wouldn't "be able to drive my grandchildren around the ranch anymore." Democratic senator from Maryland Barbara Mikulski joined Lott's objection, noting that soccer moms need big vans to be safe from road rage. Not to be outdone, Senator Zell Miller of Georgia said that the "back of a pickup truck is the think tank of rural America," where more problems are solved at the end of a long day's work than in all the halls of Washington, D.C. Ultimately, the nays carried the day. Congress chose to do nothing about gas mileage. Shortly afterward, however, it voted overwhelmingly to authorize the president to go to war in Iraq, whose oil reserves were the world's fourth largest.

Of course, America's quest for cheap oil was not the only or even the main reason for Operation Anaconda and the War in Iraq, but it was at the root of both. It was the presence of U.S. troops in Saudi Arabia and the U.S. support of the absolutist Saudi monarchy that helped trigger Osama bin Laden's ire toward America. And surely the United States would not have toppled Iraq's dictator Saddam Hussein and occupied the country if it had been in the middle of Africa with no oil, instead of in the Persian Gulf with enormous reserves.

That since then not much has changed in this state of affairs became apparent to me recently when I arrived back in Washington, D.C., after a swing through Asia and Europe. Scanning the papers while riding the airport shuttle bus, I noted a *Washington Post* headline reporting "Deadliest Month Yet in Afghanistan" (Osama, of course, slipped the Tora Bora trap and is still at large). Turning to the *New York Times*, I saw that three U.S. soldiers had been killed in Iraq the previous day. On my way home from Dulles airport, with my gas gauge registering close to empty, I stopped to fill up at my local service station. I was ashamed at the feeling of relief that came over me when the bill totaled only $60. Just a few days before in Belgium, where people take energy conservation seriously, I had spent nearly $200 to fill up my rental car.

That gap between the price of gas in America and the price in Belgium and the rest of the world is the main reason that petroleum imports, at nearly $400 billion, accounted for over half of the U.S. trade deficit in 2008, and put an extra $400 billion in the hands of many rulers who actively and passively oppose U.S. interests. That gap also represents an extra $400 billion that America had to borrow, mostly from autocratic governments. Finally, that gap means that America has less diplomatic freedom of action, and that there is less national security for the United States, and even less of the political and personal freedom that Americans have traditionally prized and sacrificed to obtain.

So the big question is, Why? Why are we in this bad situation? Why does nothing about it ever seem to change? Why are Americans willing to sacrifice for cheap oil not only their hard-won freedom, but their fortunes and the lives of their children?

A LITTLE HISTORY

It's difficult to imagine, but for just about one hundred years the United States was the equivalent of today's Saudi Arabia as far as oil and energy production are concerned. The first oil well anywhere in the world was drilled in Pennsylvania in 1859, and for many years the United States was virtually the world's only producer. In World War I, U.S. oil was arguably a more important factor in the Allied victory than American troops. And there is no doubt that World War II was won on a flood tide of U.S. oil. The unsheathing of the OPEC oil weapon in the 1970s ended not only America's dominance of energy markets, but also its effortless geopolitical and industrial dominance. Despite much rhetoric and many promises of energy independence since that time, we have not been able to kick our addiction to cheap oil. Indeed, we have increasingly defined our national security in terms of protecting the sources of cheap oil without much regard for where they may be or by whom they may be controlled. Nor do we hesitate to send our young women and men in harm's way to assure the steady flow of the black heroin. The question today is whether the threat of global warming might bring us at last to change our ways.

Cheap Energy: An American Birthright

From the time of the first colony at Jamestown and of the Pilgrims in Massachusetts until the latter half of the twentieth century, America was perhaps the country most richly endowed with inexpensive energy resources. In the sixteenth, seventeenth, and eighteenth centuries, the primary energy sources were wood, wind, and water, and nowhere was there more wood, wind, and water than in the new colonies. The Jamestown settlers and the Pilgrims in North America had the greatest of energy reserves. And this abundance of inexpensive energy largely powered the surge of economic growth that enabled America quickly to equal and then exceed the living standards of the rich European countries.

By 1820, the United States had the world's fourth-highest GDP per capita. At $1,257, it trailed only the Netherlands at $1,821, Britain at $1,707, and Belgium at $1,319. France was about even with the United States, while Germany, Italy, and Japan were well behind. As the Industrial Revolution progressed in the 1800s, a new energy era of steam, coal, and whale oil dawned. And one could say the United States was the Saudi Arabia of this age as well. It had virtually unlimited coal resources and increased production from virtually nothing in 1820 to nearly 200 million metric tons in 1900. Meanwhile, a small whaling fleet founded in New Bedford, Massachusetts, in 1755, expanded to a peak of 329 ships in 1857.

Then, on August 27, 1859, at Titusville, Pennsylvania, whale oil was instantly made obsolete by "Colonel" E. L. Drake and his drillers who, after a year of fruitless effort, finally began filling tubs and barrels with oil from the first modern oil well. Oil energy—added to that of coal, wind, and water—allowed the United States to double its standard of living over the next forty years.

The extent of the American bonanza was not clear at first. For a quarter century, the industry was fragile, uncertain, and wholly dependent on the oil fields of Pennsylvania. Indeed, in 1885, the Pennsylvania state geologist warned—presciently, as it turned out—that oil was "a temporary and vanishing phenomenon." A top executive of Standard Oil Company became so concerned that he sold some of his shares in the company at a discount of 25 percent. But no sooner had he done this than new oil was discovered at Lima, Ohio, in a field that quickly came to account for a third of U.S. production. Over the next sixty years, all concern about supplies vanished with the discovery of one giant oil field after another.

In 1893, the citizens of the small Texas town of Corsicana began drilling wells to augment their dwindling water supply. It is not recorded whether they were happy or disheartened to find oil. On January 10, 1901, the earth exploded near Beaumont, Texas, when Spindletop, the first American "gusher," sent drill pipe, rock, and oil hundreds of feet into the air as oil flowed at a phenomenal 75,000 barrels a day. Other gushers followed: Signal Hill in California, Greater Seminole in Oklahoma, and then the grandmother of them all, Dad Joiner's Black Giant in east Texas. Powered by this tsunami, the United States raced to the top of the global GDP per capita standings. Though for a moment in the 1880s oil had a scare when Thomas Edison's electric lightbulbs began replacing oil lamps, the appearance of the "horseless carriage" in 1885 saved the day. The growth of the auto industry secured the future of the oil industry and transformed the face of America and the world.

By 1913, the U.S. per capita income of $5,301 was well above the $4,921 of number 2, Great Britain, and the United States had become the world's largest economy with an industrial base far surpassing that of any other country. How could anyone doubt that cheap energy was an American birthright?

From Belleau Wood to Tokyo Bay

By the time of the United States' entry into World War I in 1917, there were 3.5 million cars on U.S. roads. By 1929, there were 23 million, or 78 percent of all the autos in the world. However, as important as oil was in driving the U.S. economy, it was probably even more important in the winning of U.S. wars and in the underpinning of American global influence and power.

At the beginning of World War I in 1914, steam-powered trains carried troops into battle, and horses pulled artillery and supply wagons. But as the war dragged on, the role of oil became increasingly decisive. The new British tanks couldn't run without oil, nor could the new trucks and troop carriers developed during the war, nor could the industries necessary for war production. In December 1917, with the German U-boat campaign of 1916–17 destroying oil tankers at an alarming rate, French Prime Minister Georges Clemenceau begged President Wilson to make more oil available immediately. Otherwise, the French leader indicated, France might be forced to make its own peace with the Germans to the detriment of the other Allied powers. Wilson responded at once with more oil and, after Russia's exit from the war in 1917, the United States ultimately wound up supplying 80 percent of Allied needs. As the director of the French Comité Général du Pétrole put it, "oil was the blood of victory." Indeed, it was the German U-boats that were forced to withdraw from the battle for lack of oil. When Britain destroyed Rumanian oil fields that had been supplying the Germans and then occupied Baku, another key source, the Germans were cut off from getting enough oil to stave off defeat.

If oil was a key part of the game in World War I, it was the whole game in World War II. Japan captured Indonesia early in the war to assure itself a source of supply. But the supply routes from Southeast Asia to Japan were long and vulnerable, and American submarines so deftly targeted the Japanese merchant fleet that over 80 percent of Japan's tankers were put out of action, with many sunk almost as soon as they were launched. In 1943 alone, Japanese oil imports fell by half. In the end, the Japanese fleet was inoperable, and the Japanese government launched a campaign directing its citizens to collect pine root for conversion into fuel. Hillsides were stripped bare of trees as production of pine root oil rose to 70,000 barrels a month. It was both a heroic and a hopeless effort. While the atom bomb may have provided the final blow, lack of oil was more crucial to Japan's defeat.

Germany's situation was only a little better. In light of its experience in World War I, it had pioneered production of synthetic oil from coal and by 1940 was producing 72,000 barrels a day—about 46 percent of its total consumption. The blitzkrieg concept was developed with fuel shortage in mind, the idea being to win quickly before the fuel ran out. The 1942 invasion of Russia particularly aimed at capturing the Russian oil fields. Indeed, Hitler failed to take Moscow largely because he had to divert a large part of his forces in the attempt to get his hands on the oil of Baku. But the poor quality of the Russian roads caused the German tanks to use twice as much fuel as normal, and his troops ran out of gas before they got to either Baku or Moscow.

In North Africa, General Erwin Rommel missed taking Cairo in large part because his tanks ran out of gas. When Russian troops captured the oil fields of Rumania, the Reich became wholly dependent on synthetic oil production, and between May and September 1944, U.S. Air Force bombing cut that from 92,000 to 5,000 barrels a day.

The Battle of the Bulge in December 1944 was Hitler's last-ditch effort; it, too, failed for lack of fuel. Indeed, once the U.S. and British navies managed to defeat the German submarine Wolf Pack in the North Atlantic in 1943, the Thousand-Year Reich was fated to last no more than another two years. The reason was that with oil flowing like a river from America, fuel was no constraint at all on the Allied efforts. In the course of the war, the Allies consumed about 7 billion barrels of oil, of which 6 billion came from the United States.

KEEPING CONTROL AFTER THE WAR

In the wake of the war, the United States remained the world's largest oil producer for some time. More important, it controlled world pricing by maintaining a production surge capability for times of crisis. The Texas Railroad Commission, which regulated output of the big Texas oil fields, maintained price stability by keeping actual production well below full capacity. It was this surge capability that had won both world wars and that the commission continued to maintain in the early postwar era.

It came in handy in 1951 when the first oil crisis arose as a result of the Iranian government's nationalization of the British Anglo-Persian Oil Company's holdings in Iran. In retaliation, London embargoed the newly nationalized company's shipments and thereby greatly curtailed the flow of Middle East oil to world markets. Thanks to the Texas Railroad Commission, however, U.S. capacity was surged and consumers were not hurt. The surge capacity proved decisive again during the second oil crisis of 1956. In response to Egyptian leader Gamal Abdel Nasser's nationalization and seizure of the Suez Canal, Britain, France, and Israel landed troops and took control of the Canal zone. The Egyptians promptly sank ships and closed the canal, thereby once again halting the flow of oil from the Middle East to Europe. The British and French had been counting on U.S. support and another surge by the Texas Railroad Commission to counteract the effect of the Egyptian action. But they had failed to consult with Washington beforehand. A surprised and furious President Eisenhower, convinced that the Anglo-French-Israeli intervention would only drive the Arabs into the hands of the Soviets, refused to make U.S. surge capacity available unless the three perpetrators withdrew their troops and handed the canal back to the Egyptians. The Europeans relented, and the Railroad Commission then broke the embargo and saved Europe again.

The surge capacity saved the day yet again during a third oil crisis, sparked by the Six-Day War, which began on June 5, 1967, when Israel launched a preemptive strike against the Egyptian and Syrian forces that had been massing on its borders. In short order the Israeli forces destroyed the Egyptian air force and took the West Bank of the Jordan River from the Jordanian army. Now the Arab countries unsheathed the "oil weapon" in an effort to force the United States and Europe to compel Israel to withdraw. On June 6, the oil ministers of the Arab countries announced an embargo, and by June 8, shipments had already been cut by 60 percent. With Europe now getting three-fourths of its oil from the Middle East, the situation was critical. Once more, however, the Texas Railroad Commission rode to the rescue by unleashing a million barrels a day of surge capacity. By July, it was clear that the "oil weapon" was really a rubber sword and that the United States could still wield the razor-edged sword of its oil surge capacity to enforce its will around the globe.

Premonitions of Doom

Those who had been paying close attention to the state of the U.S. oil supply, however, understood that a new era was fast approaching. As early as 1941, State Department official William Ferris noted that—at current rates of production, discovery, and consumption—the United States would run out of oil in the not too distant future. He called for conserving domestic oil and developing foreign imports as an alternative. In 1943, Interior Secretary Harold Ickes wrote: "We're Running Out of Oil!" The discoveries of the 1920s and 1930s had tailed off, and with consumption rising, it was apparent that the United States would soon become a net importer. Indeed, it was partly due to this understanding that as early as 1943, Washington began fostering a special relationship with Saudi Arabia and invited Prince Faisal and Prince Khalid to meet with President Roosevelt in the first high-level meeting between officials of the two countries. In February 1943, the lend-lease program was extended to Saudi Arabia based on the declaration that "the defense of Saudi Arabia is vital to the defense of the United States." A year later Commodore Andrew E. Carter of the

Army-Navy Petroleum Council reinforced the urgency of the Saudi relationship when he told Navy Secretary Frank Knox that oil reserves were inadequate and that America needed to develop new sources to prevent its security, power, and freedom from being compromised.

Soon thereafter, the United States began supplying arms to Saudi Arabia as the kingdom simultaneously commenced building a 1,200-mile oil pipeline to the Mediterranean coast. There followed in February 1945 a one-on-one, five-and-a-half-hour meeting of Roosevelt and King Abdulaziz aboard the USS *Quincy* in the Great Bitter Lake of the Suez Canal during the Cairo meeting of Churchill, Roosevelt, and Stalin. Roosevelt ingratiated himself with the king, who suffered from severe arthritis, by giving him his spare wheelchair. The two leaders sealed an agreement on a tacit alliance between the two countries—an agreement that included the king's consent for a U.S. airbase to be constructed at Dhahran. At about the same time, a State Department memo emphasized that "the oil resources of Saudi Arabia are among the greatest in the world and must remain under American control for the dual purpose of supplementing and replacing our dwindling supplies and preventing that they fall into unfriendly hands." The urgency of this effort was underscored in 1948 when, as anticipated, for the first time in its history the United States became a net oil importer. Not since the arrival of the Jamestown settlers had America been energy dependent. Now it was becoming so at a rapid clip. With the U.S. surge capacity remaining at several million barrels a day, the immediate significance of America's new net importer status was not great. Still, consumption was rising at totally unexpected rates as the world recovered from the war. In 1949, Washington renewed its lease on the Dhahran base and also promised to help create a modern Saudi Arabian army. In a move that has had momentous consequences, the new Eisenhower doctrine of 1957 committed the United States to the defense of friendly Middle Eastern powers.

The dangers of growing dependency as oil consumption continued to boom were not lost on the U.S. leadership. As between 1960 and 1972 the free world's oil consumption climbed from 19 million to more than 44 million barrels a day, a great debate arose about how to meet demand without becoming overly dependent on imports. While some officials at the State Department favored increasing imports—in order to conserve domestic supplies—other voices, including especially those of the oil companies, called for quotas to limit imports and keep domestic prices above world levels. The idea was to stimulate more discovery and to encourage conservation. Of course, such quotas and the higher prices they generated would also mean fat profits for producers.

As the Cold War heated up, concern about overdependence on imports of key commodities intensified. In 1952, a presidential commission reported that the nation was running out of critical raw materials and that "nothing less than the survival of the human spirit against the threat of Communist world domination is at stake." In July 1955, the Reciprocal Trade Agreements Act was amended to allow the president to limit imports of commodities that threatened to impair national security, and the Independent Oil Operators Association called for quotas on oil imports above the 1954 level of about 1.25 million barrels a day. That was followed in 1956 by a deal with importers for a "voluntary" 4 percent cut in import levels and a White House commitment to hold Middle East imports at their 1954 proportion of U.S. domestic production. The following year Eisenhower proposed formal import quotas, which went into effect in 1959. Critics argued that far from protecting national security, the quotas were draining America first and costing U.S. consumers over $7 billion annually while providing windfall profits to oil producers. Nevertheless, quotas remained in force for over twenty years. Whether this represented resolve to conserve for national security reasons is debatable. It certainly resulted in fat profits for the oil companies.

The government also took decisive action to spur discovery, and with foresight, to encourage the development of alternative fuels. In addition to import quotas, the domestic industry also benefited from the so-called oil depletion allowance, a kind of tax deduction for the loss of oil reserves as a result of production for consumption. While the idea was that this too would spur discovery, it would also, of course, spur low tax payments and profitability. In 1947, the Interior Department proposed a $10 billion Manhattan Project approach to develop synthetic fuel from Rocky Mountain shale oil. Eventually, $85 million was authorized for research, but the program ultimately died when it became clear that synthetic oil would not be cost-competitive without the levy of a tax on natural oil, a politically unthinkable move.

A second alternative was the development of nuclear-generated electric power. The Atomic Energy Commission was created in 1946 and after 1954 worked closely with industry and various states to promote commercialization of nuclear-generated electric power. In 1955, Arco, Idaho, became the first town powered by nuclear energy, and in 1957, the first fully commercial nuclear power plant went in at Santa Susana, California. By 1979, the sixty-eight nuclear plants operating all over the country were generating more than 20 percent of total U.S. electricity, thereby saving hundreds of millions of barrels of oil. Then on March 28, 1979, the nuclear plant at Three Mile Island in Pennsylvania experienced a partial meltdown; it not only closed the plant but also effectively stopped development of nuclear power in the United States.

The Dependence Trap

All these efforts to address overreliance on imports (the dependence trap) were partly well intentioned and effective, partly self-serving for the oil companies, and partly halfhearted. But they were all overwhelmed by the counterforce of a massive transformation in the fundamental geography of American life. When wartime gasoline rationing was lifted at the end of World War II, the cry of "fill 'er up" became the new national anthem. Between then and 1950 sales of autos exploded. For a decade and a half of depression and war Americans had scrimped and saved; now it was time to enjoy the nation's birthright of cheap energy.

If you have ever visited Flatbush in Brooklyn, you have seen a typical American suburb 1890s style. Built within a twenty-minute train ride of downtown Manhattan, it has short, straight blocks with sidewalks. Its close-set houses, stores, schools, and train stations are all within easy walking distance. Cars are not really necessary; indeed, Flatbush was not built with automobiles in mind. But the suburbs of the emerging postwar America were a different matter altogether. Essential to their viability was at least one car, and preferably two, per family.

Suburbia was both cause and effect of the creation of a car-centric American way of life. Located beyond the jurisdiction of cities, the suburbs could not connect to public transportation, and usually didn't have enough people to justify a private rail line. The only way to get to and around them was by car. Further favoring the car was the fact that while private companies had to invest in, maintain, and pay taxes on railroad lines, roads were a public good provided by the government, and taxes on gasoline were kept at very low levels. Not surprisingly, road building became a boom industry, with California breaking ground on its massive freeway system in 1947, and New Jersey soon following with the Garden State Parkway and the New Jersey Turnpike. Other states quickly followed suit. Then, in 1956, President Eisenhower inaugurated the mother of all road projects by signing the Interstate Defense Highways Act that, as I noted earlier, created our interstate superhighway network.

Think for a moment of the irony of that title. Here was a bill that would dramatically increase oil consumption at a moment when quotas were being imposed on oil imports in order to avoid excessive dependence on foreign suppliers. And this was being done by a former five-star general. I have sometimes wondered whether Eisenhower ever considered the longer-term security implications of the Highways Act. (Why did neither he nor anyone else couple it with a gas tax and a massive alternate energy development program?) He promoted it as a national security measure that would enable quick evacuation of cities under atomic attack (can you imagine getting out of LA today under an atomic attack?), but it was pushed through Congress by a vast array of lobbyists from the auto, oil, rubber, real estate, trucking, and parking industries. Eisenhower said it "would change the face of America," and it did. Public transport and railroads languished as Americans took to the subsidized roads and skies, and by 1975, the whole structure of American life had been designed to favor cars and airplanes over trains and buses, private transportation over public.

Meanwhile, by 1970, U.S. oil production had peaked at 11.3 million barrels a day, heading into steady decline, and the surge capacity was done away with in 1971 when the Texas Railroad Commission authorized full production. The quotas on imports had to be constantly increased, from 2 million barrels a day in 1967 to 6 million by 1973, over 35 percent of U.S. consumption. Under these new circumstances, the Arab producers were finally able to wield the oil weapon.

When, in 1973, the United States and Europe came to Israel's support in the Yom Kippur War, the Organization of Petroleum Exporting Countries (OPEC) called for an embargo on exports to the United

States and Europe and also agreed to cut their production by 25 percent. With the U.S. surge capacity gone, the impact was immediate, a stunning shock to Americans. Lines at gas stations often extended for a mile, and the price of crude oil quadrupled to nearly $12/barrel while the price at the pump nearly doubled. The stock market was sent into freefall, losing $97 billion in value in a few days, and state governors even called on Americans to forgo putting up Christmas lights. The state of Oregon banned all Christmas and commercial lighting outright. Meanwhile, President Nixon called on service stations to refrain from selling gas on Saturday evenings and Sundays.

The Arab and other OPEC producers saw a windfall in earnings, and the largest producer, Saudi Arabia, assumed the former role of the United States as the world's supplier of last resort. The "oil weapon" had turned out to be far more powerful than anyone had imagined. When in the wake of the overthrow of the Shah of Iran in 1979, the Iranian oil fields were temporarily closed, gas prices again soared, and the industrial countries went into deep recession; U.S. GDP fell by 6 percent and unemployment doubled to 9 percent. The public ached for its leaders to find a new energy strategy.

IN SEARCH OF A STRATEGY

Consider for a moment the enormity of what was happening and the issues at stake. The United States was spending nearly 10 percent of GDP on defense. It had an enormous military and intelligence establishment stocked with experts whose job was to anticipate and develop strategies for nullifying any threat to national security, and the famous strategist Henry Kissinger was Secretary of State. Legions of think tanks and university experts spent their lives pondering threats and countervailing strategies. Energy independence and control of the oil supply and pricing had long been identified as crucial elements of America's global power and national security, far more important than any weapons systems or troop deployments. If their loss was not a national security matter of the highest priority, a matter calling for extraordinary measures, it was hard to imagine what might be.

Certainly the response in Japan and Europe reflected that degree of urgency. Japan's powerful Ministry of International Trade and Industry (MITI) took elevators out of service at its headquarters building and put the thermostat at 60 degrees in the winter and 80 degrees in the summer. Of course, these measures were symbolic, but they set an example that enabled other tough measures. On the supply side, Japan moved to widespread adoption of nuclear electric generators and also shifted from oil to coal and liquid natural gas wherever possible. Even more significant, however, were the country's energy conservation measures. Gas taxes were raised far above the already high level so that the price per gallon became about $7. Electric prices were also raised substantially, and high-efficiency standards were set for new appliances and industrial machinery and processes. Most important, the Japanese government convinced its public that the future of Japan depended upon conserving energy, thereby enlisting the legendary ability of the Japanese to get just a little bit more out of nothing. Also at this time, MITI drew up the plans for shifting the entire structure of Japanese industry from energy-intensive to knowledge-intensive high-technology sectors. Indeed, MITI Vice Minister Naohiro Amaya told me at the time that the whole oil crisis had been a blessing in disguise. By 1985 Japan was using 31 percent less energy to produce a dollar of GDP and fully 51 percent less oil while growing at over 5 percent annually. Today, Japan has the lowest energy consumption per dollar of GDP of any major nation, and the hybrid gas-electric vehicles it developed in response to high gas taxes (coupled with rebates for energy-efficient models) are now selling fast in the small car markets of America.

Led by France, Europe emulated Japan by raising already high gas taxes and electric prices. Even more than Japan, France committed to nuclear power. As in Japan, all public buildings and private apartments and offices were heated to no more than 20 degrees centigrade (68 degrees F) and inspectors made unannounced visits to enforce the rules. (France is not widely air-conditioned.) The French even banned any advertising that might encourage more energy use. Efforts to develop the North Sea oil fields were accelerated with additional European government supports. As in Japan the results were dramatic. Whereas 63 percent of France's electricity in 1973 was supplied by oil, natural gas, and coal combined, oil today accounts for less than 1 percent while nuclear generates over 75 percent. Europe also shifted most cars from gasoline to diesel fuel, raised its fleet fuel economy from 28 mpg to over 35 mpg, and accelerated plans for the creation of a network of super high-speed TGV (Train à Grande Vitesse) trains. Europe's per capita electric consumption has been held to half that of the United States, and its energy consumption per dollar of GDP has fallen to about two-thirds of the American level. Further, Europe began seriously funding projects to develop wind, solar, and other alternative energy sources.

In contrast, despite its greater strategic stake, Washington's response was fitful, confused, and divided. While Americans paid lip service to energy independence and energy policy as the "moral equivalent of war," they never developed a serious, comprehensive strategy and never defined national security in terms of conservation and development of alternative energy sources. This failure did not go unmentioned. In his 1969–70 memoir, *Present at the Creation*, Dean Acheson, former secretary of state, noted that "if a fraction of our investment in the space program had been put into the development of a practical electric automobile and of nuclear power plants here and in Europe, we could have done much to solve our air pollution problems and free Europe from dependence on the Middle East." At about the same time, a State Department official said "it would be absolutely insane to become dependent upon such a volatile area [Middle East] for energy supplies," and the department outlined a plan calling for development of shale oil and continental shelf deposits, construction of an Alaska pipeline, changing the price structure of oil and natural gas, and use of taxes on oil to limit auto usage and encourage development of mass transport. But while some of these recommendations, such as the Alaska pipeline, were taken to heart, we never pursued most of them with the same consistency and purpose as we did closer ties with the Saudis and development of great military capability in the Persian Gulf and Asian sea lanes. In fact, if not in theory, America came to define national security in terms of protecting the global tanker lanes along with the Middle East oil fields and the autocratic often corrupt regimes that controlled them. In short, America's strategy was to trade blood for cheap oil.

Nixon's Last Gasp

Back in 1969, President Nixon actually had created an oil task force, though his intent in doing so was more to control raging inflation, pollution, and looming energy shortages than to bring about energy independence. In 1970 he pushed through Congress the Clean Air Act, which established the Environmental Protection Agency and created incentives for electric utilities to swap from coal to oil. Then in 1971, to control inflation in the face of the looming 1972 election, he imposed a general price freeze.

These steps, however, were countered by other moves, such as the removal of the quotas on oil imports. The task force identified the quotas as a vexing problem, driving down supplies and keeping prices well above world levels, even as they failed to induce extra domestic exploration and production. While costing American consumers dearly, the task force argued. Nixon removed the quotas, but not all price restrictions, in April 1973.

He also worked to spur increased production, calling on Congress to remove remaining legal barriers to the Alaska pipeline, and proposing a 50 percent increase in R&D spending (with a special emphasis on nuclear power). He also made a limited appeal to the public for voluntary conservation by, for instance, turning out lights and reducing the use of air-conditioning.

After the shock of the 1973 Arab embargo, Nixon stepped up his efforts, signing legislation authorizing further price, production, allocation, and marketing controls, and announcing Project Independence. Cast as being in the spirit of the Manhattan and Apollo projects, this initiative was meant to make the United States energy independent by 1980. When Nixon was forced out of office shortly thereafter by the Watergate scandal, President Ford, in his first address to Congress on August 9, 1974, promised to continue the push for Project Independence.

True to his word, in October, Ford established the Energy Research and Development Administration with a starting budget of $2.5 billion. Shortly thereafter, Congress approved $12 billion of funding for mass transit programs and made the then temporary 55 mph speed limit permanent. Later, Ford announced a $3 per barrel fee on imported oil and called for amending the Clean Air Act to return to more coal-fired electric generation. He also called for a set of incentives to encourage conservation and alternative energy development, including tax credits for the construction of electric power plants that did not use oil or gas; tax credits for the installation of home insulation; an increase of 3 cents per gallon in the gas tax; and the elimination of all oil price controls. He championed the production of 1 million barrels a day of shale oil by 1985, and a mandated floor price for oil, meant to ensure that any efforts to produce alternative energy would not be undermined by future declines in oil prices. He also proposed higher fuel efficiency standards for new cars, as well as the creation of a 1.3-billion-barrel strategic oil reserve.

Again, progress was made in half-measures. Congress approved the strategic reserve, instituted a program to help the states reduce energy consumption by 5 percent annually, legalized right turns at red lights—aimed at decreasing fuel use while cars idle unnecessarily—and mandated auto fuel efficiency standards of 27.5 mpg to be achieved by 1985. But most of Ford's recommendations went down to defeat by a Congress intent on keeping gas cheap.

Continuing the struggle, Ford pushed shortly thereafter for an Energy Independence Authority and for a ten-year plan to build 200 nuclear plants, 250 major coal mines, 150 coal-fired power plants, and 20 synthetic oil plants. Vice President Nelson Rockefeller, grandson of the founder of the modern oil industry, added a proposal for a $100 billion program to underwrite the development of synthetic fuels and other alternative energy sources. This was a truly meaty program for a comprehensive energy strategy. But again political opposition was intense, and the plans never even got onto the drawing boards. Ford then ignored the energy issue during the presidential campaign of 1976. The cause was picked up, however, by Democratic candidate Jimmy Carter.

Carter: MEOW and Malaise

In the first campaign debate of 1976, Carter opined: "I think almost every other developed nation in the world has an energy policy except us." After being elected president he made a truly concerted effort to develop a serious, comprehensive energy strategy. Unfortunately, many of his efforts were shot down, and the message he repeatedly delivered—that solving the problem of dependence would involve "some sacrifice"—caused a good deal of public disillusionment with him. Nevertheless, during his term the country made significant progress on the energy front. Many people took heed and turned their thermostats down when he explained that setting thermostats at 65 degrees during the day and 55 at night could save half the natural gas shortage being caused by that winter's frigid weather. (When Carter put the White House on those settings, Rosalynn nearly froze and begged for relief: but he stood firm and she eventually took to wearing long underwear in the winter.)

More significant, he put forward a detailed program, developed under the guidance of former secretary of defense James Schlesinger. It had 113 specific components, including the reduction of gasoline consumption by 10 percent, halving oil imports, increasing coal production by two thirds, insulating 90 percent of homes and all new buildings, and using solar energy in more than 2.5 million homes. The plan also called for a 50 cent increase in taxes on gasoline and provided tax credits for the installation of home solar water heaters and insulation. Striking at the problem of rapidly rising automobile usage, the plan also called for more funding for mass transit projects and tougher fuel efficiency standards, to be implemented after the original 1985 target of 27.5 mpg had been met. A key element was an $88 billion Energy Security Corporation to develop alternative energy sources (shale oil, coal liquids, solar, gasohol, unconventional natural gas) and expand the construction of nuclear power plants beyond the forty new plants that had been ordered in 1974.

To pitch this program to the public Carter turned to his former navy boss and nuclear submarine developer Admiral Hyman Rickover for advice. Rickover advised calling for sacrifices for the common good and said that the energy challenge should be considered (in the words of William James) "the moral equivalent of war." The White House also released a CIA assessment of the country's energy future, which predicted that, due to declines anticipated in world production of oil, "greatly increased conservation" would be the only way to prevent further energy crises. Carter invested a great deal of political capital in the plan, presenting it to the public on April 18, 1977, in a prime-time television address in which he described the energy challenge as a problem "unprecedented in our history," and, with the exception of preventing war, the greatest challenge we would face in our lifetimes. As Rickover had suggested, he called it the moral equivalent of war and stressed that we must not be "selfish or timid if we hope to have a decent world for our children and grandchildren." He continued that "our decision about energy will test the character of the American people and the ability of the president and the Congress to govern." He addressed those who doubted the gravity of the problem or who blamed it all on greedy oil companies by emphasizing again and again that we were using up our energy resources at an unsustainable rate and that our nation's "independence of economic and political action is becoming increasingly constrained." He warned of future gas lines and embargoes and of dependence on Middle East suppliers, stressing that new oil from Alaska's North Slope would be only a short-lived palliative. He especially warned that economic and political disaster would inevitably follow if we continued to drive oversized cars with only one passenger and to live in oversized, underinsulated houses. Consequently, Carter urged, the solution must be conservation and the development of alternative sources of energy. In particular he focused on the target of reducing oil imports by 1985 to 6 million barrels a day from the 9 million of 1977. "Conservation," he said, "is the only way that we can buy a barrel of oil for about $2. It costs $13 to waste it."

Once again, entrenched resistance to the message flared up, with the speech and the plan both garnering decidedly mixed reviews. While some praised Carter for his political courage, critics noted that the acronym for moral equivalent of war is a cat's MEOW. In the end, the legislation that was passed did not contain any new taxes on gasoline or any further toughening of the auto fuel standards. Still, it was a significant achievement, and it put the country on a new energy footing. It was now the express policy of the U.S. government to force the country to break its oil habit through a combination of conservation and alternative fuel development. There was now a serious plan to achieve the goals of Nixon's Project Independence.

Despite so many ups and downs, and so much political wrangling, the net result of the Nixon-Ford-Carter efforts at conservation and alternative fuel development were impressive. In 1977, the United States imported 8.6 million barrels of oil a day. By 1982, that number was 4.3 million, half as much. Moreover, the OPEC share of our imports had dropped from 34 percent to 17 percent, and the Arab OPEC share was down to only 6 percent. Some of this was due to the recessions of 1980 and 1981–1982, of course, and a million of that 4.3-million-barrel-per-day decline in imports was due not to conservation but to the increase of domestic supply that had started to come from Alaska. The rest of the decline, however, resulted from better auto gas mileage (saving 600,000 barrels per day), from better building insulation (saving 900,000 barrels a day), and from switching virtually all of the roughly 20 percent of our oil-fired electric power generation to nuclear, coal, and solar. Though not nearly as impressive as the achievements of Japan and Europe, the United States had made serious progress in gaining control of its energy future. But this progress was soon to be dramatically reversed.

REGRESSION

The tide of progress, so long fought for, turned abruptly when Ronald Reagan defeated Jimmy Carter in the 1980 election, a defeat due in large part to the national trauma of the Iranian hostage crisis. In his last State of the Union message, Carter emphasized that the Iranian revolution, as well as the Russian invasion of Afghanistan, which was launched on December 24, 1979, "have dramatized a very important lesson: our excessive dependence on foreign oil is a clear and present danger to our nation's security." But Ronald Reagan had campaigned hard on the argument that the main problem for America was not the energy threat but too much government intervention in the economy.

Even though two Republican presidents and Republicans in Congress had supported the various energy bills and programs that had at last generated substantial success, the government was, in the words of Reagan's budget director David Stockman, "about to get new marching orders: dismantle it, all of it." Stockman had earlier elaborated his views in a 1979 *Washington Post* article arguing that "one of the most pernicious forces loose in Washington is the widely shared belief in the need for national energy independence." Free trade and the unfettered production of capitalist wealth were, he emphasized, more important than reducing the risk of depending on foreign oil. That statement set the tone for the conduct of our energy policy—and the formulation of our national security strategy—ever since. Rather than strive for energy independence, we would strive for a six-hundred-ship navy.

Among Reagan's first acts as president were returning to the old practice of leaving the White House lights on at night and removing the solar panels from the White House roof. I was Counselor to the Secretary of Commerce at the time, and I vividly remember the frenzy that developed around dismantling programs like that for developing synthetic fuels which had been pilloried during the election campaign as government white elephants. To get an idea of the impact of just that one reversal, note that Canada, which is the world's number 6 producer of oil, persevered with its own such project, and today 20 percent of the oil it produces and exports is synthetic.

Federal funding for energy conservation was cut by 70 percent, energy R&D was slashed by 64 percent, and the proposals for higher efficiency standards for new vehicles were dropped as the administration also called for ending the 55 mph speed limit. For Reagan the answer to energy dependence and high energy prices was all about supply. New tax incentives and the opening to oil exploration of the outer continental shelf and vast areas in the national parks were used to spur drilling and enhanced domestic crude oil production. And, in fact, supplies did increase and prices began to drop. But this was mostly because of the Alaskan production, a major expansion of production in the North Sea, Mexico, Malaysia, Nigeria, and elsewhere, and a new Saudi policy of pumping enough to keep prices at a level that made investment in alternative energy sources unattractive. Indeed, in 1986 Vice President George H. W. Bush was dispatched to plead with the Saudis to stop flooding the market as their overproduction was jeopardizing the financial viability of the whole American industry. Of course, consumers loved it. Drivers who had paid $1.40 per gallon in 1981 found themselves paying only 80 cents in 1986.

As prices fell and our leaders ridiculed the need for any kind of government energy policy, the progress achieved by Nixon, Ford, and Carter was substantially reversed. Neither synthetic fuel development nor conventional drilling any longer made sense from a profit standpoint, and both virtually halted. The gas mileage of new cars and light trucks began to decline, and oil imports, having reached their lowest level since 1978, suddenly jumped in 1986 by over a million barrels a day, increasing their share of U.S. consumption from 27 percent to 33 percent in just one year. The average horsepower of new vehicles rose steadily after 1982, and renewable energy use fell steadily from 10 percent of U.S. energy consumption in 1984 to 7.6 percent in 1997.

Neither President George H. W. Bush nor President Bill Clinton did much to change these trends. Bush did nothing materially to alter the Reagan policies and used releases from the Strategic Petroleum Reserve to dampen any higher prices that might result from his intervention against Iraq in Kuwait. Clinton made a halfhearted stab at an energy tax (called the BTU tax), but settled for an insignificant 4.3 cent increase in the gasoline tax. He made no move to increase auto fuel efficiency or to do much beyond a bit more research for alternative fuels. Clinton did negotiate to reduce greenhouse gas emissions under the Kyoto agreement but refrained from presenting the deal to the Senate for ratification because he believed there was no chance of obtaining it. He also allowed energy R&D spending to fall below even the levels of the Reagan years. In 1978–79, they had exceeded such spending on space and health; now spending on space was three times and on health five times that of energy. When Clinton left the White House at the end of the century, imports accounted for nearly 55 percent of U.S. oil consumption, which itself had risen substantially since Jimmy Carter's efforts to cap it.

The decision to dismantle the Independence Project and leave the country's energy future to the market was not only foolish energy policy, it was terrible national security policy. What were the generals in the Pentagon and the high-powered experts at the National Security Council thinking? In fact, if not in explicitly expressed policy, a key result was that, as noted earlier, the U.S. government came to define national security largely in terms of protecting the global tanker lanes and the Middle East oil fields, and in order to do both, we became entangled in the dangerous and shortsighted game of propping up the autocratic and often corrupt regimes that controlled them.

During the Reagan era, the special relationship with Saudi Arabia got even more special, a policy that has been supported ever since, with dangerous repercussions. In 1981, Washington agreed to supply its super-secret AWACS (Airborne Warning and Control System) to Saudi Arabia despite strong opposition in Congress and from Israel. In return, the Saudis, who already sold oil at a $1-a-barrel discount to the United States, provided off-the-books funding for U.S. undercover activity in Nicaragua, Iran, and Afghanistan. (Let's not forget that Osama bin Laden got his start as a leader of the U.S.-backed mujahedeen in Afghanistan.) At the same time, Reagan promised that "there is no way we'd stand by and see Saudi Arabia taken over by someone who would shut off the oil."

Although it declared formal neutrality in the Iraq-Iran War, the United States tilted toward Saddam Hussein's Baghdad when the Iranians appeared to be getting the upper hand; and then Donald Rumsfeld was sent as a special envoy to ask Saddam how America could help. The administration eventually worked out a deal to provide U.S. satellite photos and other support to the Iraqis. This was all by way of ensuring that the Shia Iranians were kept well clear of the Saudi oil fields whose population is also largely Shiites.

In 1987, the United States was forced to put the American flag on Kuwaiti ships and convoy them in order to prevent the Iranians from dominating the Gulf. When the Iraqi military used poison gas in 1988, there was no outcry about "weapons of mass destruction" from Washington. Nor was there an apology in 1989 when the cruiser USS *Vincennes* mistakenly shot down an Iranian airliner in Iranian air space and killed 290 people, including 66 children. By then, the cost of maintaining U.S. naval forces in the Gulf and keeping the shipping lanes open amounted to about $50 billion annually, but none of the Americans who absolutely opposed any gasoline taxes or fuel efficiency standards ever complained about these hefty expenditures.

The United States was forced to spend a good deal more when Saddam subsequently invaded Kuwait and we launched the Gulf War because, in the words of President George H. W. Bush, "Our jobs, our way of life, our own freedom, and the freedom of friendly countries around the world would all suffer if control of the world's great oil reserves fell into the hands of Saddam Hussein."

It was another instance of the domino theory, and the dominoes continued to fall. Even in defeat Saddam remained a threat, and Washington insisted on maintaining large deployments of U.S. troops on Saudi territory as a deterrent. The prolonged American presence there sparked heated resentment among some Saudis, especially from one Osama bin Laden and the strict Wahabi religious sect that dominates Saudi Arabian Islam. Indeed, there was a double irony here: Owing to America's need for Saudi oil, that oil had to be protected. At the same time, the flow of U.S. dollars that paid for the oil also financed the Wahabists' dissemination of a militant, anti-Western brand of Islam well beyond their borders. It also financed Osama bin Laden's al-Qaeda and its September 11, 2001, attack on the United States.

By the time George W. Bush became president in January 2001, oil imports had risen to more than 55 percent of U.S. consumption and the energy trade deficit was running at about $110 billion annually as imports approached 15 million barrels a day—equivalent to the entire production of Russia and Saudi Arabia. Moreover, the market was tightening and prices were rising as OPEC cut back on production. Gas at the pump had gone over $2 a gallon. While this increase might have been cause for serious reconsideration of the approach the country had been pursuing, the Bush administration not only maintained but reconfirmed its course.

Estimates at this time showed that to maintain sufficient global supply at affordable prices, the Gulf's output would have to rise by 85 percent by 2020. So the administration concluded that the United States not only had to protect the Gulf, but also had to encourage a maximum extraction strategy. Its two-pronged approach became to beef up U.S. military forces in the region and to exploit the close ties between the Bush family and the Saudi royal family. On more than one occasion, Vice President Cheney was sent to plead with the Saudis to increase their pumping as a way of abating rising U.S. prices.

But events of the past few years demonstrate that pleading will not ultimately solve the problem. In the spring of 2008, the price of oil soared to over $150 per barrel and many predicted it would soon hit the $200 mark. The U.S. trade deficit in oil climbed to over $300 billion. The global economy was booming, and countries like China, India, Indonesia, and Brazil were not only growing rapidly but burning oil ever more rapidly. Their increasing demand, coupled with a projected increase in world population from the current 7 billion people to an estimated 9.3 billion by 2015, will drive global consumption from the present 80 million barrels a day to over 120 million barrels a day. The Middle East presently contains 63 percent of world oil reserves, and within ten years will contain 70 percent unless massive new fields are soon discovered elsewhere. This will give enormous leverage to the Saudis and other Middle East producers. And while the price of oil fell in 2009 to under $40 a barrel in the wake of the Great Recession, as of early 2010 it was already back to $80. With any recovery of even modest global growth, prices will be back over $100 per barrel and the cost of protecting the oil fields will also climb astronomically.

It really is time to recognize that Nixon, Ford, and Carter were right. There is only once choice: conservation plus alternative energy.

9

Competing in the New World

The big issue now is how we can prevent the United States from declining too quickly.

—CHINESE LEADERS

We did the opposite of what the American economists advised.

—NAOHIRO AMAYA, VICE MINISTER, JAPAN MINISTRY
OF INTERNATIONAL TRADE AND INDUSTRY

On the day after Christmas 2009, a gleaming new train nosed slowly out of southern China's Guangzhou station for its maiden run. Once clear of the city, the engineer turned on the juice, and three hours and 660 miles later, the Harmony Express pulled into the central China city of Wuhan, having clocked an average speed of 220 miles per hour with spurts of up to 240 mph. As a kind of Christmas–New Years' gift, the Guangzhou Railway Group had just given China the world's fastest train. Just a few days before this event, the *New York Times* had reported that in the next decade China would build more nuclear power reactors than the rest of the world combined. Two days after the event, the United Arab Emirates announced that a South Korean–led consortium had beaten out both a Japanese and a French-led consortium for a $20 billion contract to build the first nuclear power reactors in the Middle East.

Needless to say, the United States had a lead entry in none of these events. To be sure, the venerable American name Westinghouse was mentioned. But it was as a subsidiary of its new Japanese owner, Toshiba, which in turn was part of the Korean consortium. More significant for America was a story, also in the December 16 *New York*

Times, from the old Westinghouse hometown of Pittsburgh. There, it was reported, the city council had decided to tax students on their university tuition in an effort to raise the money necessary to finance the municipal employees' pension fund. This was just the latest in a series of similar stories. For example, the state of Michigan announced that it would cut state funding of higher education by more than 60 percent. Not to be outdone, the state of Hawaii cut back on secondary education by cutting an already short school year by the equivalent of three weeks. Those were just a couple of the highlights of similar cuts being made by forty-two states plus the District of Columbia. There was what some observers considered a piece of good news, however. The *Times* of December 16 also reported that in the wake of its government bailout, top investment bank Goldman Sachs was prospering as if there had never been a crisis.

In an apparently unrelated but actually very pertinent development, the Number 1 People's Court of Beijing handed down a Christmas Day sentence of eleven years in prison to longtime dissident Liu Xiaobo. He was convicted of "inciting subversion of state power" by posting articles that called for political reform on the internet and by circulating a petition calling for the abolition of "subversion" in China's criminal code.

These reports, along with many others mentioned earlier, signal the advent of a new age and of a world turning upside down, with China and much of Asia moving toward the top as America loses its effortless supremacy or even any supremacy. They also reveal realities about globalization, about much American mythology, and about the present competitive and strategic circumstances that are leading the United States into a trap that we Americans must recognize and confront if we are to avoid the fate of Great Britain and if we are to answer Craig Barrett's question of how his grandchildren—and ours—will earn a living.

THE NEW UPSIDE-DOWN WORLD

What we are seeing here is, in part, the natural return of China and the rest of Asia to their historical position as a major part, perhaps even eventually the largest part, of the world economy. There is not necessarily anything wrong with that. We in America who have been so fortunate cannot begrudge Asia getting rich, especially since, under the right circumstances, it could be good for us. But we are also watching an unnatural displacement and decline of America. Many analysts and pundits tell us that our decline is relative and natural. They argue that with only 5 percent of global population, America cannot expect indefinitely to account for 25 percent of world output, and that we should not fret about countries with giant populations like China and India surpassing the United States in GDP. And, if our decline were, in fact, merely relative, as the pundits argue, then, indeed, we should not fret. But our decline is not just a matter of losing our share of global GDP. Our situation is not that of a player maintaining a competitive but perhaps relatively less dominant position as the positions of other players improve. No, for we are not maintaining a strong, competitive position. Some U.S. companies may be doing so, but our country's position is eroding absolutely as well as relatively. In short, we're losing in situations where we ought to be winning at least some of the time, and as we do so, we're heading down in virtually every way. The Chinese see this development clearly even if we don't. Indeed, one Chinese leader recently emphasized that the big issue now is "how we can prevent the United States from declining too quickly."

Losing Where We Should Be Winning

Consider the Harmony Express. China has now joined the big three of France, Germany, and Japan as a bullet train maker and operator. The big three may have suffered a relative decline in terms of their share of global bullet train production and operation, but they are maintaining a strong, competitive position. The United States, on the other hand, has no position. It is simply not in the game, but not because of any technological, financial, natural resource, topographical, or human resource reason. It could be if it really wanted to be. However, for a variety of complicated factors, the United States has simply chosen not to play.

Okay, I know that trains and railroads may be a special case in America. So let's look at aircraft and aerospace, where we have long ruled the roost. I have watched over the past thirty years as the U.S.-produced content of a Boeing jet has gone from around 70 percent to around 30 percent and as American companies wishing to launch satellites have turned from U.S. rockets to the French, Russians, and

Chinese for the boost into space. Again, it is not a matter of relative decline but of absolute decline. We just don't have the rockets anymore. I have watched as investment in semiconductor fabrication facilities in the United States has almost dried up.

Or take green industries. In November 2009, I happened to be visiting my ninety-three-year-old mother in Wilmington, Delaware. On her coffee table, I spied the Delaware *News Journal,* a paper for which I was once a reporter. The lead story reported that GE was planning to shutter its solar panel plant in Glasgow, Delaware. Long ballyhooed as the world industry leader in crystalline silicon panels, the plant was said to no longer be able to compete with more technologically advanced and less expensive Chinese producers. Again, this was not a case of relative decline, of losing an order or two while holding on to a strong position. In the mid-1980s, America absolutely dominated photovoltaic solar panel production. Now, although a few U.S. firms are still competing and some German, Chinese, and Japanese companies are investing in U.S.-based production, industry dominance has shifted to Germany, China, and Japan—not because of low labor costs (Germany has the world's highest labor costs) or because these countries have some natural comparative advantage stemming from peculiarly advantageous resource endowments, but because they have done more than we to push the technology and to achieve bigger economies of scale. Again, this is not a relative decline for America. Germany and Japan may be experiencing a relative decline as China increases its share in this industry, but the United States is suffering a debacle.

Moreover, this is happening throughout all the so-called green industries. In November 2009, the Information Technology and Innovation Foundation (ITIF) reported ("Rising Tigers, Sleeping Giant") that Asia's "clean technology tigers" (China, Japan, and South Korea) have already passed the United States in the production of virtually all clean-energy technologies and that over the next five years, the governments of these countries will out-invest the United States by 3 to 1 in these sectors. These investments will attract a further wave of private sector investment and thereby solidify the "first mover" advantages of these tigers in the clean-energy sectors, making them the likely dominant producers. As for the United States, ITIF said it will probably import the vast bulk of the clean-energy technology it employs, thus switching its energy dependence from the Middle East oil producers to the East Asian wind, solar, and battery producers. Many of the energy tigers' investments are aimed at fostering development of clean-technology industries as major leaders of export growth. By 2012, for example, China, Japan, and South Korea plan to produce 1.6 million gas-electric or electric vehicles annually compared to only 267,000 for North America.

Of great significance here is the first-mover phenomenon, which derives from the presence of economies of scale. In none of these industries is excellence a matter of climate, natural resources, or low labor costs. The keys are capital, technology, and policy. In theory, capital-rich countries like the United States should have some advantage, but, in fact, any country that can allocate the capital or attract it could become a major player in these industries. But the winners will be the countries that manage to grow their industries rapidly, because then, with the lower costs that arise from being large scale, they will be able to lock out potential newcomers by underpricing them. Today America still has a chance of being a player in at least some of these industries. In five years, entry will be prohibitively expensive unless some strategic action is taken now.

Losing the Industrial and Technological Commons

I stumbled across another kind of example while speaking to the Association of Wood Office Furniture Manufacturers a few years ago. When I asked one of the CEOs what was selling, he told me that he had a line of cherry office furniture that was just flying out of the showroom. Where do you make it? I asked. Well, he said, the cherry trees are cut in West Virginia and the logs are then shipped to Germany, where the veneer is peeled. From there the veneer goes to China, where it is glued to the furniture frame, and then the furniture comes back to Wisconsin, from where we market and distribute it. Amazed, I asked why the veneer was peeled in Germany. Surely, I thought, veneer peeling can be done in America. After all, it is not rocket science, and Germany has far higher labor costs than we do. But the answer was that the Germans just do veneer peeling better; indeed, enough better to warrant the cost of shipping those logs and then the veneer around the world. I'm still wondering why Americans can't do veneer, but somewhere along the line, we lost those skills or didn't keep them up to speed.

Another more significant example of the same thing is Amazon's Kindle electronic reader, one of the 2009 Christmas season's bestsellers. The key innovation that makes this product possible is the electronic ink invented and made in the United States by Cambridge, Massachusetts–based E Ink Corporation. Nevertheless, the Kindle cannot be made in the United States because the special glass of the display, and virtually all the other key components like its semiconductor chips and its battery, are made only in Taiwan, Korea, Japan, and China. Thus, of the $185 total estimated manufacturing value added per Kindle, only $40 to $50 is added in the United States, and that may soon decline to zero. Some analysts believe that E Ink's production and R&D will also soon be moved to Asia, not because of cheap labor (the product is not labor intensive), but because Asia has a more friendly investment, tax, and regulatory environment and offers various direct and indirect export subsidies, including undervalued currencies.

This suggests the most significant aspect of the above examples. The next e ink is unlikely to be developed in America, because we will lack the supporting components and skills of the innovation ecosystem. The special displays are made with lithographic equipment originally used to produce semiconductors, a technology that left the United States for Asia in the 1980s and 1990s as Japan and then Korea and Taiwan targeted the semiconductor and semiconductor equipment industries for strategic development. The battery technology that powers the Kindle left America with the consumer electronics industry in the 1960s and '70s. Much of the glass technology also left with the consumer electronics industry. As Silicon Valley entrepreneur, corporate director, and author Richard Elkus says, "Eventually, everything is related to everything else."

These were not just losses of market share or of a few factories and jobs. They were losses of what Harvard Business School's Gary Pisano and Willy Shih call the "industrial commons." Like the common pastures and fields of medieval times or the common transportation infrastructure that supports modern life, the industrial commons is the collective operational capabilities that underpin new product and process development in the United States. Their loss represents not a relative shift but an absolute subtraction from the total assets of the productive base of the economy. Perhaps the most important loss of this type was signaled by the November 9, 2009, issue of *Business Week*, which reported that employment of U.S. scientists and engineers had fallen by 6.3 percent over the past year as opposed to a 4.1 percent decline in overall employment—apparently a result of American corporations transferring more of their R&D to India and China. For a country that says its future is in high technology and innovation and that it is moving to "higher ground" as India and China do the low-tech and mid-tech production, this was a shocker. Clearly, the world is turning upside down, with China and India doing the R&D and America apparently moving to lower-tech endeavors.

Services and Innovation

Of course, many U.S.-based producers still maintain strong positions in a number of industries, and new and innovative companies like Google, Apple, and Human Genome Sciences, Inc., are creating whole new industries or industry segments. But they are not creating enough in the United States to offset the impact of the losses in other industries. If they were, we wouldn't have a trade deficit, and there wouldn't be any talk about the days of the dollar's hegemony being numbered.

Innovation is great, and it is a great American strength. And, in my view, the greatest innovator of our time is Steve Jobs and his company, Apple. His latest hit, the iPhone, has revolutionized yet another industry and created a huge profit stream for Apple. Yet the iPhone is a big contributor to our trade deficit and our mounting international debt because it is made mostly outside the United States. Like the cherry office furniture, the idea and design are done here, as are the marketing and servicing, but the parts and assembly are all done abroad. So the more iPhones that are sold, the bigger our deficit gets and the more we go into debt, putting more pressure on the dollar. The argument is often made that the manufacturing aspects of the iPhone are low-margin operations and that all the profit is in the design and marketing. This may be true regarding labor-intensive iPhone assembly. But we'd still be better off if some of the components were made in America as well.

I'm not talking about trying to do the labor-intensive stuff here. That clearly wouldn't be sensible. But the chips and the batteries and the displays aren't labor intensive. It's not that Japan has some magic resources that we don't have. It's that we have lost the skills and the economies of scale. Further, we have seen in case after case that design, engineering, and even marketing eventually follow manufacture. This has happened most recently with laptop computers, the design as well as the manufacture of which have now migrated to Taiwan and elsewhere in Asia. There is no reason why the iPhone can't go the same way. I'll go into the whys and wherefores of this later, but my point here is that innovation may be a necessary but not sufficient answer to keeping America near the top.

It is often argued that just as agriculture shrank as a percentage of our economy while manufacturing rose during the twentieth century, so in this century will services grow to take over from manufacturing. It is a credible argument because it has, in fact, been happening. I have already noted the fact, however, that under current circumstances, services exports are very unlikely to solve our trade deficit, since provision of tradable services seems to be going the way of the production of tradable goods—abroad. So here I want to focus on another aspect of our situation. Let's look at upstate New York, which has a long tradition of manufacturing in machine tools, air conditioning, furniture, auto parts, and appliances, but also has a history of innovation and high technology with companies such as Eastman Kodak, Xerox, and Bausch and Lomb. The area has been hard hit by competition from China and other parts of Asia in virtually all of its manufacturing and technology sectors. As a result, employment has shifted heavily into service industries. From 1990 to 2005, manufacturing employment declined by about 400,000 jobs while employment in education and health services gained about 450,000 jobs. So services took over nicely from manufacturing and high tech. But here's the catch: the average salary for manufacturing jobs in New York in 2008 was $62,000, while for jobs in education and health services it was $46,000. This is not to say that we can't be prosperous with the right combination of service and innovative technology industries, but it is to say that we do not now have that combination—and don't seem to be on the road to getting it. Indeed, we seem to be on the road to ruin.

TWO VIEWS OF THE WORLD

Our dire situation has come about in large part because of two very different world views the existence and significance of which we have been painfully slow to recognize. One view is ours, the other is that of

China, Japan, Korea, Singapore, Taiwan, Finland, France, Ireland, and much of the rest of the world.

The View from Washington

The view from Washington was well articulated at a White House meeting I attended in the fall of 2009. The subject was how to revitalize the Midwestern economy that had been so hard hit by the economic crisis and especially the failure of GM and Chrysler. One idea was to foster green industries as the replacement for auto and auto parts manufacturing. Could wind turbines, batteries, and solar panels be made in old auto plants? was one question. But another was: If not, can we just build new plants to produce the green products? My answer was: "yes" and "yes" if you are prepared to jump-start these operations with some tax breaks, free land, capital grants, and government orders. That immediately sparked an intense discussion. Most of the economists present objected that such measures would constitute an industrial policy and a breach of the sacred taboo against government "picking winners and losers." Moreover, they said, it would involve subsidizing production that, initially at least, would have a higher cost than in countries such as Denmark, Japan, Korea, and Germany, where large-scale production was already taking place. In other words, producers in those countries have already achieved certain economies of scale and coasted down the cost curve, meaning that even though U.S. competitors could equal or beat those costs eventually, they couldn't do so initially. The argument of the economists was—and remember that these were officials trying to create jobs and reduce our trade deficit—that we could buy the wind turbines, batteries, and solar panels cheaper from foreign producers and should do so because to do otherwise would constitute protectionism and misallocation of resources. That response, of course, left unanswered the question of how to revitalize the Midwestern economy by doing something with the shuttered auto plants. But it revealed perfectly the dream world in which American policy has been made and promoted for the past sixty-five years.

In this world, the focus is transactional and short term. One considers the price to be paid and the benefit to be obtained only on an immediate basis and only in terms of the narrow benefit to the consumer. Foreign economies of scale are seen as something to be taken advantage of in terms of obtaining lower buying prices. But we never consider taking advantage of the ultimate size of the American market to achieve economies of scale for domestic production by simply jump-starting a U.S.-based operation or inducing foreign suppliers to produce in the United States. Most important, global corporations compete in this world, but countries do not compete economically, and if they try to do so, they only damage their own economy. A final key element is the view that subsidies by foreign governments to their exporters or dumping by the exporters in the U.S. market are not so much to be frowned upon as welcomed as a gift to American consumers. If the gift happens to knock out a key domestic industry, there is no reason to fret, because it doesn't matter what we make and the workers can easily find jobs in some other industry. Finally, in this world, the rules of the WTO and the IMF are seen to be based upon these premises, and all the members of these two institutions are understood to have embraced them upon joining.

The View from Most of the Rest of the World

The statement by former MITI vice minister Naohiro Amaya in my epigraph, which he made to me nearly thirty years ago, perfectly expresses the view of most of the rest of the world. When Japan and then Korea and Taiwan embarked on development of their semiconductor industries, these countries either had no semiconductor producers or the ones they had were technologically behind and had higher costs than the U.S. producers. The Washington logic was for them to import from America and export something like ladies' blouses or kids' tennis shoes. The logic in Tokyo, Seoul, and Taipei, however, was to catch up. They thought they could become competitive once they got over the initial learning stage and could achieve economies of scale. They were right, and now each country has a big trade surplus in semiconductors and has taken leadership away from U.S. producers in key sectors. By the same token, the French, British, and Germans didn't forget about building commercial aircraft because the Americans were way ahead. They too decided to catch up, and the catch-up story has been repeated in many other industries by many other countries. China is now repeating it.

The leaders of these countries believe that countries do compete. They understand the huge importance of economies of scale, of imperfect competition, of first-mover advantages, and of the critical role of linkages between things like consumer electronic batteries and new electric car batteries. They use markets to achieve certain ends, but they don't worship markets. They are members of the WTO and the IMF, but they don't interpret the provisions of either body as restricting their strategic promotion of the long-term economic interests of their societies. Indeed, for them, economic and technological development are as important as geopolitics and national security are for the United States. In fact, for them, economic development is national security. Let me show you how seriously they take it.

INDUSTRIAL POLICY DRAGON, REINDEER, AND TIGER

Most of the world's leading economies are guided by strategic industrial policies that aim to achieve a desired overall structure and direction for the economy. Here I will discuss three—China, Finland, and Taiwan—which are representative of many others.

China: The Dragon

In his November 2009 discussions with China's president, Hu Jintao, President Obama pledged closer technical collaboration on and accelerated safety approval of China's planned ARJ21 commuter jet. When I read of this promise, I wondered what must have been going through Hu's mind at the time. Obama's commitment was that of a leader who puts geopolitical interests first and who, in keeping with American economic orthodoxy, thinks that countries don't compete economically. He knew he was soon going to approve some arms sales to Taiwan that were bound to irritate Hu, so maybe a little technical help on commuter jet development would soften the blow, or maybe it would induce China to be a little more helpful in dealing with North Korea. Whatever consideration Obama had in mind, it's for sure that Hu and his colleagues don't think that way. Just a few months before, China's prime minister, Wen Jiabao, had laid out China's vision for developing and producing its own commercial jets in competition with

Boeing in a speech titled "Let the Large Aircraft of China Fly in the Blue Sky." *The Economist* expressed the conventional Anglo-American wisdom on this in an editorial arguing that it would be a costly mistake for China to try to overtake the much more advanced and established Boeing and Airbus. Wen, however, emphasized: "We must succeed in doing this, and the dream of many generations will come true."

But aircraft are only the tip of the Chinese industrial policy iceberg. A small but fundamental point to note in this connection is that in contrast to most American government leaders who are lawyers or economists, most Chinese leaders have been educated as engineers. They preside over the development of a continuing series of five-year economic visions and plans by government ministries that do intensive analysis of the history and plans of other successful developing countries like Korea, Singapore, Ireland, and Japan. They think strategically about which industries will achieve rapid economies of scale, about the linkages that enable one industry to foster another, about the most desirable sector-by-sector structure of the entire economy. Based on this analysis, they allocate tax, investment, training, and other resources and incentives to guide and induce development along the desired lines.

So, for example, in the eleventh five-year plan now in force, some of the industries designated as strategic include: autos, auto parts, armaments, power generation and distribution, oil and petrochemicals, construction, machine tools, information technology, optics, photonics, clean energy, aviation, steel, machinery, telecommunications, shipping, and coal. Among other things, these industries will receive subsidized land, energy, and water and the value-added tax (VAT) may be rebated on exports. There may also be tax holidays and outright capital grants as well as R&D incentives. These plans include especially incentives to attract targeted foreign companies with advanced technology capabilities. Thus, for example, Intel recently announced a major new fabrication facility for China that will entail an investment of about $3 billion to $5 billion. Intel has said that the various Chinese financial incentives will result in an additional $1 billion of profits over ten years as compared to operating the same facility in the United States. At the initiation of this project in the Great Hall of the People, in Beijing, Intel CEO Paul Otellini made an interesting comment. Intel's goal, he said, "is to support a transition from 'manufactured in China' to 'innovated in China.' " Innovation, of course, is what the conventional wisdom says America is supposed to do.

In addition to designating priority industries, the Chinese government directly owns or controls about 200,000 enterprises that are under the oversight of the State-owned Assets Supervision and Administration Commission (SASAC). Think of it as the world's largest equity fund, whose sole owner is the Chinese government. It has designated five priority sectors for future development: national security, monopolies of natural resources, provision of key public goods and services, critical resources, and core enterprises of pillars and high-tech industries. It has also announced that China will create thirty to fifty large corporations with international competitive power. A cluster of state-owned enterprises (SOEs) in what the Chinese call "lifeline" sectors—including oil, coal, petrochemicals, metallurgy, power, telecommunications, defense, ocean shipping, air transport, scientific instruments, and related industries—will remain under absolute state control.

This industrial activity is supplemented by the world's largest sovereign wealth funds with assets of more than $1.8 trillion even after the recent economic crisis. These funds have already made major investments in U.S. banks such as Morgan Stanley and the Blackstone Group, and of course they can facilitate investment by China's national champions in a wide variety of industries.

Although China has actively solicited foreign investment, it acts in a variety of ways to guide that investment so as to ensure transfer of technology to China and to foster further development of China-based value-added production. Thus foreign enterprises must gain approval for investment, an approval that often requires foreign companies to enter into joint ventures or to do certain kinds of production in China. "Buy Chinese" and local content rules are in effect in a number of industries, including telecommunications and clean energy. Technical standards, such as those for wireless communications, are also used to promote domestic industry development. In the wake of the economic crisis, China's stimulus program stipulated that stimulus money had to be used to buy goods and services made and provided in China. And, of course, the biggest policy boost for Chinese production is Beijing's policy of intervening in international currency markets to keep the

RMB undervalued by about 40 percent versus the U.S. dollar. That, combined with the incentives noted above, provides enormous advantages for China's producers, and is the most dramatic evidence of both the fact that China is competing as a country and that it sees that competition as a matter of the highest strategic priority. For China, geopolitics and geo-economics are the same thing.

A final powerful element of China's industrial policy strategy that I should mention is the 863 Program, a project launched in March 1986 (863 is the year and date of the project's birth) by China's then paramount leader Deng Xiaoping to drive its technological catch-up effort. In 2001 this program began to focus intensely on energy, especially new or green energy, setting targets for installing wind turbines, solar panels, hydroelectric dams, and other renewable resources. In 2006 the 863 Program drove China to double its wind power capacity, and then it doubled again the following year and again the year after that. In 2003 China had virtually no solar power industry. By 2008, it was making more solar cells than any other country and taking customers away from American and other foreign companies that had originally invented the technology. In October 2009, President Hu commented that China must "seize preemptive opportunities in the new round of the global energy revolution." (Can you imagine an American president making such a statement?) In response, U.S. Assistant Secretary of Energy David Sandalow acknowledged that "unless the U.S. makes investments, we are not competitive in the clean-tech sector in the years and decades to come." Not only did 863 provide funding but it also required that wind farms, for example, use locally manufactured equipment. The fact that this requirement went into effect in 2003 and was dropped in 2009 is instructive. In 2003, China was a high-cost producer. By 2009, it had achieved such economies of scale and advanced in technology sufficiently that it was the low-cost producer. Dropping the "buy Chinese" rule then had no effect. By now everyone was buying Chinese because they were the cheapest and of good quality.

Interestingly, the 863 Program was fashioned after similar programs at the U.S. National Institutes of Health and the Pentagon's Defense Advanced Research Projects Agency. Since the program got rolling in 1987, its budget has grown by more than fifty times. By way of comparison, President Carter in 1977 quadrupled U.S. public investment in energy research, and by 1987, the United States was the unchallenged leader, installing more than 50 percent of the world's solar cells. That effort, however, was not sustained.

Finland: The Intrepid Reindeer

You probably don't think of Finland as either a "tiger" or a "dragon," but it is just as focused on the importance of an economic strategy as China or any of the Asian tigers. Long a quasi-satellite of the Soviet Union, Finland faced economic disaster when the Soviets collapsed in 1991 and the major export market of the Finns evaporated. Unaccustomed to the more exacting standards of Western markets, Finnish industry went into sharp contraction. Indeed, the GDP fell by more than 10 percent. In response, the Finnish state actively promoted the development of modern industries and created a culture of innovation through a series of public policies and institutions that have transformed Finland from a largely agrarian and natural-resource-based economy into one of the most modern, high-tech economies in the world.

Finland early on decided that it had to adopt a high-technology-centered strategy. The command center of that strategy is the Science and Technology Policy Council chaired by the prime minister, and including the ministers of education, trade, and industry, who serve as vice chairs. The council also includes representatives from academia, private industry, and labor, as well as the heads of Tekes and the Academy of Finland. Tekes is central to the activities decided on by the council because it is the major state agency for funding R&D. It readily admits to "picking winners and losers" and argues that every government does so, the only question being whether it does so haphazardly or on some reasonable basis. Tekes's criteria for support of projects include: potential for export, job creation, productivity and value-added increases, and spillover effects on the surrounding communities and industrial clusters. Tekes keeps close tabs on what is happening around the world and maintains offices in Brussels, Washington, D.C., Silicon Valley, Beijing, Shanghai, and Tokyo. It plays a significant role in the R&D programs of every major Finnish company as well as in the funding of start-ups.

But the Finnish strategy is not just about funding high-tech R&D. Education is a critical element, and extensive planning goes into link-ing the potential needs of industry to the resource allocation of the schools and universities. Finland perennially scores near the top on comparative international student testing in part because it lavishes attention and talent on its educational system. It also fosters collaboration among the schools, government, and industry with a variety of exchange and cross-funding systems.

The biggest Finnish success of recent years, of course, has been Nokia, which transformed itself from a manufacturer of paper and rubber boots into the world's dominant maker of mobile phones and equipment. While remarkable corporate managers engineered this transformation, the government played a major role through early military procurement and establishment of the Nordic Mobile Telephone technical standard that was the forerunner of today's global GSM standard.

A final point is that more than 75 percent of Finnish workers are union members, including company CEOs as well as line workers. In addition, regular consultations between the unions, the employers, and the government create agreements on inflation targets, wage and salary increases, and other broad economic objectives. The focus is on stakeholders, and a clear definition of an overall national economic interest influences decisions throughout the society.

Taiwan: The Tiger

Taiwan today is the number two semiconductor-producing country in the world. From 1952 to 2005, it recorded the world's second fastest economic growth with an average annual increase in real GDP of 7 percent, just behind Singapore's 7.5 percent. From its beginning, the Taiwan government developed detailed four-year development plans, and its approach was straightforwardly interventionist. The government identified promising investment opportunities and arranged low-interest loans and foreign aid funds to support them. Initially, textiles were especially favored, with the government itself supplying cotton and materials to the factories and then buying up all the output. The success of these efforts resulted in many Taiwanese producers becoming contract producers for American and other foreign companies. Similar programs were mounted in other industries, and while the domestic market remained highly protected, special tax incentives and financial grants were made available to foreign and domestic companies that built factories in Taiwan and produced for export. At the same time, emphasis was placed on developing steel, shipbuilding, and petrochemical industries, with the government sometimes owning all or part of a company.

These efforts were all organized under the aegis of what today is known as the Council on Economic Planning and Development, which includes all the key government ministers and has an elite staff and sizable budget of its own. It oversees, among other entities, the Science and Technology Development Council and the Industrial Technology and Research Institute, which were to prove key to the effort to move Taiwan from mid-tech to high-tech beginning in the early 1980s. It was then that the Taiwanese bureaucrats identified semiconductors as an important industry and technology of the future and decided to foster the industry's development in Taiwan—in other words, to pick a winner. To create a plan, they hired Morris Chang, a Shanghai native who, after thirty years of working in Dallas for Texas Instruments, had just retired as president of America's General Instrument Corporation. Chang came up with the idea of a semiconductor foundry that would make computer chips from many different semiconductor producers, thereby allowing them to avoid the high-capital costs of building their own factories. The Taiwan government liked the idea and backed it with an initial $110 million. The rest is history. By 2009, there were about sixty semiconductor fabrication facilities in Taiwan, and Taiwanese technology companies had branched out from semiconductors to laptop computers, flat panel displays, and their indigenous chip design.

Taiwan is now entering a new stage of its Plan for National Development in the New Century. It begins with a vision of a "Green Silicon Island" that will build the new "Taiwan Dream" based on "openness, innovation, compassion, inclusiveness, and harmony with nature." The Taiwan that will emerge will have "a creative mind, a just heart, a bold maritime spirit, a vigorous circulatory system, and a sustainable lifestyle." Concretely, what this means is that Taiwan aims to raise the contribution of technical progress to GDP from 33.4 percent to 52 percent by 2015, to become the foremost internet economy in Asia, to create a green island and green society, and to build Asia's most efficient air-rail-road infrastructure.

Although in America, it is often said that government can't pick winners, I wouldn't want to bet against Taiwan's latest plans. More important, however, is the point that there are many countries out there, not just Taiwan, that measure and plan the contribution of technical progress to GDP. Virtually all the countries of Asia and most of those in Europe think and act in these ways to a greater or lesser extent, in stark contrast to the U.S. approach.

THE NEW AMERICAN WAY

As I have explained, the United States in the past thought and acted pretty much like China, Finland, and Taiwan. But for the last half century, and especially since the presidency of Ronald Reagan, we have not only turned away from the notion of an economic strategy but also have actively condemned it. In making our own policies in international institutions and negotiations, we have considered government guidance or support of economic strategies and industrial policies as not only wasteful and counterproductive but also as downright bad. Our view was well described by Reagan's famous comment noted in chapter 1—that far from being a solution, government is the problem. So we have apotheosized the pure free market, the business CEO, and, above all, the entrepreneur. We have attributed all of our economic successes to these factors and all of our setbacks to misguided government intervention. So deeply ingrained is this attitude that a sure laugh line for any public speaker is to say to the audience: "I'm from the government and I'm here to help." Ha, ha. No one in the audience believes the government can do anything except screw up. So we pride ourselves on not having and not wanting any economic strategy, and heaven forbid that anyone should allow the words "industrial policy" to escape their lips. Our mantra has been that competition and market forces are the great drivers of economic and technological progress. But is that in fact true, and is it really the case that we don't have an economic strategy or industrial policies?

Let's take the concrete example of telecommunications and fast broadband internet service, and compare Korea and the United States. Fifteen years ago, we had telecommunications service far superior to Korea's, which was actually pretty bad. Today Koreans laugh at our cell phones and our internet. We call it fast broadband, but for them our 3.9 megabits per second (Mbps) average speed is no better than snail mail compared to their 49.5 Mbps. As I mentioned in chapter 1, during one of my recent trips to Korea, my traveling companion on Korea's bullet train watched his favorite soap operas all the way from Seoul to Busan with nary a flicker as we moved at 200 miles per hour through the rugged mountains and tunnels of the spine of Korea. Using his phone, I also managed, without interruption, to call my wife, who was then in Maui. Could I call my wife in Maui without interruption from a train tunnel in the United States? Could I even get a call through to start with?

So what happened to make the United States and Korea trade places in the telecommunications league standings? Well, in the 1990s, the Koreans were feeling like the meat in the competitive sandwich. On top of them was Japan with a strong lead in high-technology industries; coming up fast from below was China with a low-cost advantage in the low- and medium-tech industries that were then Korea's mainstay. In considering how to respond, the Korean policy makers concluded that digital telecommunications and the internet were possible game changers and that Korea could get a competitive edge if it built the world's best and fastest telecommunications network. Many Americans automatically assume that an industrial policy like Korea's promotion of fast, reliable telecommunications must entail heavy government subsidies to favored industries and companies. But, in fact, while Korea used some tax incentives to induce investment in broadband internet deployment, the main tools were regulatory or, to say it more precisely, the removal or addition of regulations to do away with bottlenecks or compel cooperation. Thus, for example, the government coordinated arrangements between builders of houses, owners of apartment buildings, the telephone companies, and the equipment producers for setting technical standards and getting agreement on internet speeds, deployment objectives, and timetables.

The key was that Korea was determined to achieve the broadest possible deployment of the highest speed internet capability. It used many tools. For instance, Korean taxpayers were given a small break if they filed electronically. This created demand and economies of scale for broadband deployment and production of broadband equipment. Many similar measures were used. Korea also used the tool of promoting competition between service suppliers and equipment makers, but it didn't worship that tool. If competition wasn't resulting in rapid deployment of high-speed broadband and of high-speed, high-quality mobile phone capability, then policy makers saw to it that competitors were cajoled or forced to do more. Korea didn't want a process. It wanted results, and it got them. And it got them without spending a lot of public money.

In contrast, the United States did not have any particular goals for telecommunications and broadband in the 1990s except to have more competition. It was thought that competition would spur technological innovation and rapid deployment of the broadband internet as well as of cell phone capability and use. Our Federal Communications Commission (FCC) oversees the telephone service providers as well as the allocation of the radio spectrum necessary for cell phone communication. So the FCC must make decisions of one kind or another about how the spectrum will be allocated and about the rules governing the telecommunications services. In other words, we will have a policy. The only question is what kind of policy it will be. For the past thirty years, the policy has been to create more competition by breaking up AT&T, creating the Baby Bells, spinning off AT&T's Western Electric production arm and its iconic Bell Labs (the inventor of the transistor and much else) into separate operating companies, and trying to foster the startup of entirely new telecom providers. More competition, it was firmly believed, would automatically lead to continued U.S. telecom leadership.

Wrong. In the first place, it wasn't so easy just to dictate that there would be more competition. Only one phone line or cable can go into a house. It's not hard for the company who controls either one to deter new competitors. Moreover, switches and transformers and the like have to be located in appropriate locations, which aren't always easy to duplicate. In addition, the companies all had claims under the law and regulations and lots of lawyers. So the United States did, in fact, get a lot of competition, but it was more of the legal sort than of the technology development sort. In fact, the way the competition rules worked, there were actually incentives *not* to deploy new, faster internet capacity. To make a long story short, the United States wound up without much more competition and also without competitive telecom services. In the name of not having an industrial policy, we had a kind of antiindustrial policy that has undermined our competitiveness.

To take another example, let's go back to China's 863 Project and our own DARPA and clean energy programs. In 1987, when 863 started rolling, the United States was, as I have noted, the unchallenged leader in clean technology. We then made more than 50 percent of the world's solar cells and were installing about 90 percent of the wind power. At the same time, DARPA had made the United States the sole possessor of the internet technology and was pushing ahead on flat panel displays, high-definition television, and other so-called dual-use technology that had potentially commercial as well as military uses.

We've seen what 863 has done for China since then. The momentum was very different in America. Having campaigned on a promise to abolish the Department of Energy, President Reagan cut the department's investment in research way back so that by 2006 it was spending one-sixth of what it spent in 1979. DARPA was also cut back and told to focus strictly on military-use technology and to forget about anything that might have commercial uses, since that would be taken care of by private sector R&D. Of course, it was at this time that private sector R&D began to suffer as well in the face of intense competition from Japan and then from the Tigers and China. Nevertheless, our ability to assess this competition was substantially reduced when the Congressional Office of Technology Assessment (similar to the Congressional Budget Office) was closed in 1995. In any case, in 2005 the National Academies called for creation of an Advanced Research Projects Agency–Energy, or ARPA-E, to be modeled on DARPA and to spark an effort to regain the American lead in clean technology. But the first Bush administration rejected the proposal as "an expansion of government" into an area "more appropriately left to the private sector."

So, having determined to leave telecom and energy to the "free" market, we are lagging badly in competitiveness in those areas. On the other hand, it is interesting that between 1979 and 2006, federal spending on the National Institutes of Health (NIH) and medical research nearly quadrupled. Especially in the area of biotechnology (as in the area of national security), the United States now spends more than the rest of the world combined. Is it then a coincidence that we are by far the world leader in biotechnology and in the commercialization of biotechnology?

I could go on, but I think several points are clear. Although the United States eschews a formal economic strategy and any kind of stated industrial policy, we have such policies. Indeed, we can't avoid them. The FCC must choose how to regulate telecommunications. The choice of focusing on competition (a process) rather than on deployment (a result) is a form of industrial policy—or perhaps of antiindustrial policy. The same holds for treatment of DARPA, ARPA-E, and the NIH and for many other agencies and programs. The U.S. government is very large, spends an enormous amount of money, and sets standards and regulations that have an enormous impact on the business environment, on the shape of various industries, and on the conditions of consumer life. We cannot avoid having a de facto economic strategy and de facto industrial policies of all kinds. So let's take a quick look at our de facto strategy.

Let's start with agriculture. Despite all our talk of leaving things to the private sector, the last thing we will ever do is get rid of the agricultural subsidies that now cost us $50 billion annually and that provide, for example, about $160,000 per U.S. cotton farm, despite the fact that America is the high-cost international cotton producer. As noted above, we also highly subsidize medical research and are not likely to stop. We have long subsidized home buying and home construction through the lending of Fannie Mae and Freddie Mac and, of course, with the mortgage interest tax write-off. Our low taxation of gasoline and public provision of roads, skyways, and airports have favored driving and flying over taking the train, and, of course, have been a great boon to the oil companies. Our taxation of savings and dividends penalizes saving, while the home equity loan, with its mortgage tax write-off, subsidizes consumption, particularly of consumer durables. This, coupled with our tolerance of dumping, currency manipulation, and other trade-distorting activities by our trading partners, has favored the offshoring of U.S.-based production, as have the asymmetrical trade agreements we have concluded for geopolitical reasons.

Most striking of all is the extraordinary support we have given to one industry over the past thirty years. It is so striking that I fear we must call it for what it has been—a clear industrial policy to target development of the financial services sector. Consider that from 1929 to 1988, the profits of the U.S. financial sector averaged annually

1.2 percent of GDP and never rose above 1.7 percent in any year. From 1988 until 2005, they averaged 3.3 percent of GDP. In 1980 the financial sector's share of business profits was 6 percent. By 1990, it was 30 percent, and by 2005, it had soared to 40 percent, although it fell back to 30 percent in 2007 as the crisis began to break upon us. Even more striking is the pay per worker in the finance sector. In 1948 it was 105 percent of average worker pay. That proportion, though unchanged in 1980, was, by 1990, 130 percent, climbed to 165 percent in 2000, and soared to 185 percent in 2007 as Wall Street sold trillions of dollars of securities backed by "ninja" (no income, no job) mortgages. As former IMF chief economist Simon Johnson has emphasized, measures such as regulation of derivative instruments that could have stopped the 2008–9 economic crisis but would have limited financial sector profits, were prevented. Hedge fund managers who made literally billions of dollars benefited from special income tax breaks. The Glass-Steagall Act and virtually all other bank regulatory acts were abolished or weakened. Indeed, as I write, Federal Reserve Chairman Ben Bernanke is saying that lack of Fed oversight of the banking industry caused the crisis. Just as an example, in 2004 the SEC changed its net capital rule that a bank had to have $1 of capital for every $12 of liabilities. Under the new rule, any bank with assets of more than $5 billion could use its own model of risk to determine an appropriate ratio. Bear Sterns, for one, went from $1 of assets to $33 of liabilities. That, of course, is what broke the bank.

So why did finance become so favored? A couple of numbers tell a lot. From 1998 to 2008, the finance industry spent $1.78 billion on political campaign contributions and another $3.4 billion on lobbying. As Simon Johnson says, the Wall Street–Washington corridor is rich and crowded. The writer Pat Choate has even coined a new name for the United States: Goldman Sachsony.

In this light, America's economic strategy is clear. It is to overconsume, and to promote weapons production, financial services, construction, medical research and services, agriculture, and oil and gas consumption and production. Further, it is both to offshore production and provision of all tradable manufacturing and services as well as, increasingly, high-technology R&D, and to expand the domestic retail, food service, and personal medical services industries. At the macro level, the strategy is to run up massive debt and borrow as much and as long as possible.

In terms of international competitiveness, the United States benefits from its fundamental nature. It has a very stable political system, a real rule of law, a relatively low level of corruption, a high average level of education, strong incentives for entrepreneurial activity, lots of second-chance opportunities, leadership in many technologies and industries, and a diversified economic base. But these factors are offset by some surprising negatives. For instance, while we think of Scandinavia as the citadel of high taxes, the United States, in fact, has higher taxes on business than do the Nordic countries and, indeed, than almost all other countries. As already noted, America's advanced infrastructure is lagging, and even its legacy infrastructure is deteriorating. The fact that there are no investment incentives at the national level and only small ones at the state level, coupled with a strong dollar relative to manipulated Asian currencies and the high business taxes, makes America unattractive for investment. So the funny thing is that while America should be very competitive, it currently is not and is becoming less so.

THE DYNAMICS OF A WORLD THAT IS HALF FREE TRADE AND HALF MERCANTILIST

So you see, to paraphrase Abraham Lincoln, the world in which we live is half free trade and half mercantilist. Half or more of the countries have a clearly defined national economic interest, an economic strategy focused on export-led growth, and a series of industrial policies to fulfill the strategy. The rest, mostly us and the Brits, have no defined national economic interest, no formal strategy, and a bunch of de facto industrial policies that are uncoordinated and often contradictory. This is significant especially in the arena of trade negotiations and globalization.

Consider the Doha Round of WTO multilateral trade negotiations or the U.S.-Korea Free Trade Agreement negotiations. Before these talks begin, the foreign negotiators already have an economic strategy and a series of industrial policy objectives that define their objectives for the talks. They are not looking for something vague like "open markets." Rather, they are looking for specific, concrete results in terms of lower tariffs or lifting of regulations in sectors like autos or semiconductors, which they have targeted for development because of a belief that those sectors will lead to higher productivity, faster growth, and more extensive technological advances. So, for example, Korean negotiators will want both to get lower U.S. tariffs on imports of autos and to shield their producers from U.S. prosecution for theft of intellectual property. Of course, the foreign negotiators will have consulted with their industries and labor unions, but they will have done so on the basis of a governmentally defined national economic interest and not on the basis of which interest group shouts loudest.

In contrast, the American negotiators have no governmentally defined national economic interest and have done no analysis of what negotiating results might lead to the greatest increase in American exports or the greatest decrease in the U.S. trade deficit or to any other particular benefit for their country. Their negotiating agenda will have been largely determined by the wish lists they have received from various industries and members of Congress and the negotiating priorities by how politically influential the presenters of the wish lists are. So, for example, in the talks with Korea, getting the Koreans to reduce their tariffs and quotas on U.S. beef exports have been a high priority—not because beef exports add much in any way to the United States' economy but because Senator Max Baucus of beef-producing Montana is chairman of the Senate Finance Committee, which has jurisdiction over the ultimate Senate approval of any free-trade deal.

It's against this background that I recently had a conversation with an old Korean friend who has also been one of his nation's trade policy makers. He knew that I was skeptical of the value to America of the proposed U.S.-Korea Free Trade Agreement and tried to persuade me to favor it by emphasizing the big concessions that Korea had made, especially in the area of auto tariffs and intellectual property protection. I agreed with him that Korea had indeed been unprecedentedly forthcoming and had gone a long way to meeting the U.S. requests. But I asked: "Do you honestly believe that this deal will significantly increase U.S. exports to Korea or reduce the U.S. trade deficit with Korea?" He replied: "Frankly speaking, no." Indeed, we both knew that, if anything, the deal would increase the U.S. deficit. Yet the American negotiators have been calling the proposed agreement a great negotiating victory because they think they have been procedurally successful.

Let's look at how this half free–half mercantilist world works between the United States and China. Around the time of President Obama's November 2009 visit to China, GE announced that it was forming a joint venture with China's AVIC (Aviation Corp. of China, an offshoot of the state-owned Commercial Aircraft Corp. of China) to not only develop and supply avionics to China's budding aircraft industry but also to use the joint venture to produce and market globally. Further, it was explained that Washington had given all necessary technology export approvals. Now, GE is a longtime player in aviation and avionics and a leader in the field. AVIC is not. Avionics are just the sophisticated, high-tech kinds of products in which the United States is supposed to have a comparative advantage, the exports of which are supposed to reduce our trade deficit, and the production of which is supposed to provide the jobs for our grandchildren.

One could understand that GE might announce a contract to export avionics to China for its newly planned commercial jets. And one could understand that Washington would be pleased by such an announcement. But why a joint venture with AVIC? What does AVIC bring to the party? The Chinese government's blessing is the answer. This commercial jet of China's is very much an industrial policy project aimed at making China a powerhouse in aircraft and avionics production. China is going to be a big aircraft market, and the Chinese authorities know that and know that all the avionics makers will want to sell to that market. They are therefore in a position to require, either formally or informally, that any avionics maker who wants to sell to them must do so through a joint venture to which that maker transfers lots of technology to help boost China's indigenous development effort.

GE or any other company may not want to do that, but the deal is basically half a loaf or none. So the supplier goes for half a loaf. But once the technology is transferred, the other dynamics we have been discussing kick in. China achieves economies of scale and gets its production costs down. Together with its undervalued currency and the investment subsidies the joint venture gets from the government, the Chinese production facility becomes the world's low-cost, high-tech (by dint of the tech transfer) location, and China adds another export industry to its belt as the U.S. trade deficit gets a bit bigger.

Now, the big question is, Why does Washington give the tech transfer clearances (these clearances apply only to products with a possible military use) for these deals, and why does it accept these deals and even cheer them? The answer is that the government officials also think half a loaf is better than none, even if that half will come back to bite them later. But why don't they think in terms of reciprocity? If the Chinese require or strongly hint that it would be a good idea for our exporters to do joint ventures on avionics, why don't we do likewise for their computer exporters? The answer is that that would be protectionist. And so here you have the results of unilateral, nonreciprocal, simplistic free-trade doctrine.

The Dynamics

Dynamics similar to these operate in all the neomercantilist markets. The structure of our present globalization is such that a combination of currency undervaluation, explicit or implicit requirements and incentives to invest and transfer technology as a condition of market access, and explicit industry targeting policies exists in most of the major markets—especially in Asia—to a greater or lesser extent. This important fact negates all the remedies normally proposed by American conventional wisdom for regaining our competitiveness, especially the two major ones: improved U.S. education and more and better innovation.

While both of these aims are highly desirable, they alone cannot reverse the current dynamics of globalization. While the American education system has many flaws, which we have already discussed, the American workforce is still the best educated workforce in the world. Very interesting is the fact, noted earlier, that the share of the workforce with a college degree doubled from 15 percent to 30 percent between 1973 and 2005, while the high school dropout rate over the same period fell from 29 percent to 10 percent. That is a huge improvement in education. It is difficult to imagine a greater improvement. Yet it is precisely during this period that our trade deficits and the erosion of our technological, industrial, and R&D leadership have accelerated. Do we need better education? Of course, but will it solve the problem by itself? Absolutely not.

By the same token, neither will innovation. Recent studies have shown that 80 percent of engineering tasks in product development can relatively easily be offshored. And that seems to have been confirmed by the report in *Business Week* noted earlier that unemployment among U.S. scientists and engineers has risen more rapidly than general unemployment during the recent crisis, as American companies sent more of their R&D to India and China.

WHO STANDS FOR THE AVERAGE AMERICAN FAMILY?

The answer to the above question in terms of the national economic interest is pretty much "no one." This is largely due to the assumption of economic orthodoxy that countries don't compete economically. Consequently, the economic decisions that in most countries are made based—like our national security and geopolitical decisions—on careful consideration of the objective national interest are, in America, made largely on the basis of lobbying.

Among the lobbies, the one that comes closest to articulating the interest of the average American family and thus the objective interest of America is organized labor. The reason is obvious. Union members are American workers, and American workers mostly can't go offshore for jobs. Since they have to work for a living and have to work here, they have a primary interest in the competitiveness of the United States in producing products and providing services for the domestic and international markets. In the words of the Young Commission, American workers very much want U.S.-based production to "meet the test of the global marketplace while raising standards of living." Their livelihood depends on this. However, the fact that organized labor is now such a small percentage of the workforce (12.4 percent) makes it difficult for labor leaders to claim to speak for the whole American workforce or even for the average family. A second problem is that because U.S. unions are organized along industry lines, their inevitable sector interest militates against a broader interest. So they are one of the lobbies. However, I would say that in my experience, they are the lobby most likely to be speaking for the people, and this is certainly true in the arena of international trade and globalization.

Lobbying is closely tied to the U.S. electoral system. As elections have become dominated by the media, they have become astronomically expensive, and the winning candidates are usually those who can raise the most money. Corporate lobbies have most of the money, and under lax U.S. campaign finance rules, they gain enormous leverage over legislation and policy. Our recent health care debate and legislation is a good example. Every other developed country in the world has more comprehensive, and in many cases, such as France, better quality health care than the United States at half the cost. Moreover, because their systems are nationally and not employer based, health care costs for Japanese and European companies are minimal, whereas for U.S.-based employers they are a major cost factor. Of course, there is a great fear of socialism in America, and no one wants to be like those "socialist" Europeans. But no one has ever accused the Japanese or Koreans of being socialist, and in any case, they seem to know how to compete with our capitalist system. So why can't we at least be like them on health care? Powerful, deep-pocketed lobbies is, of course, the answer.

Consider also the case of the banks. Even under quasi-government ownership, the big financial institutions have been left free to continue practicing highly questionable forms of business, such as high-speed trading, and they have lobbied aggressively against regulation of the derivatives business that was at the heart of the meltdown. We need to understand that the interests of Wall Street, and therefore of much of Washington, have not been and will not be those of Main Street. Wall Street doesn't care about trade deficits, has bought into the idea that making things is passé as we move to the "higher ground" of services (including especially financial services), abhors taxes, and thinks the growing gap between rich and poor is a sign of the strength of the U.S. economy. Yet the financial system is not being fundamentally reformed or even reregulated very much, and the big banks that were "too big to fail" have gotten bigger and are presumably even more likely to be bailed out of an emergency than before the crisis.

But lobbying is not just a matter of influencing major legislation or major government regulatory actions. Indeed, it is much more a matter of thousands of unknown and seemingly insignificant meetings with midlevel bureaucrats and congressional staffers, of handing over wish lists, of providing the government with industry information it doesn't generate itself because those who believe government is the problem have abolished all the industry data gathering and analyzing arms of the government, and of using political influence to remove bureaucrats who might object to certain corporate objectives. In this game, big business wins out over small business, rich business wins out over poorer business, and foreign interests represented by good Washington lobbyists often win out over American interests.

THE TRAP

As a consequence of all these factors, the United States, and, indeed, the world find themselves in a nasty trap. Even at its current reduced level of about $500 billion, or 3 percent of GDP, in the wake of the Great Recession, the U.S. trade deficit is problematic and will likely become more so with any kind of economic recovery. Its financing already requires a daily inflow to the United States of $4 billion to $5 billion of foreign capital a day, a number that could easily pop to $8 billion. China and other big holders of U.S. debt are expressing increasing unease over holding too many dollars and are even calling for a new global currency, as most analysts admit that the present situation is clearly not indefinitely sustainable. Moreover, the U.S. federal budget deficit and national debt are racing into uncharted waters and obviously must be brought under some kind of control to avoid ultimately unsustainable interest costs, but also because the federal deficit reduces net national saving and exacerbates the trade deficit. Yet unemployment is high and threatens to remain so despite huge federal deficit spending. Indeed, further spending to help reduce unemployment is probably not possible.

To add to this mix, U.S. geopolitical concerns cost a lot of money and take priority over economic issues. So spending on them will further constrain economic stimulus spending. Just to complicate matters a bit more, despite its unilateral defense of key allies and huge buying from possible adversaries, America's national security policies work to accommodate the economic strategies of both our friends and our possible adversaries while undermining our own productive and technological base. If the trade situation gets bad enough to really cause a shift away from the dollar, our ability to maintain our far-flung deployments will collapse because we have no means to export enough to earn the foreign currency necessary to pay for them. Finally, our increasing reliance on imported oil means both higher trade deficits with economic recovery and higher trade deficits just with the passage of time as our own production declines. In any case, none of this adds to employment or to our grandchildren's livelihoods.

The key to solving all these problems is to reverse the dynamics of our present form of globalization and, in particular, of the U.S. trade deficit. If we can start running a trade surplus, or even a lot smaller deficit, we can create employment without the need for federal deficit spending. We can thereby help increase savings and further reduce the trade deficit. The new jobs will generate tax revenue and further reduce the federal deficit. The dollar will strengthen and talk of alternatives will cease. Then we can play a more robust geopolitical game. Sounds simple, but there are a few problems.

The conventional prescription here is for the Chinese, Japanese, Koreans, Southeast Asians, and Germans (the major non–oil producing trade surplus countries) to save less, export less, and consume more domestically while at the same time the United States saves more, produces more, exports more, and consumes less. However elegant as a theoretical solution, it is not going to happen through enlightened self-interest and sophisticated negotiation. Just for starters, the Germans do not at all believe that they need to consume more. I was in the room in 1984 when Japan's Prime Minister Nakasone promised that Japan would become an importing superpower. Well, twenty-six years later, Japan is still dependent on export-led growth. The Chinese are not going to change their currency policy in any significant way, nor are they going to abandon their industrial catch-up policies, and even though they recognize the need to stimulate domestic consumption, it will be hard to do because of the deep structural and political problems of their economy. As for us Americans, while we are actually saving more and consuming less as a result of the Great Recession, we are not changing the fundamental production and export-import dynamics. The only way to do this is to produce more of what we consume and export more of what we produce. Further, we will simply have to produce and export more manufactured goods. The trade deficit is so big in manufactures that we simply will not be able to overcome it with services and R&D. But an export-led growth policy of our own puts us on a collision course with China, much of the rest of Asia, and even possibly with the EU.

Above all, we need to create jobs, and as both Columbia University's Jeff Sachs and *U.S. News and World Report*'s Mort Zuckerman have recently said, "jobs just don't happen." The free market by itself is no longer, if it ever did, going to produce those jobs. In the face of the difficult dynamics of globalization, of the division of the world into half free trade and half mercantilist, and of the present collision course of ourselves and most of Asia, we need to explicitly define our national economic interest and to devise a strategy to further it.

10

Playing to Win

Sí se puede (Yes, we can).

I have spilled a lot of ink explaining America's problems and deficiencies in everything from education to corporate management to international trade to science and technology and much else besides. And I hope I have convinced you of their seriousness and of the necessity of addressing them urgently. But there is good news: the problems are far from irreparable. Indeed, as I will show in a moment, they can be repaired with relative ease. Consider the global competition among nations as similar to a game of bridge. Each of the countries has a hand of cards and has to decide how to play them. Ask yourself which hand you'd prefer to play: China's, Japan's, India's, Germany's, the EU's, or America's? Each has some good cards and some bad cards. China is on a roll right now, but its system tends toward chronic overinvestment, and its population will soon begin to age very rapidly. The Chinese will likely get old before they get rich, and they will be continually plagued by corruption. Germany has unparalleled engineering skills, good labor-management-government coordination, and high savings and investment rates. But the population is already aging and shrinking, and Germany is going to have to bear the burden of structural weaknesses in the EU. India has great talent, but its population may outgrow its economy. So, if I were choosing, I'd want to play the American hand. With all its weaknesses, the American hand is still the best. But, as anyone who has ever played bridge knows, it is very possible to have a good hand and lose—by playing the cards badly. We have been playing our cards badly and need a whole set of new policies and programs. But the most important thing we need to do is to change our mind-set.

What America makes will make (or unmake) America. In this case, "make" refers not only to the production of goods, but also to provision of critical services and to development of sophisticated high-tech systems. It is the whole productive base that we must revitalize and keep competitive. But doing so will require that, from the president on down, our leaders declare that they understand that countries do compete and that they are going to ensure that America is competitive in a broad range of key industries. They must declare their intent that America will indeed produce things like advanced batteries, wind turbines, solar cells, computer chips, advanced search engines, cyber systems, and much else. They must make it clear that they will match the financial investment incentives, infrastructure investments, and government encouragement of other countries with regard to promising industries and that, in the spirit of Alexander Hamilton, they intend for America to make more than dung.

THE TYRANNY OF ORTHODOXY

Referring to the difficulty of supplanting old theories with ideas based on new observations, the great German physicist Max Planck once lamented that "science advances one funeral at a time." A similar sentiment led John Maynard Keynes famously to quip that "practical men who believe themselves quite exempt from any intellectual influences, are usually the slaves of some defunct economist."

We tend to rely on experts to guide our thinking on the many topics and issues about which our knowledge is limited. Indeed, we cannot do otherwise, and therefore, we very much want our experts to know what they're talking about. We reassure ourselves about their correctness by frequently invoking the unanimity or near unanimity of expert opinion in phrases like: "most doctors think that . . ." or "despite their many differences, all economists agree that . . ." or "virtually all scientists have concluded that . . ." And we resist giving up on the consensus view even as evidence mounts that the experts may be wrong.

The recent death of Robert McNamara, secretary of defense under presidents Kennedy and Johnson, reminded me of the immense power of this kind of group think. A Harvard Business School "whiz kid" who helped mastermind the logistics in World War II and became Ford Motor Company CEO at age forty-four, McNamara was a key early protagonist of the domino theory and the war in Vietnam. Widely perceived to be brilliant, he eventually acknowledged that the war had been a great mistake. He bore the burden of that mistake to his grave and will be forever known in history as a smart guy whose errors and arrogance resulted in the unnecessary deaths of hundreds of thousands of people. But, as I noted earlier, McNamara was not alone. In his great book *The Best and the Brightest* (1972), David Halberstam catalogued how virtually the entire American leadership elite got it wrong. In retrospect we know how foolish and superficial the domino theory was, but the establishment brooked no dissent at the time. As Max Planck might have said, it took a funeral, or perhaps I should say over 58,000 funerals, to advance the thinking of the experts.

This phenomenon isn't new, of course. In the Middle Ages, scientists and theologians under the thrall of the Ptolemaic theory of an earth-centered universe tied themselves in knots proving that Galileo's (and Copernicus's as well) concept of the earth moving around the sun could not possibly be correct. Indeed, Galileo was tried by the Inquisition, forced publicly to recant his views, and placed under house arrest. In the 1920s, in America, General Billy Mitchell was demoted and court-martialed for promoting the notion of strategic use of airpower. In particular, virtually all of the brass and military experts at the time argued that Mitchell was wrong to claim that bombers could sink battleships—despite the fact that in tests organized by the navy, Mitchell's bombers had sunk every ship the navy sent into their sights including the "unsinkable" ex-German battleship *Ostfriesland* in July 1921. It took the funerals of Pearl Harbor to vindicate Mitchell and put to final rest the false doctrine of the invulnerability of battleships. Or take the reaction to the advent of the Great Depression. Virtually all economists agreed at the time that the federal government should balance its budget while the Federal Reserve should tighten lending and cut back on the money supply. The Keynesian notion of using government deficit spending as a kind of economic pump priming was widely condemned as heretical until the unprecedented deficits of World War II did just what Keynes had argued deficits would do.

Consider also the recent episode that I mentioned in the introduction—the hubris and eventual collapse of Lehman Brothers. All the masters of the universe on Wall Street had their value-at-risk models. There was no problem. "Be happy," they said. They were all smart with degrees from the best schools, all rich, and experienced—and all wrong. Finally, an entrepreneur, investor, writer, and editor tells about a speech he gave to two hundred finance professors. When he asked how many of them taught the efficient-market hypothesis (EMH), nearly all raised their hands. When he asked how many of them believed it, only two hands went up.

I know full well how difficult it is to go against the establishment; how brutally the apostles of denial will fight to maintain their credibility and that of their orthodoxy; and how often orthodoxy prevails even in the face of strong evidence of error. But if America is to have any chance of revitalizing itself—of ceasing to export, say, "loads of dung"—we must be willing both to consider the possibility that the experts and the conventional wisdom may be wrong and to find ways out of the hole we have been digging.

The Role of Government

As I noted earlier, a sure opening laugh line for a speaker before any American audience is: "Good evening. I'm from the government, and I'm here to help." The inevitable answering roar of mirth means the audience doesn't believe for one minute that the government can ever do anything to be helpful. One part of the American brain permanently perceives the government as at best a blundering, idiotic bureaucracy and at worst a power-mad oppressor bent on total control of the smallest details of life. This image is constantly fed by political and media commentary. For instance, in 2009 the U.S. government came to the rescue of General Motors, Chrysler, and, in one way or another, a large part of the extended automotive industry, not to mention the insurance and banking industries. Throughout this process, officials from the president on down have constantly repeated that the government is not good at running things and that they don't want the government actually to manage or interfere with the management of these entities, even though the government is their major shareholder. Indeed, they seem to be promising that the government will abdicate its responsibility as a shareholder.

In the great debate over the future shape of health care in this country, a major issue is the concern of many people that the government role in the provision of health care and medical insurance will

284 | THE BETRAYAL OF AMERICAN PROSPERITY

be greatly enlarged. Some fear the government will ration their health care or even take it away completely. House of Representatives minority leader John Boehner commented derogatorily in one interview that "If you want your health care to feel like the post office, just turn it over to the government."

Well, my local post office works pretty well. In fact, it works a lot better than many of the private doctors' offices and hospitals I visit. Furthermore, my medical care and payments are already being rationed and dictated by a faceless, private medical bureaucracy that presents me with endless telephone menus whenever I try to contact it. Maybe it's true that the government wouldn't be good at running AIG, Bank of America, or General Motors. But hey, their shareholders and private sector executives were the ones who ran them into the ground and made it necessary to bail them out in the first place. Could the government really do worse? Don't get me wrong. I'm not really calling for socialization. In fact, I'll be very happy to see GM and the others pay off the taxpayers and become competitive in the marketplace again. But I believe it is essential for the revitalization of America that Americans stop automatically dissing their government.

In fact, a bizarre schizophrenia characterizes the relationship between the American people and the American government—as was wonderfully articulated by the man at a recent town hall meeting who shouted at his congressman to "keep the government's hands off my Medicare." Statements like that, which make you wonder whether to laugh or cry, reveal the essential irrationality of the discussion. In this case, the guy loved what the government was doing for him as long as he didn't know it was the government doing it. Or take an old classmate with whom I recently had dinner. First, he objected to any expansion of the government role in medicine and to any new taxes to pay for insurance coverage of those who are presently uninsured. Then, in discussing his own health problems, he noted that as a veteran he uses the Veterans Administration hospitals and emphasized how efficiently they are run and how great their treatment is.

This same disconnect manifests itself in many other areas. Many farmers who pride themselves on their rugged independence actually survive and even, in some cases (e.g., cotton farmers), thrive on government agriculture subsidies. Business leaders who are quick to move operations to foreign tax havens want the government to spend more on R&D. Americans who oppose big government in education or medicine want even bigger military forces and ever more support for our troops. It seems to be the case that Americans don't like government except when they like government or don't know it's government.

The truth is that the story of America's development into the world's leading country is one of private sector–government partnership. Sometimes as a kind of experiment I will ask an audience if anyone knows who invented the internet. The guesses usually include Bill Gates, Steve Jobs, Intel, AT&T, and Google. They never include the right answer: the U.S. government. Or even more correctly, the long partnership between the Defense Advanced Research Projects Agency (DARPA), the National Science Foundation, our research universities, and companies like Bolt, Beranek and Newman. From the American System and the Erie Canal to the construction of the railroads to the development of aviation to the mobilization for the world wars to the founding of companies like RCA to the atomic bomb and nuclear energy, to the moon landing and the internet, American industry and government have worked hand in glove to achieve unprecedented progress.

As a veteran of the trade wars with Japan in the 1980s, I am often asked what happened to Japan. The questioner usually doesn't pause for my response but hastens to tell me how good old American entrepreneurs and businessmen pulled up their socks and improved their quality and productivity to overcome their Japanese competitors. Of course, while there is truth in what they say, it's not the whole truth. The U.S. government also concluded a deal with Japan to devalue the dollar and to guarantee U.S. semiconductor producers a 20 percent share of the Japanese market. It also launched the High Speed Computing Initiative, invested $1 billion in the Sematech 50/50 government-industry semiconductor consortium, and initiated an antidumping action that prevented Japanese producers from selling below cost in the U.S. market. What happened to Japan was an American public-private partnership aimed at recovering American industrial and technological leadership. While the actions of the companies were important, they would not have been successful without the government's actions as well.

The first step on the way out of our present predicament should be to reread our own history. And not only to reread it, but to broadcast and promote it to diverse audiences so that a wide cross-section of leaders and ordinary citizens understand the complex and subtle interaction between the government and the private sector that has always underpinned American success.

Turn Away from False Gods: Teach Reality

One positive result of the recent Great Recession is the blow it has struck to the efficient-market hypothesis (EMH) and rational expectations (RE) school of thought. In the wake of the crisis, many prominent economists and commentators—such as Paul Krugman, Justin Fox, and Warren Buffett—have echoed Robert Shiller in his prescient critiques of the theory, and there are now many efforts under way to achieve better oversight and regulation of financial markets in recognition of the failure of so-called efficient markets. They may abandon at least this false god in favor of dealing with harsh, complex reality.

But the efficient-markets god was linked to the gods of shareholder value, industry nonintervention, and laissez-faire globalization in a broader market fundamentalist faith. These other gods may have been a bit damaged by the fall of EMH, but they have not been displaced. If the American Dream is to survive, they too must go. Surely the Great Recession has demonstrated the emptiness of shareholder value as the sole guiding principle for CEO decision making. As we noted in chapter 7, when the going got really difficult, it was not the shareholders but the stakeholders of troubled corporations who bore the ultimate risk and who were called upon to serve as economic rescuers. This is not to say that shareholders don't count. But a sole focus on increasing shareholder value too easily becomes, in fact, a focus on increasing shareholder value in the short term, and too often, as in the case of Scott Paper Company, to no value in the long term. Professor Jensen and the apostles of shareholder value protest that serving the competing interests of stakeholders risks ultimately serving no interest because performance cannot readily be measured by some common yardstick. Yet our recent experience indicates that the standard quantitative yardstick measurements more often obscure than reveal true performance. The truth is that we know good performance by its look and feel over time because management is much more art than science.

Similarly, the doctrine that government should refrain from industrial policy intervention in the economy because it "cannot pick winners and losers" fails to stand up under close examination. Again, the history of the United States that I've reviewed demonstrates the key role government has played in picking winners like the telegraph, the interchangeable-parts assembly line, aerospace, RCA, the transistor and semiconductor, computers, GPS, the internet, and much more. In my view Steve Jobs is the greatest entrepreneur of our time, having consistently developed groundbreaking new products and industries. But virtually everything Jobs has developed—the mouse, Mac/Windows displays, operating systems, touch screens—began in or received support from a government office. Indeed, in view of the fact that private industry's record of picking winning new products and systems is no better than 10 percent, the record of the government seems to be at least as good and perhaps superior. But that is the wrong way to look at things.

For starters, the government doesn't decide what wins or loses. The market does that. Government makes choices about investing in various lines of endeavor, and it is compelled to do that. The government has a budget that it has to spend. It can't spend on everything. So just like any person or company, it has to make choices about what it spends on. Take, for example, the budget of the National Institutes of Health (NIH) at $30.5 billion. The NIH has to decide whether to spend on biotech research, and if yes, then on which projects. Likewise, the Defense Department has to decide which kinds of new metals or nano-tech processes to develop and which research groups are most likely to get results. The Federal Communications Commission has to decide how to allocate radio bandwidths and for what purposes. None of these choices can be avoided, and whether they are so labeled, they are, in fact, industrial policy decisions. They will shape the structure of industries and of the entire economy.

The truth is that the government cannot avoid industrial policies. The only question is whether such choices and policies will be guided by some overarching strategy and principles or solely by idiosyncrasy and political trade-offs. It is imperative that our thinkers, leaders, and media make clear the necessity of these industrial policy choices.

Laissez-faire globalization is the false god that will be most reluctantly abandoned. Even as experts and pundits have turned on the efficient-markets god and, to some extent, on the tyranny of shareholder value, they have rushed to reaffirm laissez-faire globalization. Any U.S. antidumping or other unfair trade action inevitably elicits stern warnings against Smoot-Hawley protectionism, and every debate over whether to conclude a free trade agreement is said to be a "test" of the government's commitment to free trade. This is strange in view of the general abandonment of the efficient-market notion; because the laissez-faire globalization doctrine also rests on the notion of the automatically optimizing and self-adjusting market and is thus merely a special case of the efficient-market hypothesis. Thus, if the efficient-market hypothesis is flawed, so also must be the laissez-faire globalization notion. And, indeed, we have seen that it is flawed. For one thing, it is often discussed under the rubric of free trade. This discussion has its own difficulties because as we have seen, neoclassical free trade is only fully valid as a doctrine under very narrow and increasingly unrealistic assumptions such as perfect markets, the absence of economies of scale, and international immobility of capital and technology. But even more important is the fact that globalization involves far more than trade.

Indeed, globalization is really more about investment and technology transfer than it is about trade. To imagine that a U.S. policy of laissez-faire globalization will optimize global investment flows and technology transfers for America is truly to be capable like the White Queen in *Alice in Wonderland* of imagining six impossible things before breakfast. Again, our thinkers, leaders, and media must explain and publicize the truth about laissez-faire globalization so that we can invest our energies toward keeping the American promise.

HAVE A VISION: THE GOALS OF COMPETITIVENESS

Successful individuals, organizations, and countries typically have an idea of where they want to go and the milestones they need to reach along the way to getting there. For example, Israel has a vision of its future entitled Israel 2028. China, Singapore, and the EU each have their own versions of such plans. In the past, the United States also had visions and goals—to become a major industrial power, to surpass the British and other Europeans, to assert world technological leadership, and to prevail in the Cold War. But for some time we have been without a real organizing vision or objective.

We have stimulus and monetary policies and programs for the reform of health care and the reduction of greenhouse gas emissions. But there is a big hole in our policy array. How are we going to make a living in the future? Where exactly are the jobs going to come from and what kind of jobs will they be? President Obama has said that America should build autos and make the batteries that may provide the major fuel of the car of the future. That sounds like at least a piece of a vision. Maybe we should revisit the vision put forth by John Young's Council on Competitiveness in 1986. Recall that the council called for the United States to be a competitive country, defined as "a nation which can under free and fair market conditions, produce goods and services that meet the test of international markets while simultaneously maintaining or expanding the real incomes of its citizens."

But of course, more is required. Not only must the president and Congress articulate a vision, there must also be a process for realizing that vision. A long time ago, the congressional Office of Technology Assessment did a spectacular job of assessing the technological capabilities and trends of the major countries. It was abolished in 1995. To replace it now, Congress should establish an Office of Competitive Assessment to provide a nonpartisan, expert view of the relative capabilities, strengths, and weaknesses of the world's leading economies. In addition, the National Economic Council should be charged with developing and articulating the national economic vision and with reviewing legislative and policy proposals with regard to their likely impact on the realization of the vision. For example, does Patent Office policy optimize U.S. innovation and technological leadership? Is the FCC's focus on fostering ever more competition stimulating or hindering increased deployment and speed of the internet?

Save and Invest

The key macroeconomic weaknesses of the United States are overconsumption and low rates of saving and investment. To make the United States more competitive again we must institute tax reform to increase government revenue. Of course, spending must be kept under control, but there really is no way to fix this problem without adjusting taxes. For starters, the tax base needs to be broadened and incentives reversed. At the moment close to half the population is paying little or nothing in income taxes while the top 2 percent of earners will soon be paying a marginal rate, including state and local taxes, of over 50 percent. This is de facto a more progressive tax system than the European systems often criticized by Americans as confiscatory. We must flatten the revenue base. A good place to start would be by greatly restricting the tax deduction on home mortgages. We should limit it to one house per taxpayer and to only a portion of the loan, with wealthy taxpayers and big mortgages getting a smaller eligible portion than poor taxpayers and small loans. Taxing employer-provided health benefits would be another sensible step. But to be really serious, we should be thinking in terms of something revolutionary like a reverse income tax. That's right. Instead of keeping track of your income and paying a percentage of that in tax, you'd keep track of your expenditures and pay a progressive tax on them. That way, the more you spent, the more tax you'd pay. Of course, this tax could be tweaked to avoid burdening the poor, but there would be a minimum tax so that nearly everyone would pay something. Not only would this system generate a lot of tax revenue, but it would both discourage frivolous consumption and strongly encourage saving.

Okay, it might be a little complicated and hard for people to grasp. So let's go to a more practical solution—a value-added tax (VAT). Virtually every major country except the United States has something like this. It is essentially a sales tax that is collected at each step of the production of a product or service. It is easy to collect, difficult to evade, and generates a lot of revenue while encouraging thrift. In addition, the tax is rebated on products and services that are exported. At the moment, foreign producers have a great advantage because their taxes are rebated on their exports to the United States. But because we have no VAT and corporate income taxes are not rebated under international trade law, U.S. exporters get no tax break on their exports. Moreover, when those exports enter a foreign market, the foreign government levies the local VAT upon them. Adoption of the VAT would also enable the abolition of the tax on dividends so that corporate earnings would be taxed only once, as they are in every other major country. In addition, it could enable a reduction of U.S. corporate tax rates, which are now the world's second highest. These measures would, of course, encourage investment and make the United States more competitive as a location for global production and the creation of globally oriented jobs.

Consumer credit should also be much more tightly restricted, and home equity loans for purposes of anything but home improvement should be abolished. I know this may sound tough, but if we want to be competitive, we must understand that countries like Germany and China, who are serious about competing, don't engage in such nonsense. On top of cutting back on easy consumption credit, however, we should do all we can to encourage investment. We could revive the old Kennedy investment tax credit. We might also allow for home equity loans if that money was invested in some productive enterprise. We should get rid of the tax on interest earnings and make saving attractive in every other way possible. Our objective should be to get to a national savings rate of 20 percent of GDP and a national investment rate of about the same. If we did nothing more than this, we would greatly reduce our trade deficit and become much more competitive.

SMART GLOBALIZATION

It is imperative for us to recognize both that free trade is not always win-win and—even more important—that what we have today is not so much a trading system as a globalization system, one much more driven by international investment and technology flows than by trade flows. Further, it is imperative to acknowledge at last that while about half the countries in this system are more or less market driven, the other half are neomercantilist, and that this asymmetry means globalization is not working for the United States at the moment. That doesn't mean it can't work for us or that we should be against globalization. On the contrary, globalization could do great things for us and we should be for it. But we should be for Smart Globalization.

Normalize the Dollar

Negotiations similar to those of the Plaza Agreement of 1985 should be launched by the G20 finance ministers to coordinate a substantial (40 percent to 50 percent) revaluation of a number of managed currencies versus the dollar and the euro over the next two to three years. This revaluation would also have to entail an agreement to halt strategic currency management activities. The long-term objective of this deal would be a reversal of savings and consumption patterns in the United States and Asia. Once the current recession is behind us, Washington should promise to balance the federal budget and work to reform American consumption habits. Key Asian and oil-producing countries and Germany must be induced to increase domestic consumption. China should upgrade its social safety net, and a true liberalization of Japan's housing and consumer credit markets should be encouraged. The oil countries also need to improve their social safety nets and greatly upgrade their infrastructure.

After an initial deal on revaluation of the dollar, the IMF or a new body representing the major currencies (dollar, euro, yen, and yuan) must continue to coordinate policy and manage appropriate currency adjustment. This body's mission must be to push the global system toward balance, and to this end it should effect a transition to a more stable global currency system. One possible option would be a basket of currencies. Indeed, the IMF's Special Drawing Rights (SDRs) already offers such a currency basket made up of a weighted composite of the currencies of all the countries who are members of the IMF. An exchange of dollars for SDRs might be used as a device to get away from excessive reliance on the dollar.

If starting such discussions proves difficult, Washington could jump-start them by declaring a balance of payments emergency or filing complaints against unfair export subsidies under existing articles of the WTO. This would enable the United States to consider imposition of a surcharge on imports until such time as payments came more into reasonable balance. Washington could also call on the WTO to investigate whether tariff-cutting agreements were being undermined by the currency management policies of some countries. It could, in addition, formally call for official consultations by the IMF with certain of its members regarding their currency management practices. This, of course, would be strong medicine, but it would likely stimulate action, and it is all perfectly legal and in keeping with both the rules and spirit of open, rules-based trade.

Trade Deals Pause

No matter what one thinks is the core problem of our exploding trade deficit (e.g., low savings, currency distortions, trade deals, skill deficiencies, the tax code, foreign mercantilism), the reality of America's present condition is that we have no trade strategy and the more trade deals we do, the less competitive we seem to become. Thus, the knee-jerk promotion of more trade agreements before we address the flaws in our system simply exacerbates our problem.

The first step therefore is to do no further harm. The United States should impose a strategic pause on all trade negotiations and postpone approval of agreements with major trading partners until we have a credible strategy for reducing the current account deficit at least to the point at which it is not rising faster than our income (roughly about 2 percent of GDP) and for improving American competitiveness. This does not mean opposition to trade or to trade talks in the near future. But it does mean having a serious strategy before proceeding.

Match Targeted Financial Investment Incentives

As I have explained, many countries use special tax holidays, capital grants, and other financial incentives essentially to bribe global companies to locate factories, labs, and headquarters facilities within their borders. This practice has often resulted in the offshoring of otherwise perfectly competitive U.S.-based production and the loss of good U.S. jobs.

The U.S. government should respond in three ways. First, it should propose negotiations in the WTO to establish common rules to govern these measures. Second, Washington should establish a war chest of its own with which to selectively match the offers of other countries. Finally, the U.S. government should monitor the use of such incentives carefully and file complaints about market distortion with both the WTO and the IMF under the existing antisubsidy rules and the nullification and impairment rules. Such filings would certainly serve to incentivize negotiations.

Reform the WTO

The currently prevailing half–free trade and half-neomercantilist system of globalization must be replaced by what I will call a genuine flat world system in which all participants are truly playing the same game in roughly the same way by the same rules. This, of course, means that the WTO will have to revamp some of its most fundamental standards and that under a new WTO, export-led growth strategies and administrative and cultural protectionism would not be possible. In particular, the classic most favored nation (MFN) and national treatment standards are woefully inadequate. Under the most favored nation system, in which I extend to you the most favorable trade terms that I offer to anyone else, a problem arises when the United States has, say, a 5 percent tariff on autos imported from all countries while Korea has a 10 percent tariff.

In this case, the United States must apply the 5 percent tariff on auto imports from Korea while Korea is acting perfectly in accord with the rules by applying its 10 percent tariff on imported U.S. cars. The treatment is really very unequal and nonreciprocal, but it qualifies as free trade under today's structure. Similarly, the national treatment of an authoritarian country like China means that Yahoo submits to pressure, whereas in the United States it would refuse and file a lawsuit that it would almost certainly win against the government. In this way, national treatment that sounds fair and square can be highly discriminatory and unfair. This must be remedied by the establishment of one WTO standard of treatment.

Further, global rules and procedures must be established to break up and/or regulate both formal and informal cartels and to assure that marketing and distribution channels are open de facto as well as de jure. It will have to be possible to appeal such issues not just to national courts but also to international dispute settlement bodies. In addition, sovereign investment funds and state-controlled or guided enterprises must be subject to international scrutiny and to transparency rules that assure they are operating as real businesses and not as instruments of government welfare systems or foreign policies. I have already called for the establishment of new disciplines on the use of financial investment incentives. Let me just add that the WTO and other international institutions should not simply wait for complaints to be filed but should maintain continuous monitoring of real market developments and move to apply discipline whenever and wherever needed.

A final point here is the system for advising U.S. trade negotiators. At present there is a Trade Policy Advisory Council made up mostly of CEOs from large U.S. corporations. The premise of this council as well as of the Commerce Department's Industry Sector Advisory Councils is that the interests of these "American" companies are coincidental with those of America. But as we have seen, they often are not. Consequently, the council should be redone. CEOs of large global corporations should represent no more than 20 percent of the membership of the council. Instead, the council should include more representatives from small- and medium-sized U.S. producers, labor, and independent trade analysts.

DOMESTIC ISSUES

Rebuild the U.S. Productive Base

General Motors and Chrysler had been failing for a long time, and for a long time our government ignored what was happening to them. In the end, at great cost to all involved, Uncle Sam bailed them out because they were deemed too big to fail in the prevailing crisis circumstances. How much less costly it would have been if there had been an ongoing effort to monitor their performance and to suggest and foster course corrections far in advance of crisis. Or take the green jobs that President Obama says he wants to create. Good idea, but as I noted earlier, just saying so and just spending stimulus funds on buying windmills doesn't do more than create a few temporary construction jobs. Who really knows what it will take to create long-term jobs actually producing windmills and solar panels in the United States? At what stage of development is the relevant technology in the United States? Are the requisite technicians and engineers available? If not, what would be required to obtain them? How much investment are we talking about? And so forth.

The Department of Commerce was created precisely to be on top of this kind of thing. But an important consequence of the rise of the notion that the government is the problem has been the evisceration not only of the Commerce Department's industry analysis and promotion capabilities but also of those capacities throughout the government. They need to be re-created and enhanced. The U.S. government needs to systematically analyze every important industry sector and determine in which ones and under what circumstances U.S.-based production could be competitive in international markets.

If the proper circumstances do not obtain, the government should consider what would be required to create them and whether such re-creation could be done in a way that would produce a positive return for the U.S. economy. For example, the United States is now competitive in software design and development. But such work increasingly requires very high-speed internet availability. We know that Japan, Korea, and others already have less expensive and much higher-speed internet capacity than we do—a fact that poses a challenge to the future competitiveness of the U.S. software industry. President Obama's stimulus program included money for the telecommunications companies to expand and to enhance their high-speed internet networks, yet for various parochial reasons, the companies are not taking the money. Rejection of this funding may be good for the companies, but it is not good for the U.S. economy. We need some national institution to highlight these kinds of issues and get them resolved in ways that will optimize long-term American productivity.

In order to bring all the relevant policy entities under one roof we should establish a Department of Competitiveness, which would include the departments of Commerce, Energy, and Transportation along with the office of the United States Trade Representative, DARPA, and NASA. This department would be among the first rank in the cabinet along with the departments of State, Treasury, and Defense. It should develop a vision of the future United States economy and policies necessary to realize the national vision. It should work closely with industry to achieve and assure broad-based American leadership in key industrial, service, and technology sectors. It should also work closely with and help coordinate state and local economic development efforts and enhance funding for those programs.

Energy Independence

I know a call for energy independence will sound utopian and be dismissed in expert circles as impractical and naïve. Nevertheless, I believe it is a necessary goal. First, because I believe it can be achieved. But second, even if it can't, a much lesser degree of dependence would greatly enhance our competitiveness and our freedom of action in every respect. This is a matter of the highest national security priority and must be treated as such. We have been willing to spend whatever it takes to depose Saddam Hussein and to chase Osama bin Laden around the mountains of Afghanistan and Pakistan. We should be willing to make a similar effort to achieve energy independence.

The fastest, least expensive, and most immediately dramatic results can be achieved through energy conservation. The new Department of Competitiveness should study what other countries do industry by industry and arrange for U.S. industry teams to travel abroad to enable duplication of best energy conservation practices. Japan's Ministry of International Trade and Industry organized these kinds of programs to study American productivity in the 1950s and 1960s, and it worked. Japan caught up. We can catch up as well in energy conservation. Creating new building standards, painting roofs white, creating light-colored asphalt, planting trees and bushes on rooftops, and a thousand other energy-saving steps must all be considered and adopted.

Since 70 percent of U.S. oil imports go to transportation, increasing the fuel efficiency of the U.S. vehicle fleet is imperative. The recently adopted rules call for average miles per gallon of 35 by 2016. This is a step in the right direction, but it will still leave us far short of where the Europeans and the Japanese already are. These standards should be reviewed and revised upward each year to ensure steady pressure for improved performance. A major element of the attack on oil use should be development of lighter, stronger vehicles. The use of advanced composite materials and lightweight steel could double present hybrid car and light truck efficiency while also improving safety and performance without reducing size or comfort. Not only would a vehicle's total extra cost be repaid from fuel savings in two to three years, but the factories to produce the vehicles would be smaller, less expensive, and more energy efficient as well. Further, revenue- and size-neutral "feebates" could be used to induce customers to shift quickly to using these vehicles. The idea is that in each category of vehicle, those below a designated fuel use standard would incur a fee to be added to the sales price. This fee could then fund the rebates awarded to buyers of cars above the designated standard. The Pentagon should, as a huge guzzler of oil and a major driver of technology, take the lead in using smart procurement and targeted technology acquisition to drive development of efficiency and of new energy technologies.

We should launch an all-out effort to develop a full set of alternative energies. Nuclear energy technology is already there and can be deployed immediately. A drawback has been the ten or twelve years it typically takes to install a nuclear plant. France can do it in five or six. By standardizing designs and simplifying and preclearing regulatory requirements, it should be possible for us to match the French or even do better. Wind and solar of both the photovoltaic and heat collection varieties should be vigorously pursued. While ethanol from corn is not a good idea, because it harms food production and is viable only with huge corn subsidies, ethanol produced from sugarcane, switch grass, and other cellulosic fibers is potentially very energy- and cost-effective. We should emphasize its development and commercialization.

Finally, better use of off-peak consumption incentives for electricity usage, fully synchronized traffic lights, on-ramp metering, electronic tolls, a smart grid, and other already known techniques could complete America's declaration of energy independence.

Align Business Interests with America's Interests

Washington must give serious thought to measures that better align the interests of global corporations with those of the United States and its citizens. A good place to start is the corporate charter. Few people realize that corporations are chartered by the state, not by shareholders. Indeed, the state confers enormous benefits on corporations, including most importantly its shareholders' limited liability for losses. Without such limited liability, each shareholder would be responsible for the entirety of any losses the corporation might incur. Such a prospect would severely limit investment in corporations. The state extends this privilege because it believes the corporation will produce benefits for the society. Let me repeat that—for the society. The society includes but is not limited to shareholders. The modern corporation is a creature of the state meant for the benefit of the entire society or what we might call the stakeholders. Since it is a creature of the state, a corporation can be required by the state to act in certain preferred ways or for the attainment of certain preferred objectives.

A problem in the United States is that American corporations are literally chartered by the various state governments rather than by the United States federal government—a situation that produces a race to the bottom in the sense that the states vie with each other to be the incorporating state and get the resulting state revenues. However, the competition is in the form of offering the most nondemanding conditions for incorporation. My home state of Delaware seems to have mostly won the competition, and I am sorry to say that it has done so by demanding little in return for the benefits it confers. As a result, the formal responsibility of a CEO really is primarily to the shareholders—the stakeholders be damned. In virtually every other country in the world, corporations are chartered nationally and there are quid pro quos in terms of organization, responsibility, and performance.

Germany is the best example. There, the corporate charter establishes a supervisory board on which stakeholders representing labor, shareholders, the community, and other groups serve by overseeing the company's management and its broad strategic goals. Under this board is a second board called the management board which consists of the company's top managers and is responsible for development and execution of the business plans and operations. This structure is very effective in ensuring both attention to stakeholder interests and alignment with broad national interests. Many German companies are quite global, but they also feel an obligation to keep the interests of Germany in mind. Other countries, such as Japan, France, Finland, and Singapore, have similar arrangements. The United States needs to have them, too. Congress should compel all corporations operating in the United States to be chartered by the federal government. Whether in addition to or in place of individual state charters, there needs to be a federal charter. And this charter would establish a board structure and membership that would compel serious consideration of stakeholder interests while also enabling effective pursuit of profit and shareholder interests—just as German and Japanese companies manage to do while remaining quite competitive at the same time.

In addition to the earlier mentioned war chest for matching foreign investment, the U.S. government should offer a tax credit, like the R&D tax credit for investment that results in the creation of certain categories of desired jobs or certain desired levels of production. At the same time, the burden of social costs must be relieved. In virtually all other major countries, health care insurance is provided by the national government, not by corporate employers. European, Japanese, and Chinese companies do not bear a cost comparable with that for the health care benefits provided by U.S. corporations. Therefore, to offset this competitive disadvantage, the U.S. government should provide a compensating tax credit or tax rate reduction or some other equivalent payment. In short, every effort must be made to make the United States a desirable location for investment by both American-based and foreign companies.

By the same token, federal support of R&D and innovation should be at least doubled. But in the present global economy, simply providing funds for companies, universities, and research centers can easily be counterproductive, because the resulting products and processes are increasingly likely to be produced in other countries. Not only have American firms become global, but so have universities, with partnerships and subsidiaries around the world. Harvard, for example, now refers to itself as a "world university." In the global economy, ideas cannot and should not be stopped at the border. By their very nature, research and innovation need to be free of bureaucratic restraints. But we also need government policies that increase the chances that research and development will be channeled to production in the United States. Thus, if government is funding research, there should be some obligation for domestic commercialization of whatever results are produced.

Save the Environment, but Not at Producer Expense

It is essential that the United States lead an urgent effort to reduce greenhouse gas emissions and mitigate global warming. Sir Nicholas Stern has called global climate change history's greatest case of market failure. Only a global regulatory structure will produce a comprehensive shift to a clean energy path. The U.S. government has debated a cap and trade system similar to that of the EU, and it is possible that something like this may eventually emerge as a global regime. Our challenge is to achieve a global deal that will include developing countries like China and India. On the one hand, we must make every effort to accommodate their legitimate concern over any deal that might slow down their economic development. On the other hand, if they or any other countries opt out of a deal, there is the risk that many producers will move their operations to locations with lax carbon emission regulations. To avoid that happening, the U.S. government and others should consider either imposing a carbon surcharge on imports from those locations or providing offsetting subsidies to producers. The WTO has already indicated that a surcharge would, in principle, be perfectly acceptable under WTO rules.

Training and Education

More and better education is often prescribed as the main medicine for our competitiveness ills. Actually, it is not. But it is important and is an area in which, as I noted earlier, we are doing poorly. Why? The analysis and answers would fill several more books. Indeed, they already have. But there are four major elements that I want to emphasize here. First is the simple matter of the length of the school year. The American school year is at least a month shorter than that of any other well-educated country. Their kids get ahead of our kids for the simple reason that they spend more time in school. We need to get rid of the long summer vacation, which is a relic of the farming economy of the nineteenth century. Second, we need to pay teachers like professionals—not on the level of investment bankers, but certainly so that their income is competitive with that of ordinary accountants and lawyers. Third, we need to be serious about discipline in classrooms and permanently remove students who are disruptive and disrespectful. Finally, we need to have meaningful national curricula requirements and standards.

Many countries that have been most successful in the global economy—Sweden, the Netherlands, Denmark, Germany, Japan—have demonstrated that strong social safety nets combined with extensive worker training and incentives for reemployment can greatly enhance competitiveness. In Denmark's "Flexicurity" system, for example, workers in companies or factories suffering lost competitiveness receive retraining and a salary that begins at what they had been earning and gradually declines over time. This system provides plenty of security during a reasonable retraining period but also includes an eventual strong incentive for a person to actually find a new job. It seems to work in Denmark, a country with a high standard of living that is always ranked near the top of the competitiveness standings and that has very low unemployment. Maybe it would work in the United States as well.

One final issue American educators will have to begin addressing is the percentage of the student body coming from abroad. As I mentioned earlier, Harvard calls itself a "world university." Well and good, but would that "world university" really be viable with a majority of non-American students? If not, what is the optimum level? Given the size of the world population and the number of highly talented non-Americans, it would be easy to fill all the classes with foreigners. But would it be wise?

POLITICAL REFORM

Saving the best—or, more likely, the most dangerous and difficult to achieve—for last, let's talk politics, specifically two aspects of it: fair representation and financing. As a result of the gerrymandering of congressional districts, it is generally agreed by political analysts that nearly 400 of the 435 seats in the U.S. House of Representatives are safe seats, meaning that candidates from the opposite party have no chance of winning them. This situation makes for increasingly irresponsible politics because it fosters the overrepresentation of the so-called base of each party while dampening representation by the more moderate elements. It also greatly enhances the power of money and of the incumbent, and means that it is the primary, rather than the general election that is the decisive one. And in the primary, money really talks since the parties like to pick candidates with money or who can raise money. So the competition is really for the money, and the money is mainly in the hands of the big corporations, banks, and law firms. Hence, the competition is very much about who can garner the most big money support, and of course, the incumbent has a great advantage in this regard.

As a result, the House of Representatives is very sensitive to corporate lobbies. In the Senate, of course, the elections are always state-wide and can't be gerrymandered, but the campaigns are really, really expensive. So again, big money talks loudly, and not necessarily in the best interest of our country as a whole. This is not a healthy situation.

The solution involves two major changes. The first is to drastically overhaul the procedures for congressional districting. The Iowa system, whereby the state is carved into a series of essentially equal, symmetrical squares regardless of whether Republicans or Democrats inhabit them, should be adopted nationwide. The second is to reduce greatly the role of money in our political process. Although this has been discussed ad nauseam in the past, it's even truer today because much of the money increasingly doesn't even represent the voice of truly American interests. The way to do this is to adopt the Canadian practice under which only natural persons can make political donations, with, of course, limits on their amount. Further, we need to impose limits on the length of the campaign seasons and on the amounts of money that can be spent.

I know this seems like a lot of things to change in dramatic ways. But we must face up to the *honne,* the actual reality, of our situation, to the fact that we are not now competitive and not now meeting our obligations to the future. We must tell Craig Barrett how his—and our—grandchildren are going to earn a decent living. Beyond that we must answer the question of whether America is going to continue to be an example and a source of hope for the world or just another in a long line of faded powers and crumbling empires. We cannot respond positively by continuing in the conventional way with the conventional attitudes and policies. We must think and act outside the box. We must dispense with doctrines and affirm the pragmatism and sense of shared destiny that made America great.

Acknowledgments

I could not have written this book without the help of the hundreds of people who kindly talked with me and shared their insights and opinions. The list is too long to mention each person by name, but I wish to thank all who shared their time and thoughts in interviews and discussions. I also deeply appreciate those who record the events of our time in the first draft of history.

A number of people worked long and tirelessly in researching and helping to organize the manuscript. In particular, I am deeply indebted to longtime ESI research director and vice president Ulrika ("Riki") Swanson and to Kate Heidinger, who oversaw and coordinated the full research effort and intern army. I also want to thank Bob Cohen, my longtime college friend who can find technology data where no one else can. I am indebted to my longtime helper Gladys Greaves for her administrative support and to my indefatigable and creative intern Yana Yushkina and our research assistants Megan Brimmer, David Foster, and David Fritz. I also wish to thank my good friend and constant consultant on Asian affairs, Hiromi Murakami. My neighbor Henry Morton read part of the manuscript and was of invaluable assistance on the energy issue. Nabor Carillo also contributed valuable research assistance.

I want to thank former Sloan Foundation president and former IBM chief scientist and my longtime friend, Ralph Gomory, for his support and especially for his research on international trade under conditions of imperfect competition and cross-border investment. I also want to thank his colleague Professor Willam Baumol. Together they have done groundbreaking work that has highlighted the key weaknesses of our conventional international economic theory and policies. In this same regard, I am indebted to Silicon Valley entrepreneur and corporate director Richard Elkus, whose book, *Winner Take All,* identifies the critical importance of the linkages typically overlooked by conventional economic analysis. I must thank Nucor CEO Dan Dimicco for his insights on globalization, and I am indebted to InterMedia Partners VII managing partner Leo Hindery for his constant encouragement and for sharing his experiences and views of U.S. corporate thinking and of U.S. policymaking. Intel's former chairmen Andy Grove and Craig Barrett have generously shared their views and experiences over the years and I am indebted to them for their insights and their critique of my own thinking. Former Kodak chairman and CEO George Fisher generously shared his views and time as well.

Former Harvard Business School professor Bruce Scott provided good advice and insights on the role of the corporations as did my former boss Paul Schregel. I am also indebted to former Intel vice president Jim Jarrett as well as to my colleague of many years Paula Stern. Fellow globalization policy veterans Dana Marshall, Pat Mulloy, Kent Hughes, Mike Wessel, Congressman Sandy Levin, Senators Jeff Bingaman and Sherrod Brown, Bob Cassidy, Ira Shapiro, Charlene Barshefsky, Paul O'Day, Rob Wescott, and Arnie Nachmanoff all provided enthusiastic encouragement and gave generously of their time, ideas, and experience.

I must also thank Professor Chalmers Johnson for his mentoring and guidance over many years, and I am grateful to my sometimes business partner Claude Smadja for his unique understanding of globalization. Longtime Asia hand and Global Sources founder and chairman Merle Hinrichs has likewise provided encouragement and unusual insights into both globalization and the evolution of China.

While all of these people gave generously of their time and of their insights and understanding, the responsibility for the book and its statements is entirely my own.

Last, but very far from least, I must thank my muse, advisor, critic, editor, researcher, confidant, comforter, constant companion, best friend, and wife, Carol Ann Prestowitz.

Notes

Introduction: Loads of Dung

1 **Rome lived upon:** Winwood Reade, *The Martyrdom of Man* (New York: Asa K Butts & Co., 1874), 478.

Chapter 1: The Real State of America

14 **Indeed, former Federal Reserve Chairman:** "Greenspan Says Dollar Now Sharing Stage with Euro," *Reuters,* October 26, 2006.

14 **On the other hand:** "UN panel calls for new global reserve, credit systems to avert future crises," *UN News Centre,* September 10, 2009, http://www.un.org/apps/news/story.asp?NewsID=32020.

20 **As for productivity growth:** Dean Baker and David Rosnick, "Usable Productivity," *Growth in the United States: An International Comparison, 1980–2005,* Center for Economic and Policy Research, June 2007.

21 **OECD countries:** "Income Distribution—Inequality," *OECD Stat Extracts,* http://stats.oecd.org/Index.aspx?QueryId=11112&QueryType=View.

22 **High-speed rail:** Randy James, "A Brief History Of: High-Speed Rail," *Time,* April 20, 2009; Toh Han Shih, "Mainland Set for Train Deals in U.S. and Britain; Country's High-Speed Rail technology Gains Recognition Abroad," *South China Morning Post,* October 24, 2009.

23 **Its broadband penetration:** "2008 ITIF Broadband Rankings," Information Technology and Innovation Foundation, http://www.itif.org/files/2008BBRankings.pdf.

23 **The United States ranks:** Clyde Prestowitz, *America's Technology Future at Risk: Broadband and Investment Strategies to Refire Innovation* (Washington: Economic Strategy Institute, 2006), vi.

25 **The total five-year investment:** American Society of Civil Engineers, *Report Card for America's Infrastructure,* March 25, 2009, http://www.infrastructurereportcard.org/sites/default/files/RC2009_full_report.pdf.

25 **According to the CIA:** "Country Comparison: Life Expectancy at Birth,"

CIA, The World Factbook, https://www.cia.gov/library/publications/the-world-factbook/rankorder/2102rank.html.

25 **Singapore, for example:** *OECD Health Data 2009: Statistics and Indicators for 30 Countries* (OECD Publishing, 2009).

26 **manufacturing accounts for:** EarthTrends/World Resources Institute, "Economics, Business, and the Environment—GDP: Percent GDP from Manufacturing," http://earthtrends.wri.org/text/economics-business/variable-217.html.

26 **the relative shrinkage:** Richard McCormack, "The Plight of Manufacturing," in *Manufacturing a Better Future for America,* Richard McCormack, ed. (Washington: Alliance for American Manufacturing, 2009), 11.

26 **the American steel industry:** McCormack, "The Plight of Manufacturing," 6.

27 **constructed in the United States:** Ibid., 7.

28 **Porter insisted: "We:** Richard McCormack, "Council on Competitiveness Says U.S. Has Little to Fear But Fear Itself; By Most Measures, U.S. Is Way Ahead of Global Competitors," *Manufacturing & Technology News,* November 30, 2006.

28 **that had grown:** Bureau of Economic Analysis, U.S. Department of Commerce, "Trade in Goods and Services, 1992–Present," http://www.bea.gov/international/index.htm#trade.

29 **Thirty percent were being built:** McCormack, "The Plight of Manufacturing," 7.

29 **By 2004, that was down:** "The U.S. Chip Industry," Semiconductor Industry Association, http://www.choosetocompete.org/us_chip_industry.html.

29 **Germany's Q-Cells:** "United States Is a Bit Player in the Fast-Growing Global Solar Industry," *Manufacturing and Technology News,* September 20, 2009.

29 **in the wind energy industry:** Jay Yarow, "GE Gaining Market Share in Wind Turbine Business," *The Business Insider,* March 25, 2009.

29 **As for batteries:** Matthew L. Wald, "$2 Billion in Grants to Bolster U.S. Manufacturing of Parts for Electric Cars," *The New York Times,* August 5, 2009.

30 **Defense Science Board:** McCormack, "The Plight of Manufacturing," 56.

30 **Pentagon's Advisory Group:** President's Council of Advisors on Science and Technology, *Sustaining the Nation's Innovation Ecosystems, Information Technology Manufacturing and Competitiveness,* 2004, http://www.ostp.gov/pdf/finalpcastitmanuf_reportpackage.pdf.

30 **U.S. technological leadership:** McCormack, "The Plight of Manufacturing," 56.

30 **"industry is coming unglued":** "$600 Million Over 10 Years for IBM's 'Trusted Foundry'; Chip Industry's Shift Overseas Elicits National Security Agency, Defense Department Response," *Manufacturing and Technology News*, February 3, 2004.

31 **PCAST warned:** President's Council of Advisors on Science and Technology, *Sustaining the Nation's Innovation Ecosystems*, 2004.

31 **While it is true:** U.S. Census Bureau, "Annual 2009 Trade Highlights," http://www.census.gov/foreign-trade/statistics/highlights/annual.html

32 **could be off-shored over the next few years:** Alan S. Blinder, "How Many U.S. Jobs Might Be Offshorable?" CEPS Working Paper No. 142, March 2007.

32 **profit margins of more:** Ron Hira, "The Globalization of Research, Development and Innovation," in McCormack, ed., *Manufacturing a Better Future for America*, 170.

32 **increasing its Indian head count:** Ibid., 169.

32 **top twenty universities:** *Academic Ranking of World Universities—2009*, http://www.arwu.org/ARWU2009.jsp.

33 **doctoral degrees:** Gregory Tassey, *The Technology Imperative* (Cheltenham, UK: Edward Elgar Publishing, 2007), 78.

33 **slipped to zero:** National Center for Education Statistics, *Pursuing Excellence: Comparisons of International Eighth Grade Mathematics and Science Achievement from a U.S. Perspective, 1995 and 1999*, December 2003.

33 **R&D intensity:** *OECD Science, Technology and Industry Outlook 2008* (OECD Publishing, 2008), 24, figure 1.6.

35 **China now spends:** Tassey, *The Technology Imperative*, 131.

36 **EU is now on track:** Ibid., 79.

39 **gross inflow:** C. Fred Bergsten, "Bush Needs to Make a Decisive Change of Course," *Financial Times*, December 14, 2004, http://www.iie.com/publications/opeds/oped.cfm?ResearchID=237.

44 **As Kennedy puts it:** Paul Kennedy, *The Rise and Fall of the Great Powers: Economic Change and Conflict from 1500–2000* (New York: Random House, 1987).

Chapter 2: The Real Story of How America Got Rich

47 **address to Parliament:** Ha-Joon Chang, *Bad Samaritans: The Myth of Free Trade and the Secret History of Capitalism* (New York: Bloomsbury Press, 2008), 44.

48 **Between 1700 and 1750:** E. J. Hobsbawm, *Industry and Empire: From 1750 to the Present Day* (London: Penguin, 1990), 48.

48 "country which succeeded in monopolizing": Ibid.
50 "the friendship of Europe": Alfred E. Eckes, Jr., *Opening America's Market: U.S. Foreign Trade Policy Since 1776* (Chapel Hill: University of North Carolina Press, 1995), 2.
51 "free people ought": Ibid., 15.
51 "the produce and fabrics of America": Ibid.
52 "the system of perfect liberty": Ibid., 16.
53 Jefferson did an about-face: Ibid., 19.
53 "purchasing nothing foreign": Ibid.
53 Monroe called for more tariff increases: Ibid., 20.
54 Andrew Jackson commented: Ibid.
54 Daniel Raymond: Ibid., 17.
54 American System: Ibid., 21.
55 "abandonment of the protective policy": Ibid., 30.
55 Theodore Roosevelt emphasized: Ibid.
55 grants totaling 21 million acres: Timothy J. Botti, *Envy of the World: A History of the U.S. Economy and Big Business* (New York: Algora Publishing, 2006), 92.
56 unprecedented economic growth: Louis D. Johnston and Samuel H. Williamson, "What Was the U.S. GDP Then?" *Measuring Worth,* http://www.measuringworth.org/usgdp/.
59 America was laying track: Hobsbawm, *Industry and Empire,* 115.
59 employed 800,000 men: Richard Franklin Bensel, *The Political Economy of American Industrialization, 1877–1900* (Cambridge, England: Cambridge University Press, 2000), 295.
60 nearly half the world's steel: Hobsbawm, *Industry and Empire,* diagram 24.
60 total manufacturing: Aaron L. Friedberg, *The Weary Titan: Britain and the Experience of Relative Decline, 1895–1905* (Princeton: Princeton University Press, 1989), 26; Kennedy, *The Rise and Fall of the Great Powers,* 202.
60 advantages in economies of scale: Eckes, *Opening America's Market,* 50–51.
60 U.S. per capita income: Alfred E. Eckes, Jr., and Thomas W. Zeiler, *Globalization and the American Century* (New York: Cambridge University Press, 2003), chart A1.
61 United States had a trade surplus: Eckes, *Opening America's Market,* 51.
61 English *Daily Mail:* Eckes and Zeiler, *Globalization and the American Century,* 19.
61 "British soldiers and sailors": Ibid., 20.
62 share of total British imports: Eckes, *Opening America's Market,* 51.

62 **"Suppose an industry"**: Kennedy, *The Rise and Fall of the Great Powers,* 228–229.

63 **progression of coal production:** Friedberg, *The Weary Titan,* 56.

63 **virtual monopoly on global shipping:** Hobsbawm, *Industry and Empire,* 145.

64 **the British economy:** Ibid., 118, 152–153.

65 **"The inhabitant of London":** John Maynard Keynes, *Economic Consequences of the Peace* (New York: Harcourt, Brace and Howe, 1920), 11.

66 **The Great War:** Barry Eichengreen, "The Inter-War Economy in a European Mirror," in *The Economic History of Britain Since 1700, Volume 2: 1860–1939,* Roderick Floud and Deirdre McCloskey, eds. (Cambridge, UK: University of Cambridge Press, 1994), 232.

66 **British cotton goods production:** Hobsbawm, *Industry and Empire,* 207.

67 **Wilson had emphasized:** Eckes and Zeiler, *Globalization and the American Century,* 45.

68 **The army also placed orders:** Robert Cohen, *Picking Winners and Losers* (Washington: Economic Strategy Institute), 16.

68 **Wilson began to perceive that:** Eckes and Zeiler, *Globalization and the American Century,* 50.

69 **Owen Young:** Ibid., 51.

70 **Europe plus Japan combined:** Kennedy, *The Rise and Fall of the Great Powers,* 282.

70 **U.S. GDP fell by half:** Ibid., 329.

72 **War Production Board and the Board of Economic Warfare:** Eckes and Zeiler, *Globalization and the American Century,* 109.

72 **owned 70 percent of the world's gold:** "Money Matters: An IMF Exhibit—The Importance of Global Cooperation: Destruction and Reconstruction (1945–1958)," *International Monetary Fund,* http://www.imf .org/external/np/exr/center/mm/eng/mm_dr_01.htm.

72 **leading world creditor:** Barry Eichengreen, *Til Debt Do Us Part: The U.S. Capital Market and Foreign Lending, 1920–1955* (NBER Working Papers 2394, 1989), 59, table 8.

72 **current account surplus:** William H. Branson, Herbert Giersch, and Peter G. Peterson, *Trends in U.S. International Trade and Investment Since World War II* (NBER Working Papers 0469, 1981), 210, table 3.19.

Chapter 3: America Changes Course

75 **"right to have cuffs":** Lizabeth Cohen, *A Consumers' Republic: The Politics of Mass Consumption in Postwar America* (New York: Knopf, 2003), 3.

75 **1944 GI Bill:** Ibid., 190.

75 **"prosperity of this nation":** Ibid., 55.

75 **explosion of consumer credit:** Ibid., 123.

75 **thrift had become:** Ibid., 121.

75 **ratio of credit:** Ibid., 281.

76 **IBM was an even more significant case:** Clyde Prestowitz, *Three Billion New Capitalists: The Global Shift of Wealth and Power to the East* (New York: Basic Books, 2005), 108.

82 **David Rockefeller invoked the specter:** David Rockefeller, "Present at the Trade Wars," *The New York Times,* September 21, 2009, A23.

89 **MITI official:** Eckes, *Opening America's Market,* 171.

89 **"necessary to diversify":** Ibid.

90 **U.S. GDP and productivity grew:** Federal Reserve Board, *Flow of Funds Accounts of the United States: Annual Flows and Outstandings, 1945–1954,* December 10, 2009, http://www.federalreserve.gov/releases/z1/Current/annuals/a1945–1954.pdf; see also *Flow of Funds Accounts of the United States: Annual Flows and Outstandings, 1965–1974,* December 10, 2009, http://www.federalreserve.gov/releases/z1/Current/annuals/a1965–1974.pdf.

90 **Home ownership:** U.S. Census Bureau, "Historical Census of Housing Tables: Homeownership," December 2, 2004, http://www.census.gov/hhes/www/housing/census/historic/owner.html.

90 **Manufacturing was the driving force:** Bureau of Economic Analysis, U.S. Department of Commerce, "Gross Domestic Product by Industry Accounts, 1947–2008," http://www.bea.gov/industry/gpotables/gpo_list.cfm?anon=261151&registered=0.

90 **federal budget deficit:** Executive Office of the President of the United States, "Historical Tables: Budget of the United States Government, Fiscal Year 2008," http://www.gpoaccess.gov/usbudget/fy08/pdf/hist.pdf.

90 **Geneva Round of GATT negotiations:** Eckes, *Opening America's Market,* 161.

91 **"a thin agreement":** Ibid.

91 **"the U.S. trade surplus is a serious problem":** Ibid., 158.

91 **President's Advisory Board for Mutual Security:** Ibid.

91 **Former president Hoover feared in 1953:** Ibid., 168.

91 **"problems of local industry":** Ibid., 167.

92 **forget about the U.S. market:** Clyde Prestowitz, *Rogue Nation: American Unilateralism and the Failure of Good Intentions* (New York: Basic Books, 2004), 67.

92 **import cars from America:** Eckes, *Opening America's Market,* 171.

92 **sales of Germany's Volkswagen Beetle:** William Beaver, "Volkswagen's

American Assembly Plant: *Fahrvergnugen* Was Not Enough," *Business Horizons*, November–December 1992, http://findarticles.com/p/articles/mi_m1038/is_n6_v35/ai_13246858/.

92 the television market: "Number of TV households in America," *Television History—The First 75 Years*, http://www.tvhistory.tv/Annual_TV _Households_50–78.jpg.

92 debate on international trade policy: Eckes, *Opening America's Market*, 177.

93 "acid test": Ibid.

93 "organizing its own decline": Ibid., 179.

94 half its monetary gold: Eckes and Zeiler, *Globalization and the American Century*, 169.

94 It further warned: Eckes, *Opening America's Market*, 214.

97 television sets in 1960: Clyde Prestowitz, *Trading Places: How We Are Giving Our Future to Japan and How to Reclaim It* (New York: Basic Books, 1989), 201.

97 memory chips: Ibid., 45.

104 household debt was also rising: Botti, *Envy of the World*, 502.

109 General Electric acquired RCA: Alfred D. Chandler, Jr., *Inventing the Electronic Century: The Epic Story of the Consumer Electronics and Computer Science Industries* (New York: Free Press, 2001), 45.

110 On top of all that: Botti, *Envy of the World*, 189.

111 household liabilities: Ibid., 442.

Chapter 4: Goldilocks and Bubbles: The Faith in Efficient Markets

119 supposed watchdog: Alan Greenspan, *The Age of Turbulence: Adventures in a New World* (New York: Penguin Press, 2007), 370–373.

122 CMO bubble deflated: Charles R. Morris, *The Two Trillion Dollar Meltdown: Easy Money, High Rollers, and the Great Credit Crash* (New York: Perseus Books, 2008), 43.

122 positions in derivatives: Ibid., 54.

122 "stock prices were beginning": Greenspan, *The Age of Turbulence*, 174–175.

124 George Soros published: George Soros, "The Capitalist Threat," *The Atlantic*, Volume 279, No. 2, February 1997, 45–58.

125 GDP per capita fell: Asian Development Bank, "Key Indicators of Developing Asian and Pacific Countries," http://www.adb.org/Documents/Books/Key_Indicators/2001/rt11_ki2001.xls

127 Born warned that: Katrina vanden Heuvel, "The Woman Greenspan, Rubin & Summers Silenced," *The Nation*, October 9, 2008, http://www

.thenation.com/blogs/edcut/370925/the_woman_greenspan_rubin_sum
mers_silenced.

128 **In hearings about the measure:** Joint Hearing Before the Committee on Agriculture, Nutrition, and Forestry, United States Senate, and
the Committee on Banking, Housing, and Urban Affairs, 106th Congress, Second Session, On S.2697—The Commodity Futures Modern-
ization Act of 2000, June 21, 2000, http://ftp.resource.org/gpo.gov/
hearings/106s/70514.pdf.

130 **Nearly 21 million jobs:** "Job Growth in the 1990s: A Retrospect,"
Monthly Labor Review, Bureau of Labor Statistics, December 2000,
http://www.bls.gov/opub/mlr/2000/12/art1full.pdf.

131 **household savings:** Federal Reserve Board, *Flow of Funds Accounts of
the United States: Flows and Outstandings, Third Quarter 2002,* December 5, 2002, http://www.federalreserve.gov/releases/z1/20021205/z1
.pdf.

131 **Walmart:** Robert E. Scott, "The Wal-Mart Effect: Its Chinese Imports
Have Displaced Nearly 200,000 U.S. Jobs," *EPI Issue Brief #235,* http://
www.epi.org/publications/entry/ib235/.

132 **jumped in to clean up the mess:** Federal Reserve Board, "Open Market
Operations," http://www.federalreserve.gov/fomc/fundsrate.htm.

132 **home ownership rose:** "Census Bureau Reports on Residential Vacan-
cies and Homeownership," *U.S. Census Bureau News,* http://www.census
.gov/hhes/www/housing/hvs/qtr109/files/q109press.pdf.

132 **unemployment fell:** Bureau of Labor Statistics, "Labor Force Statistics
From the Current Population Survey," http://www.bls.gov/cps/tables.htm.

132 **housing accounted for:** John H. Makin, "Housing and Economic Recessions," American Enterprise Institute, November 2006, http://www.aei
.org/outlook/25209; Daniel Gross, "As the McMansions Go, So Goes
Job Growth," *The New York Times,* November 20, 2005, http://www
.nytimes.com/2005/11/20/business/yourmoney/20view.html.

133 **attributed the success of:** Greenspan, *The Age of Turbulence,* 366.

137 **Gary Saxonhouse:** Gary R. Saxonhouse, "What Does Japanese Trade
Structure Tell Us About Japanese Trade Policy?" *Journal of Economic
Perspectives* 7, no. 3 (Summer 1993): 21–43.

137 **Ha-Joon Chang explains:** Chang, *Bad Samaritans.*

138 **IIE's Mark Noland and:** Marcus Noland and Howard Pack, *The East
Asian Industrial Policy Experience: Implications for the Middle East,*
Institute for International Economics Working Paper 05–14 (December
2005); Marcus Noland and Howard Pack, "Industrial Policies in Japan,
Korea, and Taiwan," *Industrial Policy in an Era of Globalization* (Wash-
ington: Institute for International Economics), 2003.

139 **Japan's Lost Decade:** Baker and Rosnick, "Usable Productivity."

139 **life expectancy:** "Country Comparison: Life Expectancy at Birth," CIA, The World Factbook.

140 **McKinsey:** Manjeet Kripalani and Pete Engardio, "Rise of India," *BusinessWeek*, December 8, 2003; Global Insight, *Offshore IT Outsourcing and the U.S. Economy*, March 2004, http://www.globalinsight.com/MultiClientStudy/MultiClientStudyDetail846.htm.

141 **Lieberthal promised:** "Opening Trade," *PBS NewsHour*, November 15, 1999, http://www.pbs.org/newshour/bb/asia/july–dec99/wto_11–15.html.

141 **Peterson Institute:** Gary Clyde Hufbauer and Daniel H. Rosen, "American Access to China's Market: The Congressional Vote on PNTR," *International Economics Policy Briefs*, Number 00-3 (April 2000), http://www.iie.com/publications/pb/pb00-3.pdf.

142 **deficit ballooned:** Bureau of Economic Analysis, U.S. Department of Commerce, "Trade in Goods and Services, 1992–Present," http://www.bea.gov/international/index.htm#trade.

Chapter 5: The Irrationality of the Rational

144 **headline in the *New York Times*:** Steve Friess, "A Casino Rises in the Place of a Fallen Steel Giant," *The New York Times*, May 23, 2009, A13.

144 **1936 comment:** John Maynard Keynes, *General Theory of Employment, Interest and Money* (London: Macmillan and Co., 1964), 159.

146 **infamous injunction:** Herbert Hoover, *Memoirs* (London: Hollis and Carter, 1952), 30.

149 **magnitudes of the random price movements:** George Cooper, *The Origin of Financial Crises: Central Banks, Credit Bubbles, and the Efficient Market Fallacy* (New York: Vintage, 2008), 26.

151 **mathematical expressions:** Gerard Debreu, "The Mathematization of Economic Theory, March 1991," *American Economic Review* 81(1) (March 1991): 1–7.

152 **Psychological research:** Daniel Kahneman and Richard H. Thaler, "Economic Analysis and the Psychology of Utility: Applications to Compensation Policy," *American Economic Review* 81(2) (May 1991): 341–346.

152 **David Dreman:** David Dreman and Michael A. Berry, "Analyst Forecasting Errors and Their Implications for Security Analysis," *Financial Analysts Journal* 51(3) (May/June 1995): 30–41.

153 **numerous writings over the years:** George Soros, *The New Paradigm for Financial Markets: The Credit Crisis of 2008 and What It Means* (Philadelphia: Public Affairs, 2008), 55.

154 **Benoit Mandelbrot:** Benoit Mandelbrot and Richard L. Hudson, *The (Mis)behavior of Markets: A Fractal View of Risk, Ruin & Reward* (New York: Basic Books, 2004).

155 **Robert Lucas:** Robert Lucas, "Robert Lucas on Economics," *The Economist,* August 6, 2009.

158 **Johann Hari:** Johann Hari, "Has Market Fundamentalism Had Its Day?" *The Independent,* March 20, 2008, 46.

158 **Barry Eichengreen:** Barry Eichengreen, "The Last Temptation of Risk," *The National Interest,* May/June 2009, http://www.nationalinterest.org/Article.aspx?id=21274.

158 **Robert Shiller:** Robert Shiller, "Failure to Control the Animal Spirits," *The Financial Times,* March 8, 2009.

Chapter 6: Orthodox Free Trade: God's Diplomacy

168 **"free trade is not passé":** Paul R. Krugman, "Is Free Trade Passé?" *Journal of Economic Perspectives* 1, no. 2 (Fall 1987): 131–144.

173 **"Ricardo was wrong":** James Galbraith, *The Predator State: How Conservatives Abandoned the Free Market and Why Liberals Should Too* (New York: Free Press, 2009), 70.

174 **a nation may well decide:** Chang, *Bad Samaritans,* 81.

175 **the example of Mongolia:** Erik S. Reinert, *How Rich Countries Got Rich . . . And Why Poor Countries Stay Poor* (Philadelphia: Public Affairs, 2008), 173.

175 **a modicum of prosperity:** Ibid., 15.

179 **judiciously intervene:** James A. Brander, "Rationales for Strategic Trade and Industrial Policy," in Paul Krugman, ed., *Strategic Trade Policy and the New International Economics* (Cambridge, Mass.: MIT Press, 1986), 23.

179 **article in the fall of 1987:** Krugman, "Is Free Trade Passé?"

180 **Laura Tyson insisted:** Laura D'Andrea Tyson, *Who's Bashing Whom: Trade Conflict in High Technology Industries* (Washington: International Institute of Economics, 1993), 32.

183 **undergraduate economics students:** Paul Krugman, *Pop Internationalism* (Cambridge, Mass.: MIT Press, 1996), 5.

185 **gains from trade liberalization:** Scott C. Bradford, Paul L.E. Grieco, and Gary Clyde Hufbauer, "The Payoff to America from Global Integration," in *The United States and the World Economy: Foreign Economic Policy for the Next Decade,* C. Fred Bergsten and the International Institute for Economics (Washington, D.C.: Peterson Institute for International Economics, 2005), 68.

186 **Peterson Institute analysis:** Gary Clyde Hufbauer and Jeffrey J. Schott, *NAFTA Revisited: Achievements and Challenges* (Washington, D.C.: International Institute of Economics, 2005).

187 **globalization has cost the United States:** Peter Morici, "Girding for a Depression: Another 633,000 Jobs Lost in March," Centre for Research on Globalization, April 4, 2009, http://www.globalresearch.ca/index .php?context=va&aid=13059.

192 **acknowledged that globalization:** Lawrence Summers, "The Global Consensus on Trade Is Unraveling," *Financial Times*, August 25, 2008, http:// www.ft.com/cms/s/0/aaee141a-723c-11dd-a44a-0000779fd18c.html.

Chapter 7: Companies Without a Country

193 **told the gathered analysts:** Francesco Guerrera, "Welch Rues Short-Term Profit 'Obsession,' " *Financial Times*, March 12, 2009.

193 **GE's market capitalization:** Shawn Langlois, "Exxon's Market Cap Erupts Past $500 billion," *MarketWatch*, July 12, 2007, http://www .marketwatch.com/story/exxons-market-cap-erupts-past-500-billion.

193 **411,000 workers:** Jack Welch, *Jack: Straight from the Gut* (New York: Warner Books, 2001), 129.

194 **"A corporation's responsibilities":** George A. Steiner and John F. Steiner, *Business, Government, and Society: A Managerial Perspective, Text, and Cases* (New York: McGraw-Hill, 2006), 122.

199 **sounded a different note:** Sumantra Ghosal, "Bad Management Theories Are Destroying Good Management Practices," *Academy of Management Learning & Education* 4, no. 1 (March 2005): 75–91.

199 **Jensen propagated:** Michael C. Jensen and William H. Meckling, "Theory of the Firm: Managerial Behavior, Agency Costs, and Ownership Structure, *Journal of Financial Economics 3*, No. 4 (October 1976): 305–360.

200 **stakeholder companies:** John P. Kotter and James L. Heskett, *Corporate Culture and Performance* (New York: Free Press, 1992).

201 **"Here's the screw-up":** Francesco Guerrera, "Welch Issues Rebuke to GE's Immelt," *Financial Times*, April 16, 2008.

201 **One study noted:** Michael A. Hitt, Robert E. Hoskisson, and Jeffrey S. Harrison, "Strategic Competitiveness in the 1990s: Challenges and Opportunities for U.S. Executives," *Academy of Management Executive* 5, no. 2 (1991).

202 **Japan's expenditures:** Michael T. Jacobs, *Short-Term America: The Causes and Cures of Our Business Myopia* (Boston: Harvard Business School Press, 1991), 4.

202 **Contenders like former vice president Walter Mondale:** Kent Hughes, *Building the Next American Century: The Past and Future of American Economic Competitiveness* (Washington: Woodrow Wilson Center Press, 2005), 153.

202 **one congressional staffer:** Conversation with Kent Hughes, September 6, 2009.

203 **the standard definition:** Ibid., 162.

203 **the commission called:** Ibid., 165.

211 **A relative trickle of foreign direct investment:** Robert Reich, "Does Corporate Nationality Matter?" *Issues in Science and Technology,* Winter 1990–1991.

211 **In just the five years:** Louis Uchitelle, "U.S. Business Loosens Tie to Mother Country," *The New York Times,* May 21, 1989.

211 **annual trade deficit:** Reich, "Does Corporate Nationality Matter?"

212 **"in any country where Ford":** Ibid.

217 **compensation for CEOs:** "An End to Inequality?" *The Economist,* April 2, 2009.

217 **Walmart:** Scott, "The Wal-Mart Effect."

217 **Yet real compensation:** Social Security Administration, "National Average Wage Index," http://www.ssa.gov/OACT/COLA/AWI.html; Federal Reserve Bank of St. Louis, Productivity and Cost Databases, http://research.stlouisfed.org/fred2/categories/2.

218 **high school education:** Thomas Kochan and Beth Shulman, "A New Social Contract: Restoring Dignity and Balance to the Economy," *EPI Briefing Paper #184,* February 22, 2007.

218 **workforce with college degrees:** Clyde Prestowitz, *The Smart Globalist's Agenda: A Plan for Responsible U.S. Engagement in the World,* Demos and the Economic Strategy Institute, 2009, http://www.demos.org/pubs/globalist_070809.pdf, 8.

218 **Alan Blinder has warned:** Ibid.

218 **with the bubble years:** Gary P. Pisano and Willy C. Shih, "Restoring American Competitiveness," in *Harvard Business Review* 87, nos. 7–8 (July–August 2009).

220 **document states the following:** Council on Competitiveness, "Five for the Future," October 2007, http://www.compete.org/images/uploads/File/PDF%20Files/Five_Final_8858COC.pdf.

221 **"On the face of it":** "Welch Condemns Share Price Focus," *Financial Times,* March 12, 2009.

Chapter 8: Cheap Energy: The Great American Habit

226 **fourth-highest GDP per capita:** Prestowitz, *Rogue Nation,* 84.

226 **"temporary and vanishing phenomenon":** Daniel Yergin, *The Prize: The Epic Quest for Oil, Money, and Power* (New York: Simon & Schuster, 1991), 36.

227 **3.5 million cars:** Ibid., 208.

229 **7 billion barrels of oil:** Ibid., 379.

229 **surge capacity proved decisive:** Ibid., 567.

230 **"the defense of Saudi Arabia":** Michael T. Klare, *Blood and Oil: The Dangers and Consequences of America's Growing Dependency on Imported Petroleum* (New York: Owl Books, 2004), 29.

231 **"the oil resources of Saudi Arabia":** Ibid.

231 **free world's oil consumption:** Yergin, *The Prize,* 567.

232 **survival of the human spirit:** "Materials Supply Put Up To Industry; Paley Urges It Take Initiative From Government in Attack on 'Creeping' Shortages," *The New York Times,* September 18, 1952, 43.

232 **program ultimately died:** Ibid., 428.

234 **"change the face of America":** Ibid., 553.

234 **quotas on imports:** Ibid., 567.

235 **fell by 6 percent:** Ibid., 653.

236 **energy conservation measures:** Prestowitz, *Rogue Nation,* 96–97.

236 **France committed to nuclear power:** Yergin, *The Prize,* 655.

236 **raised its fleet fuel economy:** IEA, "Saving Oil and Reducing CO_2 Emissions in Transport: Options and Strategies," OECD/IEA 2001, 23.

237 **"fraction of our investment":** Dean Acheson, *Present at the Creation: My Years in the State Department* (New York: W.W. Norton, 1987), 568.

239 **mandated auto fuel efficiency:** Yergin, *The Prize,* 660–661.

239 **Ford pushed shortly:** Ibid., 660.

240 **a detailed program:** Jay Hakes, *A Declaration of Energy Independence: How Freedom from Foreign Oil Can Improve National Security, Our Economy, and the Environment* (Hoboken, N.J.: John Wiley & Sons, 2008), 46, note 8.

240 **"moral equivalent of war":** Yergin, *The Prize,* 663.

241 **reducing oil imports:** Hakes, *A Declaration of Energy Independence,* 45.

241 **the United States imported:** Ibid., 68.

242 **the decline, however, resulted from:** Ibid., 69–70.

242 **"dramatized a very important lesson":** Ibid., 63.

242 **"new marching orders":** Ibid., 72.

243 **note that Canada:** U.S. Energy Information Administration, "Country Analysis Brief, Canada," December 2002.

243 **funding for energy conservation:** Environmental Law Reporter, "The National Energy Plan: Hitless After the First Inning," 1997; Joseph Romm, "Needed: A No-Regrets Energy Policy," *Bulletin of Atomic Scientists* 47, no. 6 (July/August 1991).

243 **found themselves paying:** Yergin, *The Prize,* 779.

243 **share of U.S. consumption:** Energy Information Administration. "Petroleum Overview 1949–2000," *Annual Energy Review 2000,* 123; Environmental Protection Agency, "U.S. Horsepower of a New Vehicle," *Light Duty Automotive Technology and Fuel Economy Trends Through 1996,* EPA/AA/TDSG/96-01; Energy Information Administration. "U.S. Retail Price of Electricity," *Annual Energy Review, 1997,* DOE/EIA-0384, July 1998, table 8.13.

244 **imports accounted for:** U.S. Energy Information Administration, "Petroleum," *Annual Energy Review 2008,* http://www.eia.doe.gov/emeu/aer/petro.html.

245 **"there is no way":** Klare, *Blood and Oil,* 48.

245 **maintaining U.S. naval forces:** Prestowitz, *Rogue Nation,* 109.

245 **"Our jobs, our way of life":** Yergin, *The Prize,* 773.

246 **oil imports had risen:** Klare, *Blood and Oil,* 68.

246 **maintain sufficient global supply:** Ibid., 82.

246 **increasing demand coupled with:** Jad Mouawad, "Gloomy Energy Report Sets the Stage for Climate Talks," *The New York Times,* November 10, 2009.

Chapter 9: Competing in the New World

248 **Just a few days before this event:** Keith Bradsher, "Nuclear Power Expansion in China Stirs Concerns," *The New York Times,* December 16, 2009, A1.

248 **More significant for America:** Ian Urbina, "Pittsburgh Sets Vote on Adding Tax on Tuition," *New York Times,* December 16, 2009, A28.

249 **in the wake of its government bailout:** Jenny Anderson, "As Goldman Thrives, Some Say an Ethos Has Faded," *The New York Times,* December 16, 2009, A1.

249 **He was convicted of:** Jane Macartney, "Leading Chinese Dissident Liu Xiaobo to Face Trial for Subversion," *The Times* (London), December 23, 2009, http://www.timesonline.co.uk/tol/news/world/asia/article6965673.ece.

250 **The Chinese see this development clearly:** Geoff Dyer, "The Dragon Stirs," *Financial Times,* September 25, 2009.

251 **In November 2009:** Breakthrough Institute and the Information Tech-

nology and Innovation Foundation, *Rising Tigers, Sleeping Giant: Asian Nations Set to Dominate the Clean Energy Race by Out-Investing the United States,* November 2009, http://www.itif.org/files/2009-rising -tigers.pdf.

251 **The lead story reported:** Aaron Nathans, "GE to Shut Solar Plant in Glasgow," *The News Journal,* November 7, 2009.

253 **Amazon's Kindle electronic reader:** Pisano and Shih, "Restoring American Competitiveness."

253 **Perhaps the most important loss:** Michael Mandel, "The GDP Mirage," *BusinessWeek,* November 9, 2009.

255 **From 1990 to 2005:** U.S.-China Economic and Security Review Commission, *2009 Report to Congress,* November 2009, http://www.uscc .gov/annual_report/2009/annual_report_full_09.pdf, 82.

259 **it would be a costly mistake for China:** "China Takes on Boeing and Airbus," *The Economist,* May 15, 2008.

259 **in the eleventh five-year plan:** U.S.-China Economic and Security Review Commission, *2009 Report to Congress.*

259 **Intel's goal, he said:** Pat Choate, *Saving Capitalism: Keeping America Strong* (New York: Vintage Books, 2009), 74.

260 **It has also announced:** Ibid., 71.

261 **David Sandalow acknowledged:** Evan Osnos, "Green Giant: Beijing's Crash Program for Clean Energy," *The New Yorker,* December 21, 2009.

262 **You probably don't think of Finland:** Clyde Prestowitz and Ben Carliner, *Israel 2020: A Strategic Vision for Economic Development,* Economic Strategy Institute, http://www.econstrat.org/images/ESI_Research _Reports_PDF/israel_2020_strategic_vision_for_economic_development .pdf, 39.

263 **Taiwan today is:** Ibid., 114.

264 **a "Green Silicon Island":** Ibid., 121.

268 **President Reagan cut the department's investment:** Osnos, "Green Giant."

269 **agricultural subsidies that now cost us:** Environmental Working Group, "Farm Subsidy Database," http://farm.ewg.org/farm/index.php?key=nosign.

269 **Consider that from 1929 to 1988:** Floyd Norris, "To Rein in Pay, Rein in Wall St.," *The New York Times,* October 29, 2009, B1.

270 **the financial sector's share of business profits:** Simon Johnson, "The Quiet Coup," *The Atlantic Monthly,* May 2009.

274 **share of the workforce with a college degree:** Jeff Faux, "Globalization That Works for Working Americans," EPI Briefing Paper #179, January 11, 2007, http://www.sharedprosperity.org/bp179.html.

274 **80 percent of engineering tasks:** Ibid.

275 **confirmed by the report in *BusinessWeek:*** Mandel, "The GDP Mirage."

Chapter 10: Playing to Win

284 **"if you want your health care":** "Obama Takes Pitch for Health Care Reform to the Public," *PBS NewsHour,* June 11, 2009, http://www.pbs.org/newshour/bb/health/jan-june09/healthcare_06-11.html.

287 **budget of the National Institutes of Health:** National Institutes of Health, "NIH Budget," http://www.nih.gov/about/budget.htm.

290 **top 2 percent of earners:** The Tax Foundation, "If Health Surtax Is 5.4 Percent, Taxpayers in 39 States Would Pay a Top Tax Rate Over 50%," July 14, 2009, http://www.taxfoundation.org/publications/show/24863.html.

Index

About the Author

Clyde Prestowitz is the author of the bestselling and critically acclaimed books *Trading Places, Rogue Nation,* and *Three Billion New Capitalists.* He is the founder and president of the influential Economic Strategy Institute in Washington, D.C. He served as a principal trade negotiator for Asia in the Reagan administration and held the position of Counselor to the Secretary of Commerce for international trade. He also served as vice chairman of former president Bill Clinton's Commission on Trade and Investment in the Asia-Pacific Region and as a member of the advisory board of the Export-Import Bank. He has been a fellow of the World Economic Forum and has served as an advisor to major corporations and foreign and trade ministers around the world. He was an advisor on Asia and globalization for the Obama campaign. Clyde holds a B.A. in political science and economics from Swarthmore College and an M.A. in Asian studies from the University of Hawaii and the East-West Center. He also holds an M.B.A. from the Wharton Graduate School of Business. He has written hundreds of articles and op-editorials over the past twenty-five years for *The New York Times, The Wall Street Journal, Foreign Affairs, The Washington Post, The Economist,* and other leading publications. He lives with his wife, Carol, in Washington, D.C.